שמירת שבת כהלכתה

SHEMIRATH SHABBATH

*a guide to the practical
observance of the Sabbath*

Rav Yehoshua Y. Neuwirth

SHEMIRATH SHABBATH

a guide to the practical observance of the Sabbath

the English edition of

שמירת שבת כהלכתה

Sh^{e}mirath Shabbath K^{e}hilchathah

prepared by

W. GRANGEWOOD

in close collaboration with the author

I

from the second edition of the Hebrew
Volume I, Chapters 1-22

FELDHEIM

Jerusalem / New York

First published 1984
Hardcover edition: ISBN 0-87306-298-1
Paperback edition: ISBN 0-87306-375-9

Phototypeset at the Feldheim Press

Philipp Feldheim Inc.
200 Airport Executive Park
Spring Valley, NY 10977

96 East Broadway
New York, NY 10002

Feldheim Publishers Ltd
POB 6525 / Jerusalem, Israel

Printed in Israel

לזכר עולם יהיה צדיק

(תהלים קי"ב)

א"א מו"ר הרה"ג ר' **אהרן** בן הרב ר' **שאול צבי** זצלה"ה נויבירט

לפנים רב ומו"ץ בק"ק מגנצא, הלברשטט, ברלין, אמסטרדם ויפו,

מרביץ תורה ברבים ומקרב הרחוקים

אשר גדלני על ברכי התורה ובדרך האמת הנחני

ואשר בזכותו זכיתי לשבת במנוחה באהלה של תורה

נפטר י"ט שבט תשי"ח

ת. נ. צ. ב. ה.

RABBI MOSES FEINSTEIN

455 F. D. R. DRIVE

NEW YORK, N. Y. 10002

ORegon 7-1222

משה פיינשטיין

ר"מ תפארת ירושלים

בנוא יארק

בע"ה

הנה כבר נתפרסם הספר החשוב "שמירת שבת כהלכתה" שחיברו ידידי הרב הגאון מוהר"ר י. נויבירט שליט"א, ר"מ בישיבת קול תורה בירושלים עיה"ק. וכעת נדבה רוחו של הרה"ג הנ"ל לסדר תירגום של ספרו הנ"ל, כדי להועיל לאלו שאינם מורגלים בלה"ק, ללמוד מדיני שבת הנחוצים בכל שבת. והנה ידוע שיטתי שאיני נותן הסכמות על ספרי הלכה, מאחר שקשה לפני להעמיק בהם ולהגיד שאני מסכים לכל החלטתם, ובפרט אני נזהר מליתן הסכמות על ספרים שנכתבים בשפת לעזות. ובכל זאת, גם עיין בהתירגום הזה נכדי הרה"ג מוהר"ר מרדכי טענדלער שליט"א ששיבחו לפני לבהירות לשונו ולהבנת סידורו, וכבר קבל הרה"ג נויבירט החזקה "שלא יוצא מתחת ידו דבר שאינו מתוקן". ובאתי בזה לברכו שיצליחהו השי"ת בהפרצת ספרו זה, וישמרו השי"ת שלא יצא שום תקלה מספרו זה, שידוע שיש חשש כזה בכל עת שנכתב בשפת לעזות, ושיזכה לחבר עוד ספרים לתפארת השם ותורתו.

ועל זה באתי על החתום לכבוד הרה"ג המחבר בז' לחודש אייר תשמ"ג בנוא יארק.

משה פיינשטיין

RABBI JACOB I. RUDERMAN
400 MT. WILSON LANE
BALTIMORE, MD. 21208

יעקב יצחק הלוי רודרמן
באלטימאר. מד.

שמחתי לשמוע שכעת עומדים להוציא לאור מהדורא חדשה של הספר הנכבד ס׳
שמירת שבת כהלכתה מאת הרב הגאון מה״ר יהושע נויבירט שליט״א ושיהא
מעתה נמסר לפני העם גם בלשון אנגלית הנקל להם ביותר ובודאי שעל ידי זה ירבו
הלומדים מספרו ויהיה מהזוכים ומזכים את הרבים וכגון דא אין צריך למודעי כי
כבר איתמחי גברא וספרו הנ״ל זכה להתקבל ברצון בכל קצות הארץ על כן אמינא
לפעלא טבא יישר ויהי חפץ ד׳ מצליח בידו וילכו רבים לאור תורתו.

הכו״ח למען תוה״ק

יעקב יצחק הלוי רודערמאן

נר ישראל

יצחק הלוי
רודרמן
ראש הישיבה

ב"ה

RAV SIMON SCHWAB
736 WEST 186TH STREET
NEW YORK, N. Y. 10033

RES: 927-0498
OFFICE: 923-5936

שמעון שוואב
אב"ד דק"ק
קהל עדת ישרון
נוא-יארק, נ.י.

מוצאי יום הכפורים שנת תשד"מ

למכ"ת יד"נ הרב הגאון מהו"ר יהושע נויבירט שליט"א
מחבר ספר "שמירת שבת כהלכתה"

שלום ושפע רב:

מי אני ומה אני ליתן הסכמות, ובפרט לספרי-הלכה, חלילה לי מעשות ככה, ולא
אאמין שכת"ר שליט"א ביקש זאת מידי, כי ידוע לכל כי רחוק אני מזה כמטחוי-
קשת, ובפרט שספרו היקר ומאד נעלה כבר מפורסם ומוסכם מגדולי ישראל
שליט"א שקטנם עבה ממתני — אך מה שבקשני כת"ר הוא לשום עיני על
התרגום-האנגלי ללועזים בלעז; ואמרתי אחרי העיון שיפה תירגם בדיוק ובלשון
סופר מהיר, צח ובהיר, וקל לקראת ונוח להשכיל, ובלי-ספק דבר גדול עשה
בשביל אלה שלא זכו עדין לעיין בספרי-הלכה הנכתבים בלה"ק, אך נשא לבם
אותם לעשות רצון קונם ולהזהר ולהזדרז בשמירת שבת בכל דקדוקיה ובכל פרטי-
הלכותיה קטנה וגדולה, בשביל אלו התרגום האנגלי יהיה חזוק גדול להחזיר עטרת-
קדושת שבת ליושנה.

ובזה בעה"ח יום הנ"ל פה ק"ק קע"י נוא יארק
בכל לשון של ידידות והערצה מו"מ בלו"נ

שמעון שוואב

Rabbi CHAIM P. SCHEINBERG

KIRYAT MATTERSDORF

PANIM MEIROT 2.

JERUSALEM, ISRAEL

הרב חיים פנחס שיינברג

ראש ישיבת "תורה אור"

ומורה הוראה דקרית מטרסדורף

ירושלים טל.525163

בע"ה

הנה ראיתי את התרגום האנגלי של הספר החשוב "שמירת שבת כהלכתה",
ספר אשר הפליא לעשות הרב הגאון המופלג בתורה וביראת שמים טהורה מוהר"ר
יהושע ישעיה נויבירט שליט"א, בעמל רב, ביגיעה עצומה, בבקיאות גדולה,
בסברות ישרות ובסדר נפלא.

והנה הספר הזה יש בו תועלת גדולה וזכות הרבים עצומה, ותועלת מיוחדת יש
בתרגום האנגלי עבור אלה שאינם מבינים לשון הקודש, ובפרט בהלכות שבת
החמורות. אשרי חלקו שזכה לזכות הרבים לשמור שבת קודש כהלכתה.

הן אמנם כאשר הוא ספר פסקי דינים, הנני נמנע מליתן הסכמה, כי בזה צריך
לעיין היטב בכל פרט ופרט, אך כבר שבחוהו גאונים וגדולים, ואף ידי תכון עמו,
ואמינא לפעלו טובא, ואשרי חילו לאורייתא להגדיל תורה ולהאדירה, ולהוסיף
זכות הרבים בעוד ספרים מועילים.

הכו"ח לכבוד התורה ולומדיה פה עיה"ק ירושלם תובב"א
יום ח"י מנחם אב תשמ"ג

חיים פינחס שיינברג

בע"ה

כב' ידידי ומכובדי, ר' קלמן זאב גרנג'ווד לאי"ט

אחדשה"ט ושמעכ"ת,

עם גמר ההדפסה של ח"א של תירגום הספר "שמירת שבת כהלכתה" לשפה האנגלית, רצוני להביע בפניך את הוקרתי המיוחדת לעבודתך הגדולה, כולה לשם שמים.

ידוע לי, כמה יגיעה רבה יגעת וכמה שקידה נפלאה שקדת בבירור מחדש של כל הלכה לפני שנגשת לתרגם כל סעיף וסעיף, השקעת ממיטב כוחותיך, לא הנחת דבר מבלי להניח עליו את שבט הביקורת, וב"ה זכית להוציא מתחת ידיך דבר יפה ומתוקן, דבר מתוקן ומסודר, להביא ברכה ואורה לבית היהודי למען דעת את המעשה אשר יעשון לשמור תורה ומצות, איך לנהוג בהלכות שבת, כהרים התלויים בשערה, וכל זה לאלה אשר אינם מתמצאים די צורכם בלשון הקודש. גם תקנת והוספת אחרי שיחת מרעים, מקומות אשר טעונים תיקון, והסכמתי לכל אלה הדברים. ועל כל דא אומר לפעלא טבא יי0שר כוחו וחילו, ויהא רעוא מן שמיא, כי תזכה להפיץ ממעינותיך חוצה להגדיל תורה ולהאדירה, למען זיכוי הרבים, ובכל אשר תפנה תשכיל ותצליח כחפץ לבך הטוב. ויאריך ה' ימיך ושנותיך בטוב ובנעימים לרוות נחת מזרעיך שיגדלו להיות גדולים בתורה ובירא"ש, ויוסיפו אומץ וכוח בתורת ה' ועבודתו, אמן ואמן.

הנני כותב וחותם, פה עיה"ק ירושלם תובב"א,

יום של נר מצוה ותורה אור, כ"ה בכסלו תשד"מ, יום השנה של א"ז הגאון ר' יעקב אטלינגר זצ"ל מח"ס ערוך לנר לש"ס, ועוד, זכותו תגן עלינו ועל כל ישראל.

יהושע י. נויבירט

יהושע י. נויבירט

PREFACE TO THE ENGLISH EDITION

Few, if any, halachic works have attracted as much popular attention in modern times as Rabbi Y. Y. Neuwirth's *Shemirath Shabbath Kehilchathah*. For many years, the need has been felt for a parallel edition in English, in order to assist those who are more fluent in that language to use the book as a quick work of reference. Today, the swelling ranks of young people who are returning to the fold of Orthodox Judaism — after what are often generations of estrangement — demand a ready source of the basic knowledge for which they thirst. In many cases, they have no conception at all of what observing Shabbath entails, beyond a vague idea that one is not allowed to work.

This book does not deal with the many facets of Shabbath as a central concept in Judaism. It does not purport to explain the deeper meaning of the Shabbath as reflected in thousands of years of Scriptural, Talmudic and rabbinical literature. That is the task of the teacher and of other works. What this book does attempt to do is to tell the reader, in a palatable format and in comparatively simple language, what one may and what one may not do on Shabbath or a Festival. The text is written in such a way that it assumes little prior knowledge of the subject, so that many readers may, on occasion, find that, to them, some of the statements made seem superfluous.

Despite the attempt made to avoid the use of Hebrew words and expressions, which tend to create a break in the text to those who are not familiar with them, there are some occasions when it was felt that adhering too rigidly to such a principle would give rise to more problems than it would avoid. A limited number of Hebrew words and expressions has consequently been used, and they and their meanings are listed, in brief, in the Glossary.

In a work such as this, there is a considerable risk that the reader might overlook an essential qualification buried in the midst of a long sentence. For the sake of clarity, the text has been arranged in numbered and lettered paragraphs and sub-paragraphs, each generally containing not more than one or two points. The reader who is irritated by this practice is requested to bear in mind that the book is not designed to be read through lightly from cover to cover in one sitting.

A comparison with the (second) Hebrew edition will show that this book is far from being a word-for-word translation. Rather, the aim has been to provide an accurate translation of the ideas, with such modifications as are felt to be appropriate for an English edition. I have had the advantage of many, many hours of Rabbi Neuwirth's time, on a daily basis, to discuss doubtful points and especially to obtain the author's express approval of all departures from the original text. Furthermore, the English text has been meticulously and critically checked by Rabbi Yaakov Schatz, to prevent halachic discrepancies. Nevertheless, the responsibility for any errors or misunderstandings falls fairly and squarely on my shoulders, and I can but pray that such mistakes or ambiguities as there may prove to be will not mislead any readers into an unintentional desecration of the Shabbath.

The voluminous footnotes in the Hebrew original have not been included in the English edition, except where it has been felt necessary for a proper understanding of the text. The English text does, however, with rare exceptions, follow the paragraph numbering of the second Hebrew edition (whatever rearrangement of the information there may be within the paragraphs); so the reader who has the inclination can quite easily delve more deeply into any subject and follow up the sources by reference to the appropriate footnotes in the corresponding Hebrew paragraph.

A departure from the usual format for a book of this nature is the use of marginal headings. It is to be emphasized that these marginal headings are inserted only for ease of reference and must on no account be taken as in any way modifying, or being explanatory of, the text.

I cannot refrain from expressing my wonder at the amount of time and trouble expended by Mr. Yaakov Feldheim and his staff on the production of this book — far more than can be justified by the purely economic considerations of a publishing house.

One final personal observation: if this edition helps just one person to improve his observance of Shabbath in accordance with the letter and spirit of the Halacha, I will feel that all my efforts have been justified. I am deeply grateful to the Almighty and pray for His continued assistance in the full realization that, without special *siyata di-Shmaya*, my own "natural" capabilities far from qualify me for fulfilling the task I undertook.

W.G.

CONTENTS

2: Laws of cooking on Yom Tov / *pages* 29-34

3: Laws of selection on Shabbath / *pages* 35-61

4: Laws of selection on Yom Tov / *pages* 62-65

5: Laws relating to squeezing fruit on Shabbath and Yom Tov / *pages* 66-70

CONTENTS

6: Laws of grinding, chopping, crushing, and grating on Shabbath / *pages* 71-75

1 Scope of prohibition. 2 Mincers, mortars and graters forbidden. 3 Vegetable choppers and egg slicers. 4 Scope of chapter. 5 Classification of foods. 6 Cutting up fresh fruits or vegetables. 7 Spreading banana or avocado on bread. 8 Mashing bananas or tomatoes. 9 Spreading jam. 10 Cooked vegetables. 11 Bread, biscuits, chocolate, sugar and salt. 12 Precrushed foods. 13 Porridge, farina and rice. 14 Chopping eggs, meat, fish and cheese. 15 Mixing mashed banana.

7: Laws of grinding, chopping, crushing, and grating on Yom Tov / *pages* 76-79

1 Classification of foods. 2 Bananas, apples, onions and potatoes. 3 Coffee, horseradish and spices. 4 Salt and nuts. 5 Cake, cookies, bread and lumps of sugar. 6 Eggs, meat, fish and cheese. 7 Mincers and grinders.

8: Laws of kneading on Shabbath / *pages* 80-89

Introductory. 1 Conditions for applying prohibition. 2 Kneading for immediate use. 3 Kneading one substance by itself. 4 Making salads and mixing powders. 5 Pouring one substance into another. 6 Substances poured together before Shabbath. 7 Substances mixed together before Shabbath. 8 Two types of mixtures. 9 Main distinction in rules applicable to thick and thin mixtures. 10 Thick mixtures partially prepared before Shabbath. 11 Making thick mixtures on Shabbath. 12 Mixing cream and soft cheese. 13 Mixing cheese and honey. 14 Mixing lemon juice into cheese or bananas. 15 Mixing biscuit and soft cheese. 16 Mixing sugar or jam with cream or cheese. 17 Mixing butter and cocoa. 18 Milk powder. 19 Food softened by cooking. 20 Mixing cinnamon or raisins with rice. 21 Adding water to dried-up food. 22 Dipping cake, cookies or bread into liquid. 23 Chopped eggs and onions. 24 Instant powders for making liquids. 25 Instant powders for producing solid foods. 26 Thick mixtures which become thin.

9: Opening cans, bottles and other containers on Shabbath and Yom Tov / *pages* 90-97

1 Preferable course. 2 Containers normally re-used. 3 Containers not emptied on opening but not re-used. 4 Containers emptied immediately and thrown away. 5 Holes in containers. 6 Perforating containers in marked positions. 7 Slicing spout off plastic bottle. 8 Cartons of toilet paper. 9 Stapled bags. 10 Boxes sealed with gummed paper. 11 Paper seals. 12 Conditions for opening wrappings and seals. 13 Bags sealed by pliable strips. 14 Bags or parcels tied with string. 15 Strings of figs. 16 Knots in plastic bags. 17 Bottle caps which may not be removed. 18 Can lids sealed by metal strips. 19 Perforated rubber nipples and salt shakers. 20 Crown-caps and corks. 21 Releasing a vacuum. 22 Above rules also apply on Yom Tov. 23 Containers opened in a forbidden manner. 24 Labels on bottles. 25 Rolls of paper. 26 Thermos stoppers. 27 Unscrewing thermoses.

10: The use of ice and refrigerators on Shabbath and Yom Tov / *pages* 98-103

11: Various laws relating to the preparation of food on Shabbath and Yom Tov / *pages* 104-118

12: Washing dishes and cleaning the table on Shabbath and Yom Tov / *pages* 119-132

scourers. 11 Wet cloths and sponges. 12 Flax-like dish cleaners. 13 Squeegees and rubber gloves. 14a) Liquid-soap containers with fitted brushes. b) Dish-washing paste and bars of soap. 15 Brushes. 16 Pouring away dishwater. 17 Unblocking a sink. 18 Sink draining onto sown ground. 19 Water meters. 20 Exterminating insects.

21 Drying dishes. 22 Drying wet towels. 23 Sorting cutlery and dishes. 24 Polishing. 25 Sharpening knives. 26 Bent cutlery. 27 Thermoses. 28 Vessels unfit for use for religious reasons. 29 Vessels acquired from a non-Jew.

30 Shaking cloths out of a window. 31 Folding cloths. 32 Bones, peels, etc. not fit for any use. 33 Bones, peels, etc. fit for animal consumption. 34 Clearing dishes. 35 Dishwashers. 36 Clearing the table after the last meal. 37 Removing spilled liquid from a cloth with a spoon or a knife. 38 Soaking up spilled liquids. 39 Terylene cloths. 40 Cleaning hard surfaces. 41 Plastic tablecloths. 42 Plastic cloths with natural trimming or backing.

13: Laws relating to fire on Shabbath and Yom Tov / *pages* 133-149

1 Scope of prohibition on Shabbath.

2 Scope of prohibition on Yom Tov. 3 Permitted methods of lighting fire on Yom Tov. 4 When fire may be lit on Yom Tov. 5 When fire may not be lit on Yom Tov. 6 Memorial lights on Yom Tov. 7 Smoking on Yom Tov.

8 Extinguishing forbidden. 9 Prohibition against lowering a flame. 10 Lowering a flame to prevent food from spoiling. 11 Replacing spent gas cylinders. 12 Limiting the supply of gas in a cylinder. 13 Water boiling over onto gas flame. 14 Turning off gas after flame goes out. 15 Gas water heaters.

16 Putting in fuel on Yom Tov. 17 Raising the flame. 18 Smoking or defective appliances. 19 Removal of fuel tank. 20 Trimming the wick. 21 Oil-lamp wicks. 22 Replacing wick of paraffin lamp or stove.

23 Setting a timer. 24 Use of alarm clock to cut off current. 25 Adjusting timer on Shabbath to turn current on or off earlier or later. 26 Adjusting timer on Shabbath to turn current on or off a second time. 27 Adjusting timer on Yom Tov. 28 Removing plug while current is turned off. 29 Removing light bulbs while current is turned off. 30 Connecting timer on Shabbath. 31 Mending or replacing a fuse.

32 Variable-strength lighting. 33 Candles standing in a draught. 34 Turning on of ventilator

14: Washing and otherwise attending to the body on Shabbath and Yom Tov / *pages* 150-163

15: Care of clothes on Shabbath and Yom Tov
pages 164-187

CONTENTS

19: Specific laws relating to the transfer of objects from one place to another on Yom Tov, where there is no *eiruv* / *pages* 237-238

20: Categories of *muktzeh* / *pages* 239-273

21: Laws of *muktzeh* on Yom Tov / *pages* 274-276

22: General principles relating to *muktzeh* on Shabbath and Yom Tov / *pages* 277-296

chamath chesron kis. 5 Basis la-davar ha-assur. 6 Animals. 7 Fruit from which t^{e}rumoth and ma'asroth separated on Shabbath.

The Contents of Volume 2

Introduction

Shabbath is described by the Talmud (Tractate Shabbath 10b) as God's precious gift to the Jewish people from His treasure house. It is a sign to the nations of the world that God has imbued His people with part of His own sanctity. (See Exodus 31:13 and Rashi's commentary there.)

Of all the mitzvoth in the Torah, none distinguishes the Jewish people from the other nations of the world as much as the observance of God's holy Shabbath.

Throughout two thousand years of separation from its land and dispersion among the gentiles, the Jewish people has remained steadfast to the eternal truths expressed in God's Torah, handed down to Moses on Mount Sinai, and has not forgotten the precious gift it enshrines, Shabbath. It is the Shabbath which has preserved the unity of the Jewish people by imparting sanctity to the Jew and making him stand out from the profanity of the surrounding world. "Why is that man's shop closed?" "Because he observes the Shabbath." "Why isn't that man at work?" "Because he observes the Shabbath." (Mechilta to Exodus 31:14). The Torah established the identity of the Jewish people. Through the Torah the individual Jew realizes that he is but one of many organs making up a whole body, a body which he is enjoined to preserve intact, through thick and thin.

As long ago as the days of Israel's enslavement in Egypt, our greatest leader, Moses, realized that the Jews would be unable to survive as a nation unless they were welded together by a superior force which singled them out from their Egyptian neighbors. The Midrash relates how, to prevent them from assimilating with the Egyptians, he requested Pharaoh to grant them a weekly day of rest, on the pretext that this was in Pharaoh's own interest, since otherwise his slaves would die of overwork (Midrash Rabba Exodus 1). In this manner, the Jews were impressed with the knowledge that they were a distinct people, a people that lived in the hope of the promised redemption. For six days they toiled as slaves; on the seventh, they delighted—by way of utter contrast—in the study of scrolls which they had in their possession, secure in the conviction that the Almighty would rescue them, thanks to the fact that they rested on Shabbath (Midrash Rabba Exodus 5).

In his mind's eye, Moses saw the people of Israel being swallowed up among the nations and totally disappearing, and this even while they were in their own land, let alone when they were scattered in exile. What did he do? "Moses assembled the whole congregation of the Children of Israel" (Exodus 35:1) and emphasized to them the importance of observing Shabbath. The Midrash (Yalkut Shim'oni at the beginning of *parshath vayakhel*) notes that the only time the Pentateuch expressly tells us that Moses assembled the people to give them a mitzva is in connection with Shabbath. God told him to gather the people together and lecture to them in public on the laws of Shabbath, so that future generations of leaders would learn from this to gather their congregations together every Shabbath to teach them the Torah, to instruct them in the "do's and don't's" of life as a Jew. Shabbath was, thus, the instrument chosen by the Almighty to lift His children up spiritually to the level where they would sing praises to the glory of His Name.

The Mishna (Chagiga: Chapter 1, mishna 8) likens the laws of Shabbath to "mountains hanging by a hair," in that a multitude of precepts and rules, entailing the most severe penalties for their breach, depend on the slightest of indications given by a biblical verse. This is probably one of the reasons why the detailed observance of the Shabbath tends to be neglected by the populace at large more than other mitzvoth. The complications involved in the principles underlying the concept of Shabbath and in their practical application can be daunting not only for the man in the street. The Jerusalem Talmud (Tractate Shabbath: Chapter 7, halacha 2) tells us that Rabbi Yochanan and Rabbi Shimon ben Lakish spent three-and-a-half years on one chapter of Tractate Shabbath (Chapter 7, which deals with the thirty-nine major activities forbidden by the Torah on Shabbath). The Sifra (at the beginning of *parshath bechukothai*) points out that we are commanded not only to observe the Shabbath and remember it in our hearts, but also to refresh our memory by keeping it constantly on our lips. Unless one has been through the laws relating to the observance of Shabbath several times and continues to study them regularly, one has no hope of avoiding even the most elementary of pitfalls week after week.

The purpose of this work is to collect in an easily assimilable format the laws relating to Shabbath and Yom Tov, for the benefit of those who, through the sheer pressure of the daily necessity to earn a living, or for more basic reasons, are unable to cull them from the traditional sources. The author's chief concern has been to help them preserve the observance of the Shabbath as an integral part of their lives. The reader will often find passages repeated in identical or similar terms in different contexts, to save him time in leafing back and forth more than necessary. The copious cross-references enable the reader to obtain further details where relevant or to see how the point in which he is interested is treated in another connection.

Nothing could be further from the author's mind than to introduce innovations into the laws of Shabbath. Every statement in the book is based on the existing authorities, and reference to the notes to the corresponding paragraphs in the second Hebrew edition should reveal who those authorities are (as well as authorities who hold opposing views).

The author has spared no effort to consult the greatest rabbinical authorities of our time in order to ascertain the ruling of the Halacha on difficult or controversial subjects; likewise, wherever appropriate, the author has not hesitated to avail himself of the knowledge and advice, both critical and constructive, of renowned experts (all Orthodox Jews to whom the observance of the Shabbath is dear) in the fields of medicine and technology, so as to verify the precise facts to which the Halacha must be applied. Nonetheless, it must be emphasized again and again that this book cannot and must not take the place of the duly qualified rabbi who must be asked to give his ruling in the circumstances of each case. It must be remembered that circumstances change and that they vary from place to place; medical and other scientific "facts" do not remain constant. The slightest alteration in one single relevant fact can result in a total reversal of the halachic situation, making what was permissible forbidden and vice versa. This book should serve as

Introduction

a guide, to enable the reader to know when he has a problem and what to ask.

May we be privileged, by virtue of the proper observance of the Shabbath, to see the final redemption of Israel. "Rabbi Yochanan said in the name of Rabbi Shimon ben Yochai, 'Were Israel properly to observe two Shabbathoth, they would immediately be redeemed'" (Shabbath 118b). Until such time, God's only dwelling-place on this earth is within the four walls of the Halacha (Berachoth 8a).

Chapter 1

Laws of Cooking on Shabbath

INTRODUCTORY REMARKS

A. All prohibitions against cooking referred to below apply, in general, only on Shabbath.

B. On Yom Tov, any cooking required for the Festival is permitted, unless otherwise stated. (Prohibitions connected with cooking on Yom Tov are discussed in paragraphs 27 and 30 below and in Chapter 2.)

C. If the prohibition against cooking is transgressed, a qualified rabbinical authority should be consulted, since in some circumstances it is prohibited to eat the resulting food.

DEFINITION OF COOKING

1. *a.* Cooking on Shabbath is forbidden.   *scope of the*
   b. The prohibition against cooking includes   *prohibition*
      1) boiling,
      2) roasting,
      3) frying,
      4) baking and
      5) any method of preparing food* by most forms of heat, provided, in general, that heating takes place to a temperature of at least 45 degrees centigrade (113 degrees Fahrenheit).

---

*Although this chapter refers specifically to the cooking of food, the prohibition does not apply only to food, and under this heading one is, therefore, not allowed
a. to melt metal, wax or other materials,
b. to heat metal in such a way that it can become red-hot or
c. to dry clothes or wood on, or next to, a stove.

classification of vessels

2. For the purposes of this chapter, it is necessary to distinguish between different vessels, according to the manner in which they are used:

   a. K^eli rishon

      1) The pot or other vessel in which food, whether solid or liquid, has been cooked is known as a *k^eli rishon,* even if it is no longer on the fire, provided its temperature is 45 degrees centigrade or more.

      2) A pot or other vessel which is on the fire should have applied to it the restrictions which apply to a *k^eli rishon,* even if its temperature is lower than 45 degrees centigrade.

      3) It is often forbidden to empty the contents of a *k^eli rishon* onto a food or liquid.

   b. K^eli sheini

      1) Any pot or other vessel into which food is transferred from a *k^eli rishon* is known as a *k^eli sheini.*

      2) Pouring out of a *k^eli sheini* may also sometimes involve the prohibition against cooking.

   c. K^eli sh^elishi

      A pot or other vessel into which food is transferred from a *k^eli sheini* is known as a *k^eli sh^elishi.*

classification of foods

3. Distinctions must also be drawn with regard to the existing state of the food or liquid to be cooked, between

   a. a liquid which has not yet been fully cooked,

   b. a fully cooked liquid which is still warm,

   c. a fully cooked liquid which has become completely cold,

   d. a solid which has not yet been fully cooked and

   e. a fully cooked solid, whether still warm or completely cold.

cooking appliances

4. *a.* Cooking is prohibited, whether it be by means of a kerosene heater, a gas or electric stove or hotplate, a steamer, or any similar appliance.

   b. Unless otherwise mentioned, it makes no difference whether the fire is covered or uncovered.

GENERAL PRINCIPLES

5. *a.* The stage of cooking at which the prohibition is trans- *stages of* gressed depends upon whether what is being cooked is a *cooking* liquid or a solid.

   b. 1) As a rule, with liquids one transgresses the prohibition against cooking even if the liquids only reach a temperature of 45 degrees centigrade (113 degrees Fahrenheit).

     2) In the case of solids, the transgression takes place when they become one-third cooked.

   c. Additional cooking is also forbidden, up to the stage where the liquid or food is fully cooked, as we shall see below.

6. *a.* No food or liquid which has not been fully cooked may be *food or liquid* put into a *keli rishon* even if the food or liquid is hot and *not fully* the *keli rishon* is not standing on the fire. *cooked*

   b. In the circumstances set out in paragraph 53 below, the same applies in relation to a *keli sheini*.

7. *a.* The prohibition against cooking does not apply to a fully *fully cooked* cooked liquid, even if its temperature has dropped below *liquids which* 45 degrees centigrade, so long as it has not completely *are still* cooled off since being cooked. *warm*

   b. Nonetheless, such a liquid should not be poured into a pot which is standing on the fire.

8. *a.* The prohibition against cooking does apply to a fully *fully cooked* cooked liquid *liquids which*

     1) which is completely cold **or** *are cold*

     2) which, after having become completely cold, is partially warmed up again, even on Shabbath (in a permissible manner).

   b. Consequently,

     1) whether or not the *keli rishon* is standing on the fire, one may not

       a) pour such a liquid into a *keli rishon* **nor**

         b) empty into such a liquid the contents of a *kᵉli rishon*, but

   2) one may

         a) pour such a liquid into a *kᵉli sheini* **or**

         b) empty into it the contents of a *kᵉli sheini.*

distinction applied to boiled liquids

9. It follows from the two preceding paragraphs that

   a. a boiled liquid which has completely cooled off may not be put into a *kᵉli rishon*, whereas

   b. 1) a boiling liquid or

      2) a boiled liquid which has not completely cooled off

   may be put into a *kᵉli rishon* which is not standing on the fire.

fully cooked solids

10. *a.* The prohibition against cooking does not apply to a fully cooked solid, even if it is altogether cold.

   b. In spite of this, even if the solid is still warm, it should not be put into a pot or pan which is standing on the fire.

baked, fried or roasted food

11. It is forbidden to cook food even if it has already been completely baked, fried or roasted, as explained in paragraph 59 below.

KELI RISHON

when on the fire

12. *a.* 1) One is not permitted to put anything onto the fire (except in the circumstances described in paragraphs 18 to 22 below) or into a pot or pan which is on the fire.

   2) It does not matter whether it is

      a) liquid or solid,

      b) cooked or uncooked,

      c) hot or cold.

   3) The prohibition applies even if the intention is merely to warm up, or take the chill off, food and remove it from the fire before it reaches a temperature of 45 degrees centigrade (113 degrees Fahrenheit).

b. One should, therefore, not
   1) put salt or sugar or anything else into a pot standing on the fire, except in the cases mentioned in paragraph 16 below, nor
   2) warm up food by putting the dish in which it is contained into a pot of water standing on the fire.

13. a. On the other hand, one may place cold food near the fire in order to take the chill off or to warm it up, **but**   *warming food near the fire*
    b. if the food is not fully cooked, it must not be put in a position where it could reach 45 degrees centigrade,
       1) even if one leaves it there only for a very brief period of time and
       2) even if one has no intention of heating it to such an extent,
       and
    c. if the food consists of a fully cooked, but now cold, liquid, such as milk or soup, it must not be placed close enough to reach 45 degrees centigrade, unless
       1) one needs to warm it up for a baby, for a person who is unwell, or for a very urgent purpose,
       2) one's object is merely to warm it up or take the chill off **and**
       3) one is indeed careful to remove it before it reaches 45 degrees centigrade.
    d. See also paragraph 37 below.

14. a. The following may not be put into a keli rishon, even if it is not standing on the fire: *what is prohibited when off the fire*
       1) any food or liquid which has not been fully cooked;
       2) any fully cooked liquid which has become completely cold.
    b. This prohibition is applicable despite the fact that one may intend to take the food out as soon as one has warmed it a little or removed its chill.
    c. One should avoid putting the products mentioned in

paragraph 49 below into a *k^eli rishon*, even if it is not on the fire.

what is permitted when off the fire

15. The following may be put into a *k^eli rishon*, but only if it is not standing on the fire:

   a. a fully cooked solid, even if cold;

   b. a fully cooked liquid which has not yet altogether cooled off.

transferring from one pot to another

16. *a.* If the contents of two pots standing on the fire are fully cooked, one may transfer food from one to the other if that other is standing on a covered fire (as defined in paragraph 18c below).

   b. Consequently, if food in a pot standing on a covered fire is becoming dried up, one can

     1) gently pour boiling water into it from an urn which is also standing on the fire or

     2) take water out of the urn with a spoon or ladle and pour it into the pot, so long as the spoon or ladle is clean and dry. (In this connection see also paragraph 33 below.)

   c. If one wishes to use for the Friday evening meal only part of the food which has cooked in a large pot, one may empty what is not required into a smaller pot and put it on the fire for the next day's meal, provided

     1) that the smaller pot is clean and dry **and**

     2) that one complies carefully with all the rules enumerated in paragraph 18 below for putting food back on the fire.

PUTTING A KELI RISHON
BACK ON THE FIRE

ovens and stoves

17. *a.* One should not put any food into a warm oven (whether gas or electric), even if it has just been removed from the fire or from the oven itself.

   b. If food which was not fully cooked was put into the oven before Shabbath, then, in the event that the oven is opened or opens by itself, it is forbidden to close it again, as long as there is a possibility that the food in the oven has still not become fully cooked. (For ovens with thermostats see paragraph 29 below.)

   c. Putting food back onto a stove is treated more leniently, and we shall see that a distinction is made between

     1) what one **should** do, if at all practicable, and

     2) what one is **permitted** to do if one finds oneself in a situation where full compliance with all the rules has become impossible or would result in hardship.

18. Generally, a pot containing food, which has been removed from the fire, should not be put back unless the following conditions are fulfilled: *five conditions*

   a. At the time when the pot was removed there was an intention to put it back. *a. intention to replace*

   b. The pot continues to be held in the hand until replaced, although, while being held, it may be placed on the table or any other dry place except the floor. *b. holding in hand*

   c. The fire on which the pot is replaced is covered by a material, such as asbestos, on which one is not accustomed to cook during the week, but which is only used to leave pots on in order to stop them from growing cold.* (See also paragraph 25 below relating to special types of electric plates.) *c. fire covered*

   d. The food in the pot is fully cooked. (If the contents include chicken bones which after being well cooked become soft and edible, one should take care that they too have been fully cooked and are fit to eat.) *d. food fully cooked*

   e. The food has not completely cooled off and is still slightly warm. *e. food still warm*

---

* If the flame is uncovered, one may cover it on Shabbath and likewise a cover may be transferred from one flame to another; however,

a. a cover may not be placed on a flame which is strong enough to make it red-hot or white-hot and

b. one must be careful when covering a flame on Shabbath to ensure that the flame does not, as a result, become smaller, as is likely to happen in the case, for example, of a paraffin stove. (See Chapter 13, paragraph 33.)

19. If **either**

    a. one did not, when removing the pot, have the intention to put it back on the fire (a breach of condition *a* above) **or**

    b. one has let go of the pot after putting it down on the table or, for instance, on a chair (a breach of condition *b*),

then, if the food is needed, the pot may, nevertheless, be replaced, provided that, in each case, the other four conditions are fulfilled.

20. Where neither condition *a* nor condition *b* of paragraph 18 has been complied with, the pot may not be replaced on the fire, unless

    a. one would otherwise have no warm food for Shabbath **and**

    b. the remaining three conditions, which are absolutely indispensable, have been fulfilled.

21. If a pot containing fully cooked food is standing on a flame which is too small, it may be transferred onto a larger flame that is properly covered, as described in paragraph 18*c* above.

22. *a.* Often, the cover on a fire extends beyond the flame and, before Shabbath, dishes or pots are placed on it in such a way that they are not directly over the flame.

    b. Such dishes or pots may be moved and stood over the flame on Shabbath, as long as

      1) their contents are fully cooked **and**

      2) the temperature at the position from which they are being moved is at least 45 degrees centigrade (113 degrees Fahrenheit).

23. *a.* Should the flame underneath a pot containing fully cooked food go out, so long as the pot is still slightly warm one may keep it warm by standing it on top of a pot of food which is on another flame. (In this connection see also paragraph 36 below.)

b. 1) Where there is no other pot, but there is another flame, whether covered or not, one should place over it something

   a) which diminishes the heat and

   b) which makes it apparent that one is not placing the pot on the fire in the same way as one normally would during the rest of the week.

   2) Thus, one can put a metal dish upside down on the fire and stand the pot on that. (See paragraph 38 below.)

c. If the flame goes out on Shabbath and no other practical possibility exists, one may

   1) stand the pot on a fire covered in the way described in paragraph 18*c* above, or

   2) even cover a fire in such a way prior to standing the pot on it.

d. One is not, however, allowed on Shabbath to wrap a pot in a cloth to keep it warm, even though it has until now been standing on the fire. (See paragraphs 65 and 66 below.)

ELECTRIC STOVES AND PLATES

24. *a.* An electric stove is considered to be an uncovered fire for the purposes of paragraph 18 above, even if the electric elements are not visible. *electric stoves*

b. One is therefore not permitted to put back a pot of food which has been removed, unless the cooking surface is properly covered as described in paragraph 18*c*.

25. *a.* 1) This does not apply to the type of electric plate which many people are accustomed to use on Shabbath and which is designed merely to keep food warm. *special Shabbath plates*

   2) Such plates are not used for cooking and, indeed, one cannot vary their temperature.

   3) Pots may be replaced on them, even if they have no additional covering, provided that the remaining conditions in paragraph 18 above are observed.

4) A pot which is not just being replaced may not be put on a plate of this kind on Shabbath even if
   a) the food is fully cooked **and**
   b) one's sole intention is to remove the chill and no more.

b. As to covering pots standing on such an electric plate with a cloth, see paragraphs 65 and 66 below.

c. 1) Moving a pot on an electric plate of this kind into a hotter position is permitted only if
   a) the food which it contains is fully cooked **and**
   b) the temperature at the position from which it is being moved is at least 45 degrees centigrade (113 degrees Fahrenheit).

2) This question frequently arises when the beans in a pot of *cholent* prepared for Shabbath are not yet altogether cooked, in which case the pot may not be moved to a hotter position on the plate.

time-switches

26. a. Before Shabbath, cooked food may be placed on an electric stove, even if the stove is not yet operating and will start to do so only when the current is automatically connected by a time-switch on Shabbath, but the stove must be properly covered, as set out in paragraph 18c above.

b. On Shabbath itself, the food may not be put on the stove, despite the fact that the stove may not yet be operating and may be properly covered.

c. We shall see, in Chapter 31, paragraph 8, that a non-Jew may be requested to put fully cooked food on a stove which has not yet started to operate, even if
   1) the stove is not covered **and**
   2) the food has become completely cold.

Yom Tov

27. On Yom Tov,

a. one may cook, within the permitted limits, on an electric stove
   1) which has been on since before Yom Tov or

2) which has been turned on automatically by means of a time-switch, but

b. one may neither lower nor raise the temperature, since a change in either direction is usually effected by the turning off of one element and the lighting of another in its place. (See Chapter 13, paragraphs 3 and 10.)

ESCAPING GAS

28. a. One may turn off the tap of a gas burner which has gone out, so as to stop the gas from escaping. *if flame goes out*

b. Where possible, this should be done with a variation from the usual manner, for instance by turning off the tap with the back of the hand or with the elbow.

THERMOSTATICALLY CONTROLLED OVENS

29. A gas or electric oven regulated by a thermostat should not be used at all on Shabbath, since opening its door is likely to increase the size of the flame or turn on the electricity, as the case may be. *thermostats on Shabbath*

30. A thermostatically controlled oven may be used on Yom Tov, and it is allowed both *thermostats on Yom Tov*

a. to open it in order to put in, inspect or take out food and

b. to close it afterwards.

STIRRING AND TAKING FOOD
OUT OF A KELI RISHON

31. a. 1) Stirring food which is not fully cooked violates the prohibition against cooking, if it is in a *keli rishon*. *food not fully cooked*

2) The removal of any such food from a *keli rishon* with the aid of any instrument or vessel is also prohibited.

b. Both actions are forbidden,

1) whether the pot is standing on the fire (covered or otherwise) or

2) whether the pot has been removed from the fire, so

long as its temperature has not dropped below 45 degrees centigrade (113 degrees Fahrenheit).

fully cooked food
32. *a.* The prohibition against stirring the contents of a *k\u1d49li rishon* or removing food from it with the assistance of an instrument or vessel has been extended to the case where the food is fully cooked, but only if the pot is standing on the fire (whether covered or not).

b. One should
1) first remove the pot from the fire and
2) then take out as much as one needs, either with the aid of an instrument or vessel or by pouring from it into a dish or plate.
3) Finally, provided all the conditions enumerated in paragraph 18 above are satisfied, one may replace the pot on the fire.

c. If replacement of the pot on the fire would be forbidden because of the absence of a suitable cover, there is room for relaxing the prohibition and taking food out of the pot with a spoon or ladle while it is still on the fire, on condition that the food is indeed fully cooked.

boiled water
33. *a.* The rules relating to the removal of boiled water from an urn standing on the fire are more lenient.

b. 1) Warm water may be removed from the urn even with a spoon or ladle* and
2) any water which is left over in the spoon or ladle may be returned to the urn, so long as
   a) the fire is adequately covered, as defined in paragraph 18*c* above,
   b) the water being returned has not completely cooled down **and**,
   c) when the water was removed, one intended to return whatever was left over.

---

*The spoon or ladle used should be *parve*, that is to say, not one which is used for either meat or dairy dishes.

34. *a.* Whenever it is permitted to remove food or water from a *keli rishon*, one should ensure that any instrument or vessel used for the purpose is free from the remains of uncooked food or liquid. *instruments or vessels put into a keli rishon*

    b. This is so even if the food or water is being removed after the pot has been taken off the fire.

    c. See also paragraph 48 below.

COVERING A KELI RISHON

35. *a.* Unless one is absolutely sure that the food in a *keli rishon* is fully cooked, one may not cover it with a lid, a plate or anything else, either while it is still on the fire or after it has been removed, since covering the pot results, in the former case, in the intensification of the cooking process and, in the latter, in its continuation. *when permitted*

    b. If the food contains chicken bones which one can eat when they are well cooked, one ought to check that these too have become sufficiently soft to be edible (as in paragraph 18*d* above).

PLACING POTS ON TOP OF
ONE ANOTHER ON THE FIRE

36. *a.* A pot containing cold food may be placed on top of another pot standing on the fire, on Shabbath, in order to remove the chill, even if the contents are uncooked, provided that, in this position, there is no possibility of the food's reaching a temperature of 45 degrees centigrade (113 degrees Fahrenheit). *warming food on Shabbath*

    b. Fully cooked food which is still partly warm, or in the case of a solid even if it has grown completely cold or been frozen, may be placed on top of a pot standing on the fire, despite the fact that it will reach a high temperature, so long as it is not in a position where it will roast.

    c. Although in the above circumstances it is permissible to place one pot on top of another on the fire, the top pot may not be wrapped in a cloth, even if the undermost pot has been so wrapped since before Shabbath. (See paragraphs 65 and 66 below.)

dissolving fat 37. a. A pot of food containing a large quantity of congealed fat should not be put on top of another pot which is on the fire—except where this restriction would result in hardship—since in normal circumstances melting is not permitted on Shabbath.

b. Nonetheless, if fat has been melted down, there is nothing wrong with eating it.

c. Where a pot contains only a small amount of fat, which mingles with the rest of the food as it melts, there is no objection to its being placed on top of another pot on the fire.

d. One may also dissolve a sauce which it is customary to eat in a congealed state, such as fish sauce.

keeping the 38. a. One may not,
upper pot
warm

   1) under any circumstance, remove the undermost of two pots standing one on top of the other on the fire and put the upper pot on the fire in its place, **even if**

   a) the food inside is fully cooked and is hotter than 45 degrees centigrade,

   b) the fire is properly covered **and**

   c) both pots have been on the fire since before Shabbath, **nor**

   2) keep the upper pot warm by wrapping it, even before Shabbath, in a cloth. (Regarding this see also paragraphs 65 and 66 below.)

b. What one may do is transfer the upper pot onto another pot of food which is also standing on the fire (it being understood that one complies with the rules set out in paragraph 36 above).

c. If there is no such other pot, one may, even though it is Shabbath, put a metal dish upside down on the fire (as in paragraph 23 above) and place the pot on that, so long as

   1) the food inside is fully cooked and still partly warm, **and**

[14]

2) one is careful not to put a metal dish on a flame which is powerful enough to make it red-hot.

WATER HEATERS

39. *a.* 1) Electric, gas, oil and paraffin-fired water heaters or boilers are usually so constructed that, when hot water is drawn from them, cold water flows in.
2) This cold water is then heated to a high temperature inside the boiler or tank.
3) Where this is an inevitable consequence, hot water should not be removed on Shabbath even when the heater or boiler is not switched on.

when removal of hot water is forbidden

b. Hot water may be removed from a boiler or tank on Shabbath if all the following conditions are satisfied.
1) The boiler or tank must be made in such a way that hot water can be run off without its being automatically replaced by an inflow of cold water.
2) The tap through which the cold water enters the boiler or tank must in fact be properly turned off.
3) One must also be careful, when removing hot water, to keep the tap through which cold water is extracted from the boiler or heater properly turned off, in order to avoid the hot water's mixing with the cold water, thereby heating it to a forbidden degree (45 degrees centigrade or 113 degrees Fahrenheit).
4) a) Where both hot and cold water come out of the same pipe, the initial flow which comes out after the hot tap is turned on should be allowed to run to waste.
   b) If this initial flow, which might well include hitherto unboiled, cold water, were retained in a vessel or receptacle, or if the sink or basin were stopped up before it had drained out, it would be heated beyond the permitted temperature by the hot water subsequently pouring onto it from the boiler or heater (which, as explained in paragraph 41 below, is treated as a *keli rishon*).

when removal of hot water is permitted

separate hot and cold pipes

c. It is preferable to install separate hot and cold taps and pipes so that hot and cold water do not come into contact with each other inside the pipes.

lukewarm water

d. There is no need to turn off the cold water taps when removing warm water from a boiler or heater if
1) none of the water inside the apparatus is as hot as 45 degrees centigrade,
2) the apparatus is not operating when the hot water is removed **and**
3) the apparatus will not be operated during the course of Shabbath, for example by means of a time-switch.

adjustment of thermostat

e. 1) If the thermostat is adjusted before Shabbath so that the temperature of the water cannot reach 45 degrees centigrade, one is permitted to use the hot water regardless of the fact that cold water will flow into the boiler or tank and be warmed by the heater, as there is no possibility of its reaching the prohibited temperature.
2) The water heated in this way must not, however, be used on Shabbath for washing oneself, but only for washing dishes, cutlery and the like. (See Chapter 14, paragraph 2.)

thermostatically regulated urns

40. A thermostatically regulated electric urn may be used on Shabbath, so long as
a. the water inside was boiled before Shabbath and has not completely cooled down
b. no cold water enters the apparatus during Shabbath **and**
c. the tap through which water is drawn is not at the very bottom of the apparatus, since otherwise the heating element is liable to burn out when all of the water is removed and one may come to add water on Shabbath to prevent this from happening.
(See also paragraphs 39 above and 63 below.)

*water heater classed as a k*e*li rishon*

41. a. The prohibitions relating to water poured from a *k*e*li rishon* should be applied to any hot water drawn from a boiler, heater or urn, as mentioned in paragraphs 39 and

40 above, if its temperature is not less than 45 degrees centigrade.

b. This is so even if, on its way out of the apparatus, the water has to pass through a considerable length of piping.

c. The rules with regard to pouring water out of a *keli rishon* are set out in paragraphs 46 to 50 below.

42. a. Should one leave on, or mistakenly turn on, the hot-water tap of a boiler or heater in which water is being heated on Shabbath, one may not turn it off again on Shabbath, if the hot water pouring out is being replaced by cold water.

taps turned on by mistake

b. The reason for this is that stopping the outflow of hot water automatically cuts off the continuous inflow of additional cold water and this, in turn, results in the heating up of the cold water which has already flowed in.

43. a. Immediately after Shabbath, one may use hot water heated on Shabbath in a boiler, heater or urn which was turned on during Shabbath (by means of a time-switch for instance), provided that the apparatus is of a design that does not permit the easy regulation of the water temperature up or down.

use after Shabbath of water heated on Shabbath

b. This water can be used after Shabbath not only for washing dishes, but also for washing oneself or for any other purpose.

44. a. 1) On Shabbath, it is forbidden to put a bottle to heat in an electric baby-bottle warmer which can reach a temperature of 45 degrees centigrade, even if it has been on since before Shabbath.

baby-bottle warmers and heating troughs

2) It is permitted before Shabbath to place a previously boiled-up bottle in such a warmer, for use on Shabbath.

3) On Shabbath, a bottle may be put to heat in a warmer which cannot reach a temperature of 45 degrees centigrade, if it was switched on or set before Shabbath.

4) Even when it is permitted to place a bottle in a warmer

on Shabbath, if it is thermostatically controlled it must be operating when the bottle is inserted.

b. The same principles apply to the use of specially designed water troughs, heated by steam or electricity, often employed in hotel or restaurant kitchens to heat food or to keep it warm.

solar energy heaters

45. *a.* It is advisable, on Shabbath, to refrain from taking hot water out of a heater operated by solar energy, if this results in its being replaced by a flow of cold water, which will be heated up by the hot water remaining in the tank.

b. Hot water may, however, be taken from such a heater on Shabbath, if

1) it is constructed in such a way that hot water can be removed without cold water entering **and**

2) the tap on the pipe through which cold water usually enters the tank is completely turned off.

c. 1) While hot water taken from a heater operated by solar energy should, for most purposes, be treated as water removed from a *k^eli rishon* (in which connection see paragraphs 46 to 50 below),

2) it, unlike water heated by a flame or in an electric boiler, should not be put into a *k^eli rishon*, even after the latter has been removed from the fire.

POURING FROM A KELI RISHON

when forbidden

46. *a.* One is forbidden to pour from a *k^eli rishon*, even if it is not standing on the fire, onto

1) a cold liquid, whether or not previously cooked or boiled, or

2) a solid which has not been fully cooked, since this results in the cooking or boiling of the surface onto which the pouring takes place.

b. Consequently,

1) one should be careful not to pour water from a *k^eli rishon* onto tea leaves which were not boiled up before Shabbath,

2) one should not pour from a *keli rishon* into a plate or cup which is not perfectly clean and dry and

3) thin cooked cereal (porridge) should not be warmed up by having hot water poured onto it from a *keli rishon*. (A *keli sheini* should be used instead, as explained in paragraph 57 below. See also Chapter 6, paragraph 13.)

47. *a.* One may pour from a *keli rishon*, even if it is standing on the fire, onto   *when permitted*
    1) a liquid which has not completely cooled down since being fully cooked (see paragraph 7 above) or
    2) a fully cooked solid, even if now cold.
    b. Consequently,
    1) it is permitted to put still-warm tea essence into a cup and to empty hot water onto it from an urn which is on the fire (although it is desirable, if one wishes to do this, to put the pot or cup containing the tea essence on top of the urn before Shabbath, to ensure that it really does stay warm) and
    2) it is likewise permitted to warm dried-up cooked cereal (porridge) by pouring hot water into it from a *keli rishon*. (See also Chapter 6, paragraph 13.)

48. Special attention should be paid to a ladle with which food is taken out of a *keli rishon*.   *ladles*
    a. As mentioned in paragraph 34 above, when it is first inserted into the *keli rishon* it must be free of the remains of uncooked food or liquid.
    b. If it is put into the pot again, one should pay attention that any food or liquid remaining on it should not be cold.
    c. 1) Since the ladle is inserted into a *keli rishon*, and all the more so if it remains in the pot for any length of time, it should be treated as a *keli rishon*. (See, however, paragraph 59 below.)
    2) Accordingly, one may not empty the contents of the ladle onto any food or liquid which has not been fully

cooked, regardless of whether such food or liquid is hot or cold.

products cooked during manufacture

49. *a.* One should refrain from emptying water from a *k^eli rishon* onto such products as sugar, saccharin, instant coffee, soup powder, milk powder or instant cocoa, even if they have already been cooked in the process of manufacture. (See also paragraph 56 below.)

b. The hot water should first be put into a *k^eli sheini* and then these substances can be added.

warming food with hot water

50. *a.* One may warm up a bottle of milk by standing it in an empty pot and pouring boiling water over it, even from a *k^eli rishon,* and one may change the hot water as many times as necessary, in order to increase the temperature of the milk, but

1) one must be careful that the hot water does not completely cover the bottle (see paragraph 65 below),

2) it is forbidden to stand the bottle in a *k^eli rishon* which is on the fire and

3) it is also forbidden to stand the bottle in a *k^eli rishon* which is not on the fire, unless there is so much milk in the bottle that it is impossible for it to reach a temperature of 45 degrees centigrade (113 degrees Fahrenheit).

b. One is permitted to put boiling water into the hollow bottom section of a child's feeding plate, in order to heat up the food in the upper section. (See also Chapter 11, paragraph 41.)

MIXING HOT AND COLD WATER

putting hot water into cold

51. Hot water may be poured into a large quantity of cold water, even out of a *k^eli rishon* standing on the fire, provided that the cold water is not heated thereby to a temperature of 45 degrees centigrade (113 degrees Fahrenheit) or more.

pouring cold water into hot

52. *a.* Conversely, a large quantity of cold water may be poured into hot water, so long as

1) the hot water is not in a k*e*li rishon which is standing on the fire **and**

2) there is so much cold water that it cannot be heated to a temperature of 45 degrees centigrade by the hot water.

b. When pouring the cold water into the hot, one should be careful to do so in one swift action, since, if it is poured in slowly, there may be sufficient time for the hot water to warm up the first few drops of the cold water to a forbidden degree, before the rest of the cold water is added.

KELI SHEINI

53. a. There are certain foods which become cooked even in a k*e*li sheini.

uncooked food or liquid

b. As we are not sure which they are, there is a general rule that we treat the prohibition against cooking as applying to anything which is not cooked, even when put into a k*e*li sheini, if indeed the contents of the k*e*li sheini have a temperature of 45 degrees centigrade (113 degrees Fahrenheit) or more.

c. One, therefore, ought not to

1) put a raw egg into a plate containing hot food, nor

2) put tea leaves that are in a bag or a strainer, or mint leaves or ordinary cocoa, none of which have been pre-cooked, into a cup of hot milk or water which is a k*e*li sheini (see also Chapter 3, paragraph 58), nor

3) put a slice of lemon into tea which is in a k*e*li sheini.

d. There are certain exceptions to this rule, the most important of them in practice being water and oil, which may be put into a k*e*li sheini even if they have not been boiled.

54. a. Since both table salt and cooking salt are boiled during the refining process, the rules set out in paragraphs 49 and 55 are applicable to them.

salt

b. There are various ways of manufacturing salt substitutes, and the rules which apply to each brand depend on whether or not it has been boiled during processing.

c. So far as unrefined salt is concerned, the prohibitions referred to in paragraph 53 above apply.

fully cooked **55.** a. We have seen, in paragraph 8 above, that the prohibition
liquids which against cooking also applies to fully cooked liquids which
are cold have grown completely cold.

b. Such liquids may, however, be put into warm food in a *k^eli sheini*.

c. Common examples are boiled milk, and tea essence which was either boiled up before Shabbath or made before Shabbath by pouring boiling water from a *k^eli rishon* over tea leaves (that were subsequently removed).

d. Processed, sweetened lemon juice, soup essence and sterilized milk, which are cooked during the course of manufacture, fall within the same category.

e. There are grounds for the view that pasteurized milk, too, may be poured into a *k^eli sheini*.

f. The above applies also to products which were boiled in manufacture, but are no longer in a liquid state, such as sugar, saccharin, soup powder or cubes, milk powder and instant cocoa, coffee and tea.

pouring from **56.** a. It is preferable to avoid pouring the contents of a *k^eli*
a k^eli rishon *rishon* into a *k^eli sheini* containing any of the products or
into a k^eli substances mentioned in paragraph 55 above.
sheini

b. For example, one should not pour hot water from a *k^eli rishon* into a cup of tea prepared from cold essence or from instant tea powder.

KELI SHELISHI,

POURING FROM A KELI SHEINI

AND SOLIDS

k^eli sh^elishi
and pouring **57.** a. The rules relating to the prohibition against cooking are
from a k^eli relaxed in the cases of a *k^eli sh^elishi* and pouring from a
sheini *k^eli sheini*. (See paragraph 2 above for definitions.)

b. Nevertheless, there are halachic authorities who hold that one should not

1) pour the contents of a *keli sheini* having a temperature of 45 degrees centigrade (113 degrees Fahrenheit) or more over a raw egg, unboiled tea leaves or food such as herring which is so heavily salted that it cannot be eaten without rinsing, nor should one
2) put these items into a *keli shelishi* having a like temperature.

58. *a.* Solids, such as potatoes, pieces of meat or whole beans, *solids* which have a temperature of at least 45 degrees centigrade should generally be treated in the same manner as a *keli rishon.*
b. This is so even if the solids have been put into a *keli sheini* or into a *keli shelishi*, since they store the heat within themselves.
c. Consequently, one should not

1) pour cold soup (see paragraph 8 above) onto a piece of hot meat in a plate,
2) put a piece of hot meat into a plate of cold soup,
3) put butter or seasoning onto hot potatoes, nor
4) place pickled gherkin or uncooked salad on hot meat or *kugel.*
d. Nevertheless

1) one may put salt on hot food and
2) there are those who rule that tomato ketchup (which is cooked during the manufacturing process) may be poured onto hot meat.

COOKING FOOD WHICH HAS BEEN
BAKED, FRIED OR ROASTED

59. *a.* In general, as we have seen in paragraph 10 above, the *baked, fried* prohibition against cooking does not apply to an already *and roasted* fully cooked solid. *food*
b. It is, however, forbidden to cook something which has previously been baked, fried or roasted.

    c. Likewise, one may not bake, fry or roast something, even if it has previously been cooked or boiled.

    d. Thus, it is not permitted
        1) to put bread, cookies (biscuits) or matzoth into a *k^eli rishon* or *k^eli sheini* containing hot soup, tea or the like nor
        2) to pour the contents of a *k^eli rishon* onto them.

    e. For the purposes of this paragraph, there are grounds for treating a ladle or spoon which has been dipped into a *k^eli rishon*—but not left in it for any length of time—as a *k^eli sheini*, so that one would, for example, be allowed to put bread into soup which has been ladled onto a plate from a *k^eli rishon*. (Compare paragraph 48 above.)

roasting on top of a pot

60. Cooked meat without gravy may not be placed on the lid of a pot standing on the fire, since it will now roast in the dry heat.

deep frying

61. *a.* Food which has been deep fried in oil is treated, for the purposes of the rule in paragraph 59 above, as if it has been cooked in water.

    b. Consequently, noodles which have been fried in oil or ready-to-serve soup almonds may be put into a *k^eli rishon*, provided that it is not standing on the fire.

toasting

62. Toasting bread or making it into rusks is forbidden, because, even if the bread is not near enough to the fire to scorch, its texture will change and it will harden.

LEAVING POTS ON THE FIRE BEFORE SHABBATH

advisable limitations

63. *a.* 1) Many fine distinctions are made in the rules about leaving pots on the fire before Shabbath.
    2) To avoid complications, it is best to ensure
        a) that before Shabbath the pot is placed on a fire which is covered in the manner described in paragraph 18c above **and**
        b) that the contents of the pot, whether solid or

liquid, have previously been fully cooked or boiled.

b. It is permissible to leave a pot or urn even on an uncovered fire before Shabbath, *relaxation of limitations*

  1) if

    a) one does not wish to replace the pot on the fire after removing it on Shabbath **and**

    b) the contents of the pot are at least half cooked, or, if there is no other possibility, one-third cooked, before Shabbath **or**

  2) if

    a) one wishes to leave the urn on the fire without removing it during the whole of Shabbath **and**

    b) the water inside is heated to a temperature of at least 45 degrees centigrade (113 degrees Fahrenheit) before Shabbath.

c. In these two latter cases, it is, however, preferable to place the pot or the urn on the uncovered fire a considerable time before the commencement of Shabbath.

WRAPPING POTS TO KEEP THEM WARM

64. It will be seen from the following paragraphs that, in determining whether or not one is allowed to keep pots warm by wrapping them up, one distinguishes *various categories of wrapping*

a. between wrapping before Shabbath and wrapping on Shabbath,

b. between wrapping which results in an increase in the temperature and wrapping which merely preserves the existing heat,

c. between wrapping a k*e*li rishon and wrapping a k*e*li sheini and

d. between wrapping a pot containing food whose temperature is 45 degrees centigrade (113 degrees Fahrenheit) or more and wrapping a pot containing food whose temperature is less than 45 degrees centigrade.

65. a. On Shabbath, it is forbidden to wrap a pot of food on all sides in order to keep it warm, even if *basic rules*

    1) the wrapping does not bring about any increase in temperature **and**
    2) the food is fully cooked.
b. 1) One may not, even before Shabbath, wrap a pot in such a way that the temperature will increase.
    2) For example, one may not wrap a cloth around a pot which is standing on a flame (albeit covered) or on an electric plate.
c. 1) A pot of food may be kept warm by wrapping if
    a) this is done before Shabbath commences **and**
    b) the wrapping does not cause an increase in temperature, but merely preserves the existing heat.
    2) a) Consequently, before Shabbath, one may wrap a cloth around a pot which is not on the fire.
    b) This is permitted even if the pot wrapped is standing on another, steaming-hot pot, so long as the latter is not itself standing on the fire, but is losing heat all the time.
d. 1) The prohibition against wrapping applies, in general, to any method of keeping a container of food warm by completely covering it on all sides, no matter with what substance, even with other food.
    2) Thus, one may not heat an unopened can of food by totally immersing it in hot water, even if it is not standing on the fire.

permissible methods of wrapping **66.** *a.* The prohibition against wrapping is not applicable—and one may consequently wrap a pot of food, even on Shabbath, to keep it warm, whether or not it is standing on the fire—if the following three conditions are **all** satisfied:
1) either
    a) the pot is not covered on all sides **or**
    b) the material with which the pot is covered, or into which it is inserted, does not touch it on all sides;
2) the food is fully cooked;
3) it has not completely cooled off or it is a solid (for the reasons given in paragraphs 7 and 10 above).
b. Accordingly, one is allowed to put the pot into a metal

box standing on the fire, since, even if the box is closed, it
is not in contact with the walls of the pot on all sides.

   c. For the use of hot water to heat a bottle of milk for a child,
see paragraph 50 above.

67. A pot containing fully cooked food, which was wrapped in a   *rewrapping*
permissible manner prior to Shabbath, may be
   a. uncovered and then re-covered,
   b. re-covered if the covering has come off by itself,
   c. re-covered with other, warmer cloths and
   d. covered with additional cloths.

68. In case of need one may, on Shabbath, wrap even a *keli*   *wrapping a*
rishon to keep the food inside warm, so long as   *keli rishon*
   a. the temperature of the food is less than 45 degrees
centigrade **and**
   b. the wrapping is done in such a way that it retains the heat
but does not increase it.

69. *a.* Even on Shabbath, one may transfer food from a *keli*   *wrapping a*
rishon into a *keli sheini* and then wrap it in a manner   *keli sheini*
which does not increase the heat.
   b. Consequently, if the flame goes out on Shabbath and one
is afraid that the food on the stove will become too cold,
one may keep it warm by emptying it into another pot
which one then wraps in a cloth.

70. *a.* One may fill a thermos (vacuum flask) with hot water   *thermoses*
from a *keli rishon* on Shabbath, provided one ensures that
the thermos is completely dry inside before filling.
   b. Although its purpose is to retain heat, a thermos is
treated as a *keli sheini*.

71. *a.* It is, similarly, permitted to fill a hot water bottle on   *hot water*
Shabbath to warm one's bed, so long as the inside of the   *bottles*
bottle is perfectly dry.
   b. The application of a hot water bottle to a part of the body

for the relief of pain or an ailment is dealt with in Chapter 33, paragraph 15 and in Chapter 34, paragraph 11.

warming food by putting it in other food

72. *a.* The prohibition against keeping food warm by wrapping it applies in three sets of circumstances:

1) if a receptacle containing food is completely wrapped in, covered by or put inside any article or material, such as a cloth, a blanket, or a pillow;

2) if food which is not inside any receptacle is completely wrapped in, covered by or put inside any article or material (other than food), as could be done in the case of a boiled egg; or

3) if a receptacle containing food is put into other food in such a way that it is completely covered. (Compare paragraph 50 above.)

b. The prohibition does not apply if food which is not inside any receptacle is put into other food, even if the express intention in doing so is to warm it up.

c. One may, thus, warm cold meat on Shabbath by putting it into hot soup, as long as the soup is not on the fire.

COOLING

placing in cold water

73. *a.* A *k^eli sheini* containing hot food may be stood in another vessel containing cold water in order to cool it down, even if, as a result, the cold water may be warmed up slightly.

b. This may not, however, be done with a *k^eli rishon*, nor with a hot solid not in a receptacle, even if this would not warm up the cold water. (See paragraph 58 above.)

ice cubes

74. *a.* Ice cubes may be put into water or another liquid to cool it down, even though the ice will melt.

b. Nevertheless, one is not permitted to put ice into an empty cup with the object of drinking it when it has melted.

c. This prohibition applies not only on Shabbath, but also on Yom Tov.

d. See also Chapter 10, paragraphs 2 and 3.

Chapter 2

Laws of Cooking on Yom Tov

1. *a.* One may cook and bake on Yom Tov, so long as one *general* intends to eat some of the food on the same day. (See *principles* paragraphs 3 and 4 below and Chapter 28, paragraph 69.)

   b. It is, on the other hand, forbidden to cook and bake on Yom Tov for the next day, whether that day be
   1) an ordinary weekday,
   2) the second day of Rosh Hashana,
   3) *yom tov sheini shel galuyoth* (regarding which see Chapter 31, paragraphs 27 to 40), or
   4) Shabbath (except in the circumstances mentioned in paragraph 10 below).

   c. The lighting of a fire, for the purpose of cooking, on Yom Tov and the kindling of a flame from another flame which is already burning are discussed in Chapter 13, paragraphs 2 and 3.

2. *a.* Food whose taste will not deteriorate at all if it is cooked *food which* on the day before the Festival (for example, fruit soup) *will not spoil* should be prepared before Yom Tov. *if prepared*
   earlier

   b. If, however, through forgetfulness or lack of time, this was not done, one may prepare it on Yom Tov, provided one introduces some variation into the normal method employed.

   c. No such variation is necessary if the food could not have been prepared before Yom Tov, either
   1) due to there having been no physical possibility of doing so, or
   2) due to its being required on Yom Tov for unexpected guests.

   d. 1) The requirement that food which will not spoil should be prepared before Yom Tov is a rabbinical one.

2) The reason for it is that a person would otherwise be tempted to neglect the preparation of food before Yom Tov, even where this would be perfectly feasible, leaving it to be done on Yom Tov, when he would have the available time.

3) The result would be that a person would spend the whole of Yom Tov preparing food and would not leave himself any opportunity of fulfilling the positive mitzva to enjoy the Festival.

cooking more than necessary

3. *a.* 1) It is permissible to cook a pot full of meat on Yom Tov, even though one only needs one piece, since the taste of the gravy is improved by the addition of more meat.

2) This is so even if the additional meat not required for the Festival is put into the pot when it is already standing on the fire, so long as one does not actually say that the additional meat is being cooked for after Yom Tov.

b. The same applies to any other food which is improved by the cooking of a larger quantity at the same time.

heating water

4. *a.* An urn or kettle may be filled to the top with water and heated up, even if one only needs to use one cupful, on condition that

1) the urn or kettle already contains the full quantity of water to be heated when it is put on the fire, **and**

2) filling the urn or kettle with more than the required cupful of water does not entail an additional action involving effort (as would be the case if the urn or kettle were filled by the jugful rather than directly from the tap).

b. To add water which will not be used on the Festival to an urn or kettle of water which is already standing on the fire is forbidden, because this action can in no way be justified as being necessary for Yom Tov.

c. The use of water heaters on Yom Tov is discussed in paragraph 7 below.

5. *a.* One should not, on Yom Tov,

    1) bake or cook food for a non-Jew to eat,

    2) add food for a non-Jew to what one is baking or cooking for oneself, even in the same pot, nor

    3) invite a non-Jew to a meal (even if everything is ready), lest one come to cook additional food for him.

  b. On Shabbath, on the other hand, it is permitted to invite a non-Jew to a meal.

  c. One is allowed, on Yom Tov, to send a non-Jew food which one has prepared for oneself on Yom Tov or which was prepared before Yom Tov, but only if

    1) the food is delivered by a non-Jew, **or**

    2) the existence of an *eiruv* conforming with the rules set out in Chapter 17 makes it permissible for the food to be delivered by a Jew.

  d. An exception is made in the case of a non-Jewish domestic (home-help) or servant, for whom one may add food to what one is cooking for oneself, but only

    1) in the same pot,

    2) before the pot is placed on the fire **and**

    3) if one's relationship with the non-Jew is not such that one might come to cook for him or her separately.

6. *a.* Just as it is forbidden to cook for or invite a non-Jew on Yom Tov, so is it forbidden to cook for or invite a Jew who violates Shabbath in public.*

  b. A restaurateur who, before Yom Tov, receives orders for food to be eaten on the Festival should consult a qualified rabbinical authority as to what he should do with regard to cooking on Yom Tov for a non-Jew or for a person who does not observe Shabbath or Yom Tov.

7. *a.* On Yom Tov, subject to the important provisos in subparagraph *b* below, use may be made of water heaters and boilers of all types,

---

*A qualified rabbinical authority should be consulted as to the scope of this term in relation to the specific circumstances of each case.

1) whether or not they are in the process of heating the water,

2) even if they will subsequently be activated by a thermostat, and

3) regardless of the fact that cold water is replacing the hot water flowing out and will itself be heated up.

b. However,

1) it is forbidden to switch on a heating element directly and,

2) if the turning on or off of the tap causes a flame to be lit or extinguished, the heater may not be operated, since, even on Yom Tov, it is prohibited to extinguish the flame by turning off the tap. (See Chapter 13, paragraph 15.)

c. See Chapter 1, paragraphs 39 to 45 for the use of water heaters on Shabbath.

medicines   8. The preparation on Yom Tov of medicines for persons who are unwell, but not seriously ill, is dealt with in Chapter 33, paragraphs 24 and 25.

other   9. a. For the use of an electric stove on Yom Tov see Chapter 1,
references   paragraph 27 and Chapter 13, paragraphs 3 and 10.

b. For the use of a thermostatically operated stove on Yom Tov see Chapter 1, paragraph 30.

c. For the lowering of a flame for the purpose of cooking on Yom Tov see Chapter 13, paragraph 10.

d. For the use of central-heating radiators on Yom Tov see Chapter 23, paragraphs 18 to 31.

EIRUV TAVSHILIN

Yom Tov   10. a. As we have seen above, one may not bake or cook or
occurring on   prepare food on Yom Tov for the next day, even if that
Friday   next day be Shabbath.

b. Nevertheless, if, on the day before Yom Tov, one prepares or sets aside some cooked food and some bread (or matza) for the Shabbath, one may, on Yom Tov, cook or bake or prepare additional food for that Shabbath.

c. The food which is set aside or prepared before Yom Tov, for Shabbath, is known as an *eiruv tavshilin*.

11. While, in principle, the obligation to make an *eiruv tavshilin* applies to every individual, *who makes an eiruv tavshilin?*

    a. the *eiruv* made by the head of the household covers also his wife and all those living in the house with him and

    b. two or more individuals or families whose food, at the time of cooking, belongs to just one of them, or to two or more of them in common, should make only one *eiruv* between them.

12. a. If, having made an *eiruv tavshilin*, one is preparing food on Yom Tov for Shabbath, one should take care to finish well before Shabbath commences. *cooking to be finished early*

    b. However, if a delay has taken place and hardship would otherwise be caused, one may cook and prepare the food until shortly before Shabbath is due to begin, all the more so on the second day of Yom Tov.

    c. As mentioned in Chapter 1, paragraph 63, one ought, wherever possible, to ensure that food which is to be left on the fire, whether liquid or solid, is fully boiled or cooked before the commencement of Shabbath.

13. a. The *eiruv tavshilin* should be kept at least until one has finished all the cooking, baking, lighting and other preparations one is making on that Friday for Shabbath. *until when eiruv tavshilin is needed*

    b. Should the *eiruv tavshilin* be eaten or lost before that time, it once more becomes forbidden to cook, bake or make other preparations for Shabbath.

    c. It is the custom to use the bread (or matza) of the *eiruv* as one of the two loaves required for the last of the three Shabbath meals.

14. The appropriate blessing must be said when making an *eiruv tavshilin*. *blessing*

two-day Yom
Tov before
Shabbath

15. If Yom Tov is on Thursday and Friday, the *eiruv* should be made on the Wednesday, but all the cooking and baking for Shabbath should be done on the Friday and not on the Thursday.

source for
details

16. A detailed exposition of the laws relating to *eiruv tavshilin* can be found in the *Shulchan Aruch, Orach Chaim,* Chapter 527.

Chapter 3

Laws of Selection on Shabbath

INTRODUCTORY COMMENT

The laws of selection on Yom Tov are dealt with separately in Chapter 4 below.

GENERAL PRINCIPLES

1. *a.* It is, in general, forbidden to separate or sort out two kinds of articles which are mixed together.
   b. This is so no matter what the articles are,
      1) whether they are kinds of food,
      2) whether they are something other than food, such as utensils or clothes, or
      3) whether they consist of food mixed with something which one does not wish to eat.
   c. Selection is permitted if it is done in circumstances where it is considered to be in the course of the normal use of the article being selected, as explained in the next paragraph.

   distinction between forbidden and permitted selection

2. *a.* Selection is looked upon as being in the course of normal use (and is consequently permitted) if the following three conditions are all satisfied.
      1) What one wishes to use is being separated from what one does not wish to use, as distinct from the reverse.
      2) The separation takes place by hand and not by means of an instrument designed for that purpose.
      3) What is being separated is intended for immediate use and not for use at some time in the future.
   b. It is to be emphasized that what is important for the purposes of condition 1) above is not whether what is being selected is usable, but whether one wishes to use it at the time.
      1) For example, if one has a dish containing a mixture of almonds and walnuts, then,

   when selection is permitted

a) should one wish to eat just the almonds, one should
        pick them out from among the walnuts, but one
        may not remove the walnuts leaving the almonds
        in the dish.
    b) On the other hand, should one wish to eat just the
        walnuts, it is they which must be removed from
        among the almonds.
2) Similarly, when one has a pile of thick and thin
    napkins or diapers,
    a) if one wishes to use the thick ones, one may only
        select the thick ones from the pile, and
    b) if one wishes to use the thin ones, one may only
        select the thin ones.

separate objects 3. *a.* The prohibition against selection is applicable only if
    1) two kinds of articles are mixed together or
    2) two kinds of articles lie next to one another, in such a
        way that one cannot draw a clear line between them.
b. If they are quite separate from each other, the prohibition
    does not apply and there is nothing wrong with removing
    either of them, at one's discretion.

articles covered by others 4. *a.* Nevertheless, where something usable is covered by
    something of a kind which is not normally used, the
    removal of the latter from on top of the former does
    involve the prohibition against selection, even if the two
    are not mixed together.
b. However, where two kinds of articles, both of which are
    normally used, are lying one on top of the other, without
    being actually mixed together, one may remove the upper
    articles in order to reach those underneath.
c. For examples see paragraph 41 below.

intention 5. *a.* The prohibition against selection is transgressed only if
    one intends to make a forbidden selection, as where one
    removes a rotten fruit from among good fruit, with a view
    to improving the general quality of what is left.
b. The prohibition is not transgressed if it only transpires

after the selection that what one has picked out is not in
fact what one wants, as where one takes an item from a
bowl of fruit, with the object of eating it, and subsequently discovers that it is rotten.

6. *a.* The prohibition against selection is transgressed only if,
in circumstances where this is not permitted, one actually
brings about the selection of what one does not want from
what one does want, or vice versa. *act of selection*

b. The prohibition is not transgressed if the process of
selection or separation would in any case take place by
itself, without human interference, as where a bottle of
liquid is placed in an upright position, so that sediment or
dregs which were settling on the side now settle to the
bottom.

7. *a.* We have seen, and we shall see in more detail later, that,
whenever selection is permitted on Shabbath, it must be
done for immediate use, whether it consists of *for whose immediate use?*
  1) picking what one wishes to use out of what one does
    not wish to use,
  2) removing the peel or shell from fruits, vegetables or
    other foods or
  3) sorting different objects according to their type.

b. It is irrelevant whether the selection is made
  1) exclusively for one's own immediate use,
  2) for one's own immediate use together with that of
    others,
  3) solely for the immediate use of other people or
  4) for the immediate use of an animal.

8. If one has transgressed the injunction against selection, one
should consult a rabbi, since it may be forbidden to use what
one has selected or left, if one would thereby be benefiting
from an activity which is prohibited on Shabbath. *result of transgression*

SELECTING WHAT IS REQUIRED
FROM WHAT IS NOT REQUIRED

proportions not a consideration

9. *a.* As already mentioned, one should pick out what is required from what is not required and not the reverse.

   b. This is so even if there is more of what one wants than of what one does not want and it would be easier to remove the latter from the former.

partial removal of unwanted matter

10. One is in breach of the prohibition against selection even if one removes only part of the unwanted matter and leaves the remainder behind.

preferred methods of separating meat or fish from bones

11. *a.* 1) One must be careful, when preparing food on Shabbath, not to remove the bones from fish or meat.

   2) Consequently, if one wishes to prepare pickled or salted herring for serving to guests or for a *kiddush* or for the third Shabbath meal, one should either remove the bones before Shabbath or else serve the food with the bones in. (See also paragraph 62 below.)

   b. There is nothing wrong with putting meat or fish into one's mouth while it is still on the bone and removing the bone from one's mouth after chewing off the meat or fish.

   c. If this is not practicable or convenient, one can either

   1) hold the bone and eat the meat or fish off it,

   2) use one's fork to remove the meat or fish from the bone (and not, of course, the other way around) while it is still on the plate, even if, in order to do this, one holds the bone on the plate with one's hand or with one's knife,

   3) hold the bone in one hand and pull the meat or fish off it with the other, notwithstanding that one will be left holding, in one hand, a bone stripped clean of meat, or

   4) remove each bone, if there is more than one, separately, provided that one sucks it before throwing it away.

removing bones with some meat or fish still on

12. *a.* If one is unable to adopt any of the methods suggested in

the previous paragraph, as in the case of fish containing many small bones, many authorities agree that the bones may be removed together with a little of the meat or fish attached to them.

b. There are, however, authorities who take a stricter view.

13. Despite what we have stated above, there are some who are in the habit of removing bones from fish or meat in the normal way on Shabbath and they have rabbinical authorities to support them, but, if this is done, it should only be done in the process of eating and not before. *removing bones in the normal manner*

14. a. Should the food on one's plate contain bones which have no meat on them, it is forbidden to take them out, unless one intends to suck them as soon as they have been removed. *bare bones*

b. Even if they contain marrow, they should be left where they are until the end of the meal.

15. It is extremely interesting to note that the long-established custom of eating "gefilte" (stuffed) fish on Shabbath avoids all of the problems and doubts mentioned in the last few paragraphs, and bears witness to the spirit of sanctity which permeates even the most mundane features in the day-to-day life of the Jewish people. *gefilte fish*

16. a. Putting a piece of watermelon, containing seeds, into one's mouth and afterwards removing the seeds from one's mouth in no way involves an infringement of the prohibition against selection. *watermelon seeds*

b. 1) If one does not wish to do this, one may shake the seeds off the slice of watermelon, as long as this is done immediately before eating it.

2) Those who are accustomed to remove the remainder of the seeds which are still attached to the watermelon have halachic authority to support them, provided, once more, that this is done immediately before eating it.

      c. Removing the peel from a melon is dealt with in paragraph 34 below.

      d. The removal of seeds from honeydew and other melons is the subject of paragraph 33 below.

fruits with pits

17. *a.* 1) Some fruits, such as most plums and peaches, contain pits (stones) which, when removed, do not come away clean, but have pieces of fruit still attached to them.

      2) When eating a fruit of this kind, it is permissible to take out the pit with one's hand. (Compare paragraph 12 above.)

     b. 1) Other fruits, such as apricot and medlar, have pits which separate from the flesh and come away clean when removed.

      2) When eating a fruit of this kind, it is better

        a) to open it in such a way that the pit will drop out by itself **or**

        b) to remove the fruit from the pit, rather than the reverse.

      3) Some authorities allow the removal of the pit from the fruit with one's hand in this case too, so long as it is done at the actual time of eating and not before.

     c. 1) A fruit pit which

        a) is no longer in the fruit,

        b) is not fit for either human or animal consumption **and**

        c) has no remains of fruit attached to it

      is classed as *muktzeh*. (See Chapter 20, paragraph 26.)

      2) However, it is permitted to move such a pit while separating it from the fruit in the ways described above or while taking it out of one's mouth.

insects in food

18. *a.* An insect which has fallen into food or drink may not be extracted by itself, either

     1) by hand,

     2) by means of an instrument or

     3) by blowing it out.

     b. One may remove an insect either

1) by pouring it out together with some of the liquid into which it has fallen or

2) by taking it out together with a little of the food or liquid surrounding it.

c. An insect may be removed in the ways just described, even if one has no intention of immediately eating or drinking the food into which it has fallen.

d. Paragraph 36 below deals specifically with the removal of insects from lettuce leaves.

19. a. It is forbidden to pour off the whey which has collected in sour-milk or yogurt, unless one also pours off a little of the sour-milk or yogurt with it. *whey and salt water*

b. 1) Similarly, one should not pour the salt water off pickled olives, cucumbers and the like.

2) If one wishes to eat them, one should, on the contrary, remove them from the salt water, and this one may do even with the aid of a spoon (as explained in paragraph 45 below).

3) See also Chapter 9, paragraph 3d2.

20. a. Lemon or calcium or any substance having a similar effect must not be added to milk in order to turn it into cheese, since the separation of the curd from the whey is prohibited on Shabbath. *making cheese*

b. One is similarly not allowed to stand milk in a warm place to make it go sour, as one does when making cheese.

c. Regarding the straining of sour-milk, see paragraph 51 below.

21. a. Fruits or vegetables which are mixed together with any inedible matter, in such a way that most people would not eat them as they are, should be prepared and cleaned before Shabbath, since one may not *cleaning fruits or vegetables*

1) put them into water so that the waste matter should settle to the bottom or rise to the top nor

2) direct a stream of water onto the waste to wash it

away, as this too amounts to separating what is not
required from what is required.

b. Nevertheless, dirt which is stuck to fruits and vegetables,
as well as dust, insecticide and the like, may be removed,
provided that this is done immediately prior to eating,

1) by directing a stream of water onto them,
2) by taking off the dirty peel, as is often done in the case,
for instance, of radishes, or
3) by wiping it off with one's hand or a dry cloth.

c. Clean fruit may be soaked in disinfectant.

*removing
bad part of
fruit*

22. a. When eating grapes, one should remove from the bunch
only those grapes which one wishes to eat at the time,
leaving on the stalk those which one does not want.

b. On the other hand, when eating a partly bad apple, it is
permitted to cut out the bad part so that one can eat what
is left, as long as this is done immediately before eating.
(Compare paragraph 31 below regarding removal of the
peel.)

*selecting
from mixed
foods*

23. a. If different kinds of food are mixed together, as we have
already seen,

1) one may remove the variety which one wishes to eat at
the time, but
2) one may not take out the variety which one does not
wish to eat at present.

b. Consequently, if faced with a bowl of assorted fruit,

1) one should not remove the fruit which one does not at
present want, leaving in the bowl only those which one
wishes to eat, but
2) it is permitted to empty all of the fruit out of the bowl,
mixed together, and subsequently pick out the variety
which one then wishes to eat. (See also paragraph 41
below.)

c. In the same way, a person who does not like onions, for
example, should not remove the onions from a mixed
salad (unless he serves them to someone who does like

them) but should eat or remove the other vegetables and leave the onions.

24. a. 1) One is allowed to select, from among articles which are all of the same kind and quality, even those which one does not intend for immediate use. *selecting from one variety*

  2) The reason for this is that selection is prohibited only when it is of one kind from another, and not when all of the articles are of one variety and are all equally available for use (but see paragraph 27 below).

  b. It follows that,

  1) from a mixture of large and small pieces of the same kind of meat, all cooked in the same way, one may take out whichever one wishes, even if the intention is to eat those which are left,

  2) from several pieces of fish of the same variety, all prepared in the same way, for example all boiled or all fried, one may take out whichever one wishes, notwithstanding that some of them may contain more bones than others (as would be the case with pieces of tail), and

  3) from a quantity of fruit, all of the same kind and variety (for instance Jonathan apples or Conference pears), and all fresh, one may take out whichever one wishes, even if one specifically selects either the large or the small ones.

25. a. A fruit which is only partly bad may be removed from a dish of fruit which is all of the same variety and quality, even if one has no intention of eating it. *separating bad fruit from good*

  b. 1) A fruit which is altogether rotten may not be removed, even from a dish containing only identical good fruit and even if the intention is solely to prevent the rotten fruit from spoiling the rest of the fruit in the dish or from attracting insects.

  2) What one may do in this case depends on the circumstances.

  a) The good fruit adjacent to the rotten fruit may be

[43]

taken out, if, and only if, one intends to eat them right away, as explained in paragraph 62 below.

b) In the absence of such an intention, even the adjacent fruit may not be removed, but one is allowed to take out the good fruit surrounding that adjacent fruit.

selection from two kinds of articles, both serving same purpose

26. *a.* As we have seen, one may, according to one's choice, pick out either the large or the small fruit of a particular variety in a dish, even if the intention is to eat the fruit which will be left, since both large and small could serve the same purpose.

b. However, when the large or small fruit, as the case may be, of two varieties in a dish are removed, one should be careful to put them all down together and not each variety in a separate place.

similar articles serving different purposes

27. *a.* Articles of the same type which come in different sizes or colors and do not all have an identical use are treated as articles of different kinds.

b. As a result, one should take out those articles which one wishes to use at present and not the others.

c. For example,

1) if one has small and large pins and one wants to use the large ones, it is wrong to remove the small pins, leaving the large ones behind to be used, and

2) if one has clothes
   a) belonging to two different people or
   b) belonging to the same person, but serving different purposes, such as Shabbath clothes and weekday clothes,
   one should pick out those one wishes to use at present, leaving the others behind.

3) See paragraph 80 below with regard to cutlery.

matzoth

28. *a.* 1) It is permitted to take matzoth one by one out of a packet or carton containing both whole and broken matzoth, until one has found two whole matzoth

(lechem mishneh) with which to begin the Shabbath meal.

    2) The selection is in this case not prohibited, for the reasons mentioned in paragraphs 4 and 5 above.

b. 1) If, however, whole and broken matzoth are lying jumbled together, not in a packet or carton, the broken matzoth should not be extracted leaving just the whole ones for *lechem mishneh*.

    2) This would amount to removing what is not required from what is required, since the broken matzoth are not suitable for *lechem mishneh*.

    3) Nevertheless, where a number of matzoth, both broken and whole, are put on the table, all intended for the ensuing meal, one may extract the broken ones, which are not fit for *lechem mishneh*, so as to leave the whole ones, which are.

c. Should one wish to set the table using only whole matzoth for aesthetic reasons, the broken matzoth, which are not required for that meal, may be removed from among them, since they are in effect equally usable for the purpose in hand, so that the selection takes place from among articles which are all of the same kind.

d. 1) There is a custom, on Passover, not to eat that part of a matza which was doubled over when being baked.

    2) Even when Passover occurs on Shabbath, a doubled-over piece of matza can be broken off and disposed of, provided that this is done immediately prior to the meal.

    3) The practice among the particularly observant is to check their matzoth for this before the commencement of Passover, to ensure that there is not the slightest possibility of their containing anything leavened.

REMOVAL OF PEELS, SHELLS
AND OTHER WASTE MATERIAL

29. The peel or shell may be removed from fruits, vegetables, eggs and so forth, in the manner which will be described below, since

peeling in principle permitted

a. it is impossible otherwise to reach the food which one intends to eat and

b. it is part and parcel of the normal process of eating them.

edible peel or skin **30.** a. A peel or skin which is edible and which is in fact eaten by most people may be removed from food on Shabbath,

    1) even with a specially designed peeler and

    2) even if one's intention is not to eat the food right away, but to leave it for a meal later on during the same Shabbath.

b. Examples are the peel of apples, tomatoes, pears and peaches—which most people are accustomed to eat with their peel—as well as the skin of many varieties of fish and poultry.

c. Whether or not a particular skin or peel is usually eaten is a fact to be ascertained in each locality, but this can sometimes be a difficult question to answer (as in the cases of fish skin, cucumber peel and the white, interior skin under the peel of a citrus fruit).

d. There is a more stringent view, according to which even edible peels or skins should be removed only immediately before the meal and then not with an instrument specifically designed for that purpose, as in the case of inedible peels or skins, discussed in paragraph 31 below.

e. With regard to poultry, one should be careful not to remove the remains of any feathers from the skin, even if the bird is cooked, since this may come within the group of prohibitions falling under the general heading of "shearing."

inedible shells, peels or skins **31.** a. Shells, peels, and skins which most people do not normally eat may be removed on Shabbath, but

    1) not with an instrument specially made for that purpose **and**

    2) only immediately prior to the meal.

b. Examples are eggshells, the skins or peels of onions, potatoes, bananas and sausages, and peanut (ground nut) shells. (Concerning nuts in general, see paragraph 38 below.)

c. A knife is not regarded as an instrument specially made for peeling.

d. It is permissible to remove a bakery label or sticker from a loaf of bread, but care should be taken to remove it together with some of the crust, so as not to tear into any of the lettering printed on it.

e. The problem of lettering on food (for instance in the case of salami or eggs) is dealt with in Chapter 11, paragraph 10.

f. Since eggshells are not fit for consumption, even by animals, they are *muktzeh* and may not, therefore, be moved, except while being taken off the egg. (See Chapter 20, paragraph 26 and Chapter 22, paragraphs 33 to 36.)

32. a. It is forbidden to remove peas, beans and the like from *pods* their pods, since this is akin to threshing, which is prohibited on Shabbath.

b. An exception is made if the pods, as well as their contents, are edible, as in the case of pea pods when they are still fresh and green.

33. a. One may extract the seeds, when opening a honeydew or *melon seeds* other melon in which they are concentrated in the center (but not a watermelon), if this is done immediately prior to the meal.

b. The reason is that the seeds must be removed in order to reach the fruit. (Compare peeling in paragraph 31 above.)

c. The removal of the seeds from a watermelon is dealt with in paragraph 16 above.

34. The thick peel of a melon may be peeled off, even with a *melon peel* knife, provided that this is done just before the meal.

35. It is permissible to remove the stems from fruits and vege- *stalks* tables such as plums or tomatoes, but here too only just before the meal.

lettuce **36.** *a.* 1) The outside leaves of lettuce which are not fit for eating may be taken off, so that one can eat the inner leaves, as long as this is done just before the meal.

2) If the leaves have already been taken off a lettuce, one should not pick out the bad leaves which one does not wish to eat, but one may, just before the meal, pick out the good leaves.

b. 1) Lettuce leaves may be examined on Shabbath to make sure there are no insects on them.

2) a) Any large insect which is found, such as a caterpillar, may be removed, since it is a distinctly separate object and can in no way be said to be intermingled with the lettuce, so that its extraction does not fall within the prohibition against selection.

b) It is, however, preferable not to move the insect by itself, but to take it off together with a piece of the lettuce leaf.

3) a) Small insects which cling to the leaves may not be removed on their own.

b) They should be taken out together with part of the lettuce leaf.

4) a) It is in general not permitted to kill insects on Shabbath.

b) One should, therefore, not wash insects off lettuce leaves in water containing salt or vinegar, since they cannot survive in such water.

scale on citrus fruit **37.** Scale insects which are on the peel of citrus fruit, or which have in some way been transferred onto the fruit itself, may be removed in the same way as a large insect may be taken off a lettuce leaf. (See paragraph 36*b*2 above.)

cracking nuts **38.** *a.* 1) It is permissible to open nuts on Shabbath, even with a nutcracker. (Contrast paragraph 31 above, where the use of a special instrument is prohibited. In the case under discussion it is permitted, since the cracking of the shell does not complete the selection.)

2) One may also crack nuts with a hammer (if a nutcracker or other suitable instrument the normal use of which is allowed on Shabbath is not available), even though before Shabbath there was no intention to use the hammer for this purpose.

3) A stone should not be used to crack nuts, unless, prior to Shabbath, it was designated for use on a regular basis.

b. Shell which remains attached to a nut after it has been cracked and the thin, internal shell of a peanut (ground-nut) may be removed on Shabbath, provided that this is done immediately prior to the meal.

c. If a cracked nut has broken into several parts, pieces of nut being mixed with pieces of shell, one should not pick out the fragments of shell, but, on the contrary, one should select the pieces of nut, leaving the remains of the shell where they are, and this too only immediately prior to the meal.

d. Nut shells, not being fit even for animal consumption, are *muktzeh*. (For the significance of this see Chapter 20, paragraph 26 and Chapter 22, paragraphs 33 to 36.)

39. When the wrapping around a candy (sweet) is stuck to it, the candy may only be removed from its wrapping just before being eaten, since otherwise this could fall within the prohibition against selection. *wrapped candies*

40. It is allowed, in honor of guests, to peel more fruit than they can eat, in order to show hospitality. *peeling more than guests can eat*

41. a. If grapes are lying on top of plums (and similarly if any two kinds of fruit are lying one on top of the other) and one wishes to eat the plums, the grapes may be removed to reach them. *fruit underneath other fruit*

b. 1) However, if rotten fruit is lying on top of good fruit, the rotten fruit may not be removed to reach the good fruit underneath, as this renders the good fruit fit to eat.

2) In such a case, all of the fruit can be emptied out of the

dish or other container mixed together and one can then select the good fruit which one wishes to eat immediately, as in the circumstances mentioned in paragraph 23 above.

bunches of grapes, bananas and dates

42. *a.* Grapes may be plucked from a bunch, provided that
1) the bunch was severed from the vine before Shabbath
   and
2) the grapes are to be eaten immediately.*
b. Bananas can be picked off a bunch, subject to the same conditions.
c. Some authorities forbid the removal of dates from a cluster, even for immediate consumption.

card index

43. *a.* It is permissible to look through a card index in order to take out a card which is required at the time.
b. The reason for this is that the case is analogous to that of the two kinds of fruit lying on top of one another, described in paragraph 41a above.
c. The fact that in the course of one's search one may take hold of cards which one does not need is irrelevant, as is explained in paragraph 5 above.
d. One may thumb through the cards in order to find the place of a card which one has taken out and now wishes to return to the index.

SELECTION BY HAND

AND BY INSTRUMENT

selection, when permissible, to be done by hand

44. Whenever selection is permissible it should be done by hand and not with the aid of any instrument, and this is the case whether
a. something usable is being removed from something useless, for example good fruit from bad fruit, or whether
b. something usable is being removed from something else

---

*The stalk remaining after all the grapes have been removed is *muktzeh*. (See Chapter 20, paragraph 26.)

which is also usable, for example one variety of fruit from
another.

45. *a.* 1) For the purposes under discussion, a selection made
with a knife, a fork or a spoon is treated as being made
by hand if, in effect, the use of the instrument is as an
extension of the hand.

    knives, forks and spoons

2) This is so if the knife, fork or spoon, as the case may
be, is being used, for instance,
   a) to prevent one's hands from becoming soiled,
   b) because the food is too far away and one cannot
     reach it with one's fingers or
   c) to pick up a liquid, which cannot be held in the
     hand, but
3) this is not so if the use of the knife, fork or spoon
simply makes it easier to pick out what one requires, in
which case their use is forbidden.

  b. It follows from the above that one may, immediately prior
to the meal,
1) use a fork to extract meat from a stew,
2) use a fork to take meat off a bone in one's plate and
3) use a knife to peel the skin off a slice of salami.

46. *a.* The layer of cream which collects in the upper part of a
bottle of milk may be skimmed off with a spoon, as long
as the cream is eaten right away, straight from the spoon
in one's hand.

    skimming cream off milk

  b. If either
1) the cream is not to be eaten right away or
2) the cream is not to be eaten straight off the spoon in
one's hand, but is first to be transferred into another
container and then eaten from that,
it may not be skimmed off the milk, unless a little milk is
removed with it or the bottom layer of the cream is left on
the surface of the milk.

    taking skin off boiled milk

47. *a.* One is not allowed to take off the skin which forms on a

[51]

saucepan of boiled milk, unless one removes it together with some of the milk.

b. Alternatively, one may

   1) pour the milk carefully out of the saucepan, in such a way that the skin is left stuck to the side, or even

   2) keep the skin in the saucepan with a spoon, while pouring the milk out.

straining milk

48. a. 1) It is in general forbidden to strain milk so as to separate out any skin, whether the skin

     a) is floating on the surface **or**

     b) consists of small pieces mixed into the milk.

   2) Since it is not usual to drink milk with the skin still in it, the straining of the milk falls within the prohibition against separation.

   3) The skin may of course be removed together with some of the milk, as in paragraph 47 above.

b. In case of need, milk may be strained to extract pieces of skin mixed into it, but only subject to the following conditions:

   1) The milk may be strained only through something which is not usually used for straining, such as a piece of cloth.

   2) If cloth is used, one must take care not to squeeze it out, since this is prohibited on Shabbath.

   3) Any cloth used should be stretched tight while the straining takes place, so that one does not pour the milk into a depression formed in the cloth, as one would normally do were one to strain milk through a cloth on an ordinary weekday.

   4) A whole skin floating on the surface of the milk may in no circumstances be strained off, even through something which is not usually used for straining (but it may be removed together with some of the milk).

c. It is forbidden to strain milk, even through something which one is not accustomed to use for straining, in order to remove matter which is altogether inedible, such as an insect.

49. *a.* A liquid may be strained, even through a normal strainer, to remove matter which is of so little consequence that it can be considered part of the liquid, if
    1) most people usually drink it without bothering to strain it **and**
    2) the person in question usually drinks it without bothering to strain it.
    b. Thus, milk containing very small clots of cream may be strained, provided one is not particular about drinking it without straining, since most people do not bother to strain it.

liquids which may be poured through a strainer

50. The principle may be expressed in another way by saying that a liquid may not be strained to remove matter of this kind on Shabbath, if
    a. most people are particular not to drink it unstrained **or**
    b. the person in question is particular not to drink it unstrained.

liquids which may not be poured through a strainer

51. Sour-milk should not be strained through a bag so as to let the whey run off and retain the curds. (See also paragraph 20 above.)

straining off whey

52. *a.* Food may not be put into a strainer to remove any superfluous liquid which it has absorbed.
    b. Examples are toast or biscuits which have been soaked in water or milk.
    c. It is, however, permitted to squeeze unwanted liquid out of food, if indeed this is done to improve the food's flavor.

extracting liquid absorbed in food

53. *a.* 1) It is forbidden to strain fruit juice (which must of course have been squeezed before Shabbath) to remove any of the flesh of the fruit still remaining in it if most people are particular about straining (or if the person in question is particular).
    2) It is also forbidden to strain the soup or water from cooked vegetables, since neither is of so little consequence that it can be considered to be part of the other.

straining fruit juice and soup

b. These prohibitions apply
1) whether one requires the liquid without the solid, as where the intention is to obtain clear, vegetable soup by straining out the vegetables which have been cooked in it, or
2) whether one requires the solid without the liquid, as where one strains off the water in which potatoes have been cooked.

straining
noodles

54. *a.* Noodles may not be strained from the water in which they have been cooked, since it is not usual to drink this water,
b. nor may they be picked up in a perforated ladle, with the object of letting the water run out through the holes, but
c. such a ladle may be used to transfer the noodles from the saucepan to a plate, so long as
1) that is one's sole intention **and**
2) one does not pause or tarry in the process of transferring the noodles,
and in those circumstances, it is immaterial that some of the water may actually flow out.

pitting olives

55. One is not permitted to remove the pit (stone) from an olive with an instrument specifically designed for that purpose, even if it is certain that some of the flesh of the fruit will remain attached to the pit.

water filters

56. *a.* One may use a water tap fitted with a filter.
b. If the filter becomes detached, it may only be replaced on Shabbath in a provisional manner and not fixed on tightly, since this may fall within the prohibition against construction.

teapots

57. *a.* It is permissible to pour clear tea essence out of a teapot in the bottom of which there are tea leaves, even if the spout contains a strainer.
b. According to one view, it is forbidden to pour essence through the strainer in the spout if the essence is mixed with the leaves (or if the clear essence has been poured

off), but another view permits it, provided that it is for immediate use.

58. *a.* 1) Tea bags may be used to make tea on Shabbath, but only by putting them into water (or water and milk) which is already in a *keli shelishi* and, according to some authorities, the water temperature must be less than 45 degrees centigrade (113 degrees Fahrenheit) when the tea bag is inserted. (See Chapter 1, paragraphs 53 and 57 above.)

tea bags and tea strainers

    2) a) It is best to remove the tea bag with a spoon and not with one's fingers.

       b) If one were to do otherwise, there is a possibility that, after removal of the tea bag, it would be held over the liquid in the cup for long enough to allow the essence absorbed in it to drip back in, and this could be considered a forbidden separation.

b. What we have said above regarding tea bags is equally applicable to the type of tea holder made in the form of two perforated spoons which close together.

c. 1) Boiling water may be poured into a strainer containing tea leaves, upon condition that the tea leaves were boiled up before Shabbath. (See also Chapter 1, paragraph 47.)

    2) This does not involve the prohibition against selection, since

       a) the strainer separates the water from the tea leaves immediately upon its being poured in **and**

       b) the water which comes out is the same water which has just been poured in, and it was separate and drinkable even before the whole process took place.

59. *a.* It is perfectly in order to give a child to drink from a bottle with a rubber nipple (teat).

rubber nipples

b. Despite the fact that the straining action of the nipple will result in the retention of any lumps or sediment within the bottle, this is permissible, since the prohibition against selection does not apply if the separation is merely part of the act of taking food into the mouth.

salt shakers   **60.** *a.* One may shake salt out of a salt shaker (cellar) even if it also contains lumps of salt which are too large to come out through the perforations in the top and which will, consequently, be left in the salt shaker.

     b. The absorption of moisture from salt by grains of rice put into a salt shaker does not involve the prohibition against selection, although the grains should be inserted before Shabbath, as they are *muktzeh*. (See Chapter 20, paragraph 28.)

     c. It is, however, better not to shake salt out of the holes in the top of a salt shaker containing grains of rice, notwithstanding that a considerable amount of salt will remain in the salt shaker, mixed with the rice.

egg yolks   **61.** If one wishes to use the yolk of a raw egg on Shabbath, one may, just before the meal,

     a. separate it from the albumen by emptying it from shell to shell or

     b. break the egg into a plate and remove the yolk from the albumen (but not the albumen from the yolk) with one's hand (but not with an instrument).

SELECTION FOR IMMEDIATE USE

selection
forbidden if
not for
immediate
use   **62.** *a.* Even the selection of what one requires from what one does not require is forbidden, if one does not intend to use it until after a while.

     b. To put the rule positively, a selection of this kind is permitted only if one makes it immediately prior to the meal, or to the use of what one picks out (and provided, of course, that one complies with all the other rules which are applicable).

banquets   **63.** *a.* When selecting what one requires, in the permitted manner, one may select however much one needs for the meal one is about to have or for the purpose in hand.

b. This is so
1) even if one is preparing a banquet which will last for several hours,
2) even if one has invited a large number of people, so that one is occupied with the preparations, including the selection, for a considerable time beforehand and
3) even if the meal consists of numerous different courses, all of which one wishes to prepare before the guests arrive.
c. A person helping in the kitchen is not allowed to select food for a meal which is not yet due to begin, even though he wishes to do so in order to enable him to go home before the time for the meal arrives.

64. In accordance with the above rules, if pieces of boiled and fried fish are lying mixed together,   *boiled and fried fish*
  a. one may pick out whichever one wants, immediately before the meal at which they are to be eaten, but
  b. one may not separate them out for a meal which is not to be eaten until later.

65. One may take the meat out of a pot of mixed stew, even with a fork or a spoon, immediately before a meal, with the object of keeping such meat for a later course of that same meal.   *removing meat from stew*

66. One may also peel as much fruit as one will need for a meal, even if none of it will be eaten until the last course, provided that this is not done until just before the meal begins.   *peeling fruit for dessert*

67. If fruit has fallen on the ground in such a way that it has to be sorted out from the dust, mud, earth or stones, one should be careful to pick up only as much as is required to be eaten immediately. (See also paragraph 21 above and Chapter 26, paragraph 24.)   *picking up fruit which has fallen on the ground*

68. a. Clothes should not be selected until immediately before they are put on.   *clothes*
  b. One should be especially careful not to pick out in the

evening the clothes which it is intended that the children should wear the next morning. (See Chapter 15, paragraph 42.)

books   **69.** *a.* Similarly, a book should not be taken from the bookcase until just before one wishes to read it.

b. If for some reason it is more convenient to remove the book a considerable time before one requires it, one may take it out, but should then read a little of it before putting it down to be read again later.

large quantities of lettuce   **70.** It is permissible to check large quantities of lettuce on Shabbath (in the manner described in paragraph 36 above), for instance when preparing a meal in a dormitory (boarding school), despite the fact that the selection will take a considerable amount of time.

type of immediate use   **71.** Selection, even of what one requires from what one does not require and even for immediate use, is not permitted, unless that use is for the real purpose for which one intends to use the item selected, as will be made clearer in the following paragraphs.

selection for purpose of refrigeration   **72.** *a.* It is forbidden to select one kind of food from another in order to store it in the refrigerator since this is not in itself the purpose for which food is intended.

b. It is permitted if one's intention is to eat the food as soon as it has become cool, since in that case the refrigeration is part of the process of preparing the food for immediate eating, which is its true purpose.

chopped eggs and onions   **73.** The ingredients of a dish of chopped eggs and onions for a meal which is not intended to be eaten right away may not be peeled, shelled or picked out, even for the purpose of immediately proceeding with the preparation of the food, since the real object of the exercise is not to chop the eggs and onions, but to eat them. (See also Chapter 8, paragraph 23.)

74. *a.* If various bottles of drink are arranged in a refrigerator *bottles of* according to kind, the bottles in front may be removed so *drink* that one can reach the desired variety. (Compare paragraph 41 above.)

    b. If the bottles are not arranged in any order, but are simply standing side by side, jumbled together, one should take out only the variety which one wishes to drink during the meal, and that only immediately prior to the meal.

    c. However, drink may be removed from a refrigerator a sufficient time before the meal to allow it to lose its chill, if one prefers not to drink or serve it when it is too cold.

75. *a.* All the food selected on Shabbath should be eaten at the *leftovers* meal for which the selection was made.

    b. Nevertheless, if

      1) some of the food is left when one has finished eating or

      2) one changes one's mind and decides not to eat any of the food at that meal at all,

    it may be eaten at a subsequent meal and one does not thereby transgress the prohibition against selection.

SORTING

76. *a.* It is forbidden to sort into their various categories foods or *general* articles of different kinds which are mixed together. *principle*

    b. This is so even if one's intention is only to put each *governing* variety in its allotted place. *sorting*

    c. An exception occurs, and sorting is allowed, if all of the varieties selected are for immediate use (and the selection is made in a permitted manner).

77. Accordingly, one may not sort out a dish full of grapefruit *grapefruits* and oranges, if one does not wish to eat all of the fruit sorted *and oranges* at the immediately ensuing meal.

78. *a.* If one has a batch of assorted cutlery, it is not permitted *putting away*

      1) to sort it into its various categories so as to put each *cutlery* away in its allotted compartment nor

2) to pick out all the items of one variety, dry them and then put them away in their allotted compartment.

b. It is permitted to dry each piece of cutlery separately, as it comes to hand, and then directly put it into its allotted compartment.

arranging cutlery on the table

79. a. It is permitted, immediately prior to the meal at which they are to be used, to take jumbled cutlery and lay each piece on the table in the desired order.

b. Where each category of cutlery is in its own, individual, allotted compartment, one may take each category in turn, laying it out on the table in the desired order, and this may even be done a considerable time before the meal.

c. It is not, however, permitted to take different categories of cutlery out of their individual, allotted compartments, allow them to become mixed together, even in one's hand, and then sort them out again by laying the table with them in a set order, unless one does so immediately prior to the meal at which they are to be used.

separating cutlery used for meat and dairy dishes

80. a. If cutlery used for dairy food becomes mixed with cutlery used for meat dishes, one is not allowed to sort them out on Shabbath, but

b. one may pick out such items as one needs, and no more, immediately before the meal at which one uses them.

returning books to shelves

81. a. It is forbidden to sort books with the object of putting them back in their proper places in a bookcase or on a shelf, but

b. if one wishes to clear books from a table, one may pick them up, one by one, as they come to hand, and put each into its appropriate position on the shelf.

washing

82. a. It is forbidden to sort clothes which have been taken off the clothesline, but

b. one may put each article, individually, in its appropriate place (not necessarily straight into the cupboard, but even next to the cupboard, for another person to put inside), immediately after folding it (in the permitted manner, as explained in Chapter 15, paragraph 46).

83. One is not permitted to sort a jumbled collection of different toys and arrange them in the toy chest, each in its allotted place, since, every time a toy is picked up, it is for the sole purpose of sorting it out from the others, and this is of course forbidden. (See also Chapter 16, paragraph 34.) *toys*

84. Pages which have become detached from a book and are not in their right place may not be put in order and re-inserted in their correct position, unless one does so with the object of reading them immediately. *loose pages*

Chapter 4

Laws of Selection on Yom Tov

1. *a.* 1) Although, in principle, sorting is an activity which is permissible on Yom Tov, it has been prohibited in relation to articles and materials which are usually sorted in large quantities at one time, since one would then appear to be making preparations on Yom Tov for several days in advance.

2) When sorting is forbidden on Yom Tov, it is irrelevant that, in any particular case in question,
   a) one intends to sort for immediate use or
   b) there was no possibility of making the necessary preparations before Yom Tov.

b. 1) Within this category of sorting fall the prohibitions against
   a) sifting flour (subject to the exception in paragraph 12 below),
   b) making cheese (subject to the exception in paragraph 11 below) and
   c) standing milk in a warm place, to make it turn sour (thus separating the curd from the whey, as in the case of cheese-making).

2) All of these activities are forbidden on Yom Tov even if specifically required for the purpose of the Festival.

2. *a.* One is permitted to sort different kinds of food on Yom Tov, for use on the same day, so long as they are types which are normally eaten shortly after being selected and are not usually sorted in large quantities at one time, for several days' use.

b. Nevertheless, use should not be made of an instrument or utensil specially designed for sorting large quantities at one time, such as a sieve.

c. Further details are contained in the following paragraphs.

3. *a.* 1) The general rule is that, whenever sorting is allowed on

Yom Tov, it should be done in the manner which causes the least possible bother or inconvenience.

2) Thus

    a) if it is easier to remove what one does not require and to leave behind what one wishes to use, because, for example, there is less of the former or it is easier to handle, then this is what one should do, but

    b) if the reverse is the case, one should adopt the opposite course of action.

    c) If an equal amount of trouble is involved in each course, one may separate out whichever one wishes.

b. Nonetheless, if it would have been possible to make the selection before the commencement of Yom Tov, but one did not do so, it is preferable to act on Yom Tov in the same way as one would on Shabbath, by

1) picking what one wishes to use from what one does not need (irrespective of the difficulty involved) and

2) doing so only immediately prior to the meal.

4. After cracking nuts, one should remove the nuts from the shells or the shells from the nuts, whichever is easier.   *nuts*

5. One should not put lentils, beans or similar foods in water, preparatory to cooking, with the object that those with maggots inside should float to the surface.   *maggots in lentils and beans*

6. *a.* Food may be sorted or strained on Yom Tov in the normal manner adopted on an ordinary weekday, even by means of a strainer or sieve, provided that the following two conditions are fulfilled.   *when sorting is permitted in the normal manner*

1) It could not have been done before Yom Tov.

2) The food is of a kind which it is not usual to sort or sift in large quantities at one and the same time.

b. Examples are

1) the removal of skin from the surface of milk which has been boiled up on Yom Tov and

    2) straining the water off noodles which have been cooked on Yom Tov.

foreign bodies in food

7. An insect or any other foreign body which has fallen into food should be taken out together with some of the food.

lettuce

8. When preparing lettuce for a meal to be eaten on Yom Tov,

    a. one may

        1) remove the external leaves (which are not fit to eat), as in Chapter 3, paragraph 36,

        2) pick the bad leaves out from among the good and

        3) remove insects, whether large or small, although it is preferable to take them out together with a piece of lettuce leaf, rather than to move them by themselves, but

    b. one may not rinse lettuce leaves in water containing salt or vinegar, in order to remove insects, since such water will kill the insects (and this is not permitted on Yom Tov).

washing fruits or vegetables

9. With regard to washing fruits or vegetables on Yom Tov, it is preferable to follow the rules which apply on Shabbath, as set out in Chapter 3, paragraph 21.

peeling potatoes

10. Potatoes and similar vegetables may be peeled on Yom Tov, not only with a knife, but also with a peeler or scraper (so long as it is not electrically powered).

making cheese for a baby

11. Lemon juice or calcium may be added to milk in order to turn it into cheese, if one requires it to feed a baby.

sifting flour

12. *a.* As explained in paragraph 1 above, the general rule is that sifting flour is forbidden on Yom Tov, even if there was no possibility of sifting it before the Festival.

    b. An exception occurs, and sifting is permitted on Yom Tov, if

        1) the flour has already been sifted prior to Yom Tov,

but it needs to be sifted again on Yom Tov because something has fallen in, **and**

   2) the sifting (on Yom Tov) is done in a manner which is different from that normally used, for example by passing the flour through an upside-down sieve.

13. *a.* Peas, beans and the like may be removed from their pods, *pods* even if these have become dried up.

   b. However, if the pods are dried up, some authorities require the adoption of a method other than that usually followed, for instance the use of the very tips of one's fingers for taking the pods apart.

14. *a.* One may pour boiling water onto tea leaves in a strainer. *making tea*

   b. When making tea with a tea bag, one may, after removing the bag from the water, hold it over the cup, so as to allow drops of essence to drip back in.

15. Whenever selection is permissible on Yom Tov and could not *sorting for* have been made before its commencement, one may make *later in the* the selection not only for the next meal, but for any other *day* meal to be eaten

   a. on the same day of Yom Tov or even

   b. on the following day if that is Shabbath and one has made an *eiruv tavshilin* (as described in Chapter 2, paragraphs 10-16).

Chapter 5

Laws Relating to Squeezing Fruit
on Shabbath and Yom Tov

general
prohibition

1. *a.* Squeezing fruit in order to extract the juice is in general forbidden both on Shabbath and on Yom Tov.

b. Various distinctions are, however, made in the application of this rule, as will be explained.

squeezing
into an
empty vessel
or into liquid

2. *a.* No fruit may be squeezed either
   1) into an empty vessel or
   2) into a liquid.

b. This prohibition applies regardless of whether the fruit is squeezed
   1) by means of an instrument or
   2) by hand.

c. Common examples are
   1) squeezing lemons,
   2) squeezing oranges,
   3) squeezing the juice out of shredded carrots and
   4) chopping up fruit to such an extent that it becomes liquefied.

d. On the other hand, lemon may be sliced and put into a drink, such as tea or cold water, even though some of the juice will come out by itself, but
   1) it is forbidden to squeeze the lemon with one's hand or with a spoon even while it is in the drink and,
   2) on Shabbath, one must be careful that the drink should either
      a) have a temperature of less than 45 degrees centigrade (113 degrees Fahrenheit) **or**
      b) be in a *keli shelishi*. (In this latter connection, see Chapter 1, paragraphs 2, 53 and 57.)

squeezing
onto food

3. *a.* It is permissible to squeeze fruit by hand (but not with a specially designed squeezer) onto non-liquid food on

Shabbath or Yom Tov, provided that one of the following two conditions is satisfied:

1) either the food is of such a nature that it will absorb most of the juice squeezed out **or**

2) the purpose of the juice is to improve the flavor of the food.

b. For the special case of squeezing grapes on Shabbath see paragraph 4 below.

4. While the rule with respect to squeezing fruit by hand onto non-liquid food applies to all fruit, it is desirable not to squeeze grapes on Shabbath, as distinct from Yom Tov, even in the circumstances specified in paragraph 3, except for the purpose of feeding a baby.

squeezing grapes on Shabbath

5. a. By virtue of the rule in paragraph 3 above, a lemon may be squeezed onto sugar, white cheese and the like. (See Chapter 8, paragraph 14.)

squeezing lemons

b. 1) If some of the lemon pips fall into the sugar or cheese, they should not be removed alone, since this would contravene the prohibition against selection. (Compare Chapter 3, paragraph 18.)

2) One of two courses may be adopted.

a) It is preferable not to remove the pips at all, but to remove the food, leaving the pips behind.

b) Failing this, the pips should be removed together with some of the sugar or cheese.

3) It is important to note that it is forbidden to squeeze a lemon into an empty vessel, even if the intention is to mix the juice immediately with sugar or cheese.

6. a. Lemon may be squeezed onto sugar even if one's purpose is to put the juice-soaked sugar subsequently into water.

when squeezing lemon for use in liquid permitted

b. Some authorities take a stricter view and prohibit the squeezing of lemon onto sugar if indeed one intends to put it into water.

c. At all events, on Shabbath one should not put the sugar into water with a temperature of 45 degrees centigrade or more, unless the water is in a *k^eli sh^elishi* (as to which see Chapter 1, paragraphs 2, 53 and 57).

flavoring food with lemon or orange juice

7. *a.* 1) As we have seen, juice may be squeezed onto food other than a liquid, to improve its flavor, but this is subject to two provisos:
   a) the squeezing must be done by hand and not with an instrument designed for the purpose **and**
   b) all or, at least, most of the juice extracted must in fact be utilized to improve the taste of the food.
   2) This is permitted even if the juice is not absorbed in the food.

b. One is consequently allowed
   1) to squeeze a lemon onto a salad or fish and also
   2) to squeeze an orange into mashed banana for a baby. (See further Chapter 6, paragraph 8 and Chapter 8, paragraph 14.)

c. It is, however, forbidden to squeeze a lemon or an orange into an empty vessel, even if one intends to pour the juice onto food in order to improve its taste.

squeezing juice from food to improve its taste

8. *a.* One may improve the taste of food by extracting juice from it, so long as this is done immediately prior to the meal.

b. It is thus permissible to squeeze excess vinegar or salt-water out of pickled cucumber, to make it more tasty.

c. Any juice removed may be used afterwards.

dipping bread into soup

9. *a.* Bread may be dipped into soup or any other liquid and then sucked, but it is proper to eat a little of the bread each time one sucks it.

b. See Chapter 1, paragraph 59 for the prohibition against putting bread into a *k^eli rishon* or a *k^eli sheini* containing hot soup.

sucking the juice out of fruit

10. *a.* The prohibition against squeezing fruit is not transgressed if the fruit is put to one's mouth and the juice

sucked out, but one must take care not to squeeze the fruit with one's fingers while it is being sucked.

b. In this way, one may suck oranges or chew sugar cane.

c. 1) With regard to grapes, a stricter attitude should be adopted. (Compare paragraph 4 above.)

2) Consequently, if one wishes to eat grapes without their skin and their pips,

a) one should not suck the juice out of them while holding them in one's fingers, **but**

b) one should put them into one's mouth, eat the flesh and then take out what is left.

11. *a.* Juice which has oozed out of grapes on Shabbath or Yom Tov, even by itself, may not be drunk on that day.

juice oozing out of fruit by itself

b. Whether or not one may on the same day drink juice which has oozed out of other fruit by itself depends on whether or not that fruit was intended specifically for eating (as distinct from pressing).

1) If the fruit was intended specifically for eating, the juice may be drunk, and one may, for instance, drink the juice which oozes out of a grapefruit while it is being cut.

2) If the fruit was not intended specifically for eating, the juice may not be drunk on that day.

c. The reason for these restrictions is that, if it were permitted to drink the juice one might, on another occasion, actually come to squeeze it out.

d. The juice which is forbidden to be drunk may not be moved, since it is *muktzeh*. (See Chapter 20, paragraph 32.)

12. There is nothing wrong with cutting a grapefruit into halves and eating it with a spoon, provided that

cutting and eating grapefruit

a. one is careful not to squeeze the grapefruit intentionally **and**

b. one does not intend specifically to drink the juice which inevitably runs out, rather than to eat the flesh.

(See also paragraph 11 above.)

squeezing out pomegranates for a child with diarrhea

13. a. If one requires pomegranate juice for a small child suffering from diarrhea, one should try and squeeze the juice out of the pomegranates in a manner other than that usually adopted.

b. One may, thus, squeeze the fruit with a spoon, directly into the cup, but one should, so far as possible, not hold the spoon in the same way as one would on a normal weekday.

c. If one is unable to squeeze the fruit out by a method different from that normally used, then, since it is for the use of a sick child, one may squeeze it in the usual way (although not, of course, with an electrical appliance).

d. See Chapter 37, paragraph 11 concerning children suffering from acute diarrhea.

frying or baking bread or matza

14. On Yom Tov one is permitted to soak matza or bread in water in order to make it soft and then to squeeze the water out, preparatory to frying or baking.

Chapter 6

Laws of Grinding, Chopping, Crushing and Grating on Shabbath

The laws of grinding, chopping, crushing and grating on Yom Tov are dealt with separately in Chapter 7.

1. *a.* While the basis of the prohibition discussed in this chapter is grinding, it also includes
   scope of prohibition
   1) chopping up finely,
   2) crushing,
   3) mashing,
   4) shredding and
   5) any method of dividing something up into small pieces.

   b. For the purposes of this chapter and the next, there is, consequently, no difference between
   1) rubbing something down into a powder, as is done when grain is ground into flour, and
   2) squashing something into a pulp, even if it is still thick enough to cling together and form one lump, as is the case when a banana is mashed.

   c. 1) This prohibition applies not only to food, but also, for example,
      a) to the crumbling of a clod of earth,
      b) to the chopping of wood into small chips and
      c) to the sawing of wood for the purpose of making sawdust.
   2) There may well be several prohibitions involved in one activity; for instance, if one crumbles a clod of earth, one is usually also transgressing the prohibition against moving earth on Shabbath. (See Chapter 20.)
   3) See also Chapter 15, paragraphs 28 and 40.

   mincers, mortars and graters forbidden

2. *a.* Even when the activities mentioned in paragraph 1 above are permitted on Shabbath (in the circumstances set out

below), it is forbidden to use an instrument or a utensil specially designed for the purpose, such as a mincer, a mortar, a pepper-mill or a grater.

b. This is so despite the fact that one may intend to eat the food immediately after it has been prepared.

c. One should also not use a large knife specifically intended for chopping up food into small pieces.

vegetable choppers and egg slicers

3. *a.* One may not, on Shabbath, use a vegetable chopper consisting of a set of blades which are fitted with springs and revolve around an axis, thereby chopping the vegetables very thoroughly.

b. One may use an egg slicer consisting of a set of equally spaced wires or blades arranged in a frame, which are pressed down onto an egg lying in a suitably sized depression, in order to cut it into slices.

scope of chapter

4. Unless otherwise mentioned, the rest of this chapter deals only with the grinding, chopping, crushing, mashing, crumbling, shredding or squashing of food without the aid of a specially designed instrument.

classification of foods

5. It will be seen that, for the purposes of the rules discussed in this chapter, various distinctions must be made between different kinds of foods, for example:

a. between

1) food which grows from the ground and
2) food which does not grow from the ground or

b. between

1) food which has previously been ground or mashed and
2) food which has not previously been ground or mashed.

cutting up fresh fruits or vegetables

6. *a.* It is in general forbidden to grate, chop or shred raw food of a kind which grows in the ground, such as uncooked fruits or vegetables.

b. It is permissible to cut up such food with a knife, provided that

1) the resulting pieces are not too small **and**

2) the meal at which the food is to be eaten follows immediately.

c. There is good authority for allowing a person who is preparing food for a small child, or for someone who would otherwise find the food difficult to eat, to cut it even into very small pieces, so long as he does so immediately prior to the meal.

7. a. Banana, avocado and other raw fruit should not be spread on bread, as this is included in the prohibition against grinding.

spreading banana or avocado on bread

b. The prohibition does not, however, apply to a fruit which is so soft that, if one tried to pull it along, the part one is holding would come away in one's fingers.

8. a. As a rule, it is forbidden to squash or mash bananas, tomatoes and the like in the usual way.

mashing bananas or tomatoes

b. If one wishes, for example, to mash a banana for a small child, one should vary the method normally employed during the week, as by the use of a spoon or the handle of a fork (and not its prongs).

9. a. The prohibition against grinding is not applicable to fruits or vegetables which have been cooked to such an extent that they are soft and easy to mash.

spreading jam

b. As a result, one may spread jam or preserves on a slice of bread or a cracker.

10. a. Cooked potatoes and other vegetables may not be creamed or mashed very fine by being put through a strainer, even if they are very soft and easy to mash, because this is one of the uses for which a strainer is specifically intended.

cooked vegetables

b. 1) Cooked vegetables may be mashed with a fork, on condition that they were at least partly crushed out of shape before or during cooking and mash easily.

2) In this case, one may use not only the handle but even the prongs of the fork.

bread,
biscuits,
chocolate,
sugar and
salt

11. *a.* Food which is made from material which has previously been ground, such as bread, matzoth or cookies (biscuits), may be crushed or crumbled on Shabbath, but,

    1) although one may use a knife, or a similar utensil, one may not use an instrument specially designed for the purpose, such as a grater, and

    2) it must be intended for eating on the same day, although not necessarily immediately after preparation.

  b. The same rules apply also to

    1) chocolate,

    2) lumps of sugar and

    3) grains of salt which, due to the effect of moisture, have formed into a block.

  c. Rock-salt should be crushed or crumbled only with an instrument not specifically made for that purpose, such as the handle of a knife or fork, since it is quarried from the mine in blocks and not as separate crystals.

  d. 1) It is perfectly in order to slice bread, meat, salami and the like with a specially designed slicing-machine, so long, of course, as it is operated by hand and not by electricity.

    2) One may even regulate such a machine, in order to obtain slices of the desired thickness.

precrushed
foods

12. *a.* Food which grows from the ground and has been well mashed or crushed, either

    1) before Shabbath or

    2) on Shabbath, in a permitted manner, as described above,

may be divided on Shabbath into small portions, in the same way as during the rest of the week, provided that one does not use an instrument intended for that purpose.

  b. A banana which has been mashed

    1) before Shabbath or

    2) on Shabbath, in circumstances which make this permissible (see paragraph 8 above),

[74]

may, therefore, be separated into small portions on Shabbath.

13. *a.* If one wishes to prepare porridge, farina, semolina, rice (either ground or whole) or cornflour which was cooked prior to Shabbath but has since dried up, one may, on Shabbath,

   1) pour hot water over it, even from a k*e*li rishon,
   2) loosen it by stirring and
   3) dissolve any lumps by pressing them against the plate with a spoon (but, due to the prohibition against selection, one may not remove just the lumps, if one does not intend to eat them).

   b. If the porridge, farina, semolina, rice or cornflour, although cooked before Shabbath, is still of a thin consistency,

   1) hot water may be poured into it only from a k*e*li sheini or, alternatively,
   2) it may be put into hot water in a k*e*li sheini.

   c. See also Chapter 1, paragraphs 46 and 47 and, for definitions of k*e*li rishon and k*e*li sheini, Chapter 1, paragraph 2.

14. *a.* It is permissible to chop or mash food which does not grow from the ground, so long as one does not do so with an instrument specially designed for that purpose.

   b. One may, thus, mash boiled eggs or cooked meat or fish,

   1) even with the prongs of a fork and
   2) even if one does not wish to eat them until later, provided that one does intend to eat them during the course of that Shabbath. (See, however, Chapter 3, paragraph 31, compliance with which may require the food to be eaten immediately.)

   c. Cheese may be cut with a special cheese knife, since it is fit to be used as a normal piece of cutlery.

15. See Chapter 8 with regard to mixing mashed banana with cheese, biscuits and so forth.

Chapter 7

Laws of Grinding, Chopping, Crushing and Grating on Yom Tov

classification of foods

1. As will be seen below, for the purpose of applying the rules relating to grinding, chopping, crushing and grating on Yom Tov, distinctions must be made
  a. between
    1) food which grows from the ground and
    2) food which does not grow from the ground and
  b. between
    1) food which will become completely spoiled if ground, chopped, crushed or grated before the Festival,
    2) food which will not spoil altogether, but will lose some of its taste, and
    3) food which will not be adversely affected at all if prepared in this way before the Festival.

bananas, apples, onions and potatoes

2. *a.* Food which
    1) grows from the ground **and**
    2) will spoil altogether if ground, chopped, crushed or grated before the Festival
    may be so prepared on Yom Tov, in the manner adopted on a normal weekday, but only for use on that same day of Yom Tov. (See, however, paragraph 7 below, regarding the use of a kitchen mincer or grinder.)
  b. Thus,
    1) bananas may be mashed with the prongs of a fork,
    2) apples may be scraped on a grater,
    3) onions may be chopped very fine, with a large chopping-knife specially designed for the purpose, in the manner which one is accustomed to use on a normal weekday,
    4) cooked vegetables may be passed through a strainer to cream them, and

    5) boiled potatoes may be mashed, to make them into a puree.

  c. For the laws concerning Yom Tov which occurs on Friday, see Chapter 2, paragraphs 10 to 16.

3. *a.* Food which

    1) grows from the ground **and**

    2) will not spoil altogether if ground, chopped, crushed or grated before the Festival, **but**

    3) will lose some of its flavor,

  such as coffee beans, horseradish or spices, may be so prepared on Yom Tov, but

    1) only in a manner which varies from that usually adopted on a normal weekday **and**

    2) only for use on that same day of Yom Tov.

  (See paragraph 7 below, regarding the use of a kitchen mincer or grinder.)

  b. Thus, for example, if one is accustomed, on a normal weekday, to grate horseradish on a grater held over a plate, one should, on Yom Tov, grate it

    1) over a piece of paper or

    2) over a cloth or

    3) over a plate, but with the grater held upside down.

coffee, horseradish and spices

4. *a.* Food which

    1) grows from the ground **and**

    2) will not spoil at all or lose any of its flavor if ground, chopped, crushed or grated before the Festival,

  such as nuts or blocks of rock-salt*, should be ground, chopped, crushed or grated before Yom Tov.

  b. If, nonetheless, one is faced on Yom Tov with a situation where the food has not been so prepared before the Festival, one may then proceed to grind, chop, crush or grate it, even with the aid of a specially designed instrument, but

salt and nuts

----

*For the purposes of these rules deposits of rock-salt are regarded as growing from the ground.

1) not with an instrument which is normally used to prepare food for several days ahead **and**

2) only in a manner which varies from that usually adopted on an ordinary weekday **and**

3) only for use on that same day of Yom Tov.

*cake,
cookies,
bread and
lumps of
sugar*

5. *a.* The following rules apply with regard to food which
   1) grows from the ground **and**
   2) is made from material that has previously been broken down or from separate crystals or particles that have formed into a block,

   such as lumps of sugar or baked foods made from ground grain.

   b. One may regrind, crush or crumble such food on Yom Tov, provided it is required for that day of Yom Tov, and one may even do so
   1) in the manner usually adopted on an ordinary weekday and
   2) with the aid of a specially designed instrument (other than an instrument normally used to prepare food for several days ahead).

   c. See paragraph 7 below for use of a kitchen mincer or grinder.

   d. After the food has been ground, crushed or crumbled, those pieces which have not been properly broken down should not be picked out by themselves, due to the prohibition against selection, but one may remove them together with a little of the ground food.

*eggs, meat,
fish and
cheese*

6. *a.* Subject to what is stated in paragraph 7 below, it is perfectly in order to mash, chop, mince or grate food which does not grow from the ground, such as eggs, meat, fish or hard cheese.

   b. This may be done in the manner normally adopted during the week, for instance with the prongs of a fork.

   c. It is immaterial whether or not the food would lose any of its flavor if prepared earlier.

7. *a.* Meat, fish, coffee, matzoth and other foods which are *mincers and* commonly ground in a mincer or grinder should, prefer- *grinders* ably, be put through the mincer or grinder before Yom Tov.

  b. If one did not do so, one may put them through a household mincer on Yom Tov; however,

    1) one should not, of course, use an electrically operated machine,

    2) one should not use a large, commercial mincer, of the type used in shops to prepare considerable quantities of food at the same time,

    3) a variation should be made in the manner normally used for grinding meat and fish, for example by mincing it onto paper or a cloth, and

    4) it is best not to put coffee through a coffee-grinder at all.

  c. Baked food prepared from ground grain, such as matzoth, may be ground in a mincer in the normal way on Yom Tov in case of need.

  d. 1) A household mincer whose use is permitted, as stated above, may be assembled and dismantled on Yom Tov.

    2) See Chapter 12, paragraph 1 concerning the rinsing or washing of a mincer on Yom Tov.

Chapter 8

Laws of Kneading on Shabbath

introductory A. This chapter deals only with the kneading of food on Shabbath.

B. The kneading of food on Yom Tov, so long as it is for consumption on the same day, is perfectly in order.

C. 1. The prohibition against kneading applies also to materials which are inedible.
   2. Examples are pouring water onto earth or cement or mixing them with water. (Actual kneading is not necessary for the prohibition to apply, provided that the conditions set out below, in paragraph 1, are present.)
   3. The kneading of matter other than food is forbidden both on Shabbath and on Yom Tov.

D. See also Chapter 16, paragraph 4.

conditions for applying prohibition 1. The prohibition against kneading is in no way applicable unless the following three conditions are all fulfilled:
   a. Two separate substances are being combined.
   b. Either
      1) each of these substances is comprised of soft, pliable matter, such as dough, or of small particles (whether because that is its natural state or because it has been ground down or chopped fine), or has a stiff consistency, such as thick honey,

      or

      2) one such substance takes one of these forms and the other is a liquid.
   c. The substances combine in such a way that they mingle together and fuse into one mixture, regardless of whether this is
      1) a result of the action of a liquid naturally present in one or both of the substances,

2) because one of the substances is itself a liquid or

3) due to the natural consistency of the substances being mixed, for example,

   a) honey and soft cheese or

   b) butter and cocoa powder.

(For a better understanding of these conditions, which are difficult to comprehend in the abstract, reference should be made to the numerous examples contained below in this chapter.)

2. When kneading is forbidden, it may not be done even immediately prior to the meal at which the food being prepared is to be eaten.

kneading for immediate use

3. *a.* It follows from condition *a* in paragraph 1 above that it is permissible to knead one substance by itself.

   b. Thus,

   1) one may crush a banana for a small child with the handle of a fork (but not with the prongs, as explained in Chapter 6, paragraph 8), until it turns into a soft pulp, and

   2) there are authorities who allow one to knead already baked crumbs, so long as one does not add water to them. (See also paragraph 22 below.)

kneading one substance by itself

4. *a.* 1) It follows from conditions *b* and *c* in paragraph 1 above that it is permissible to mix together substances of such a nature that they do not fuse into one mixture, even if they contain a liquid.

   2) Thus

   a) one may pour oil, vinegar or mayonnaise onto vegetables, such as potatoes, which have been cut up (so long as the pieces are not too small), and add salt and seasonings, to prepare a salad, and

   b) one may, similarly, make fruit salad.

   b. 1) It follows from condition *c* in paragraph 1 above that it is permissible to mix together two substances which

making salads and mixing powders

will not fuse into one mixture due to the absence of a liquid.

2) Thus, one may mix granulated sugar with cocoa powder or cinnamon.

pouring one substance into another

5. *a.* The prohibition against kneading is applicable even if one does not actually knead or directly mix the two substances together, but simply pours the one into the other and they mingle and stick to each other by themselves.

b. If one of the substances is a liquid it makes no difference whether one pours the liquid into the other substance or puts the other substance into the liquid.

c. Consequently, one may neither
1) pour water into flour nor
2) put flour into water,
even without mixing them together.

substances poured together before Shabbath

6. Two substances of the kind described in paragraph 1 above should not be mixed or kneaded together on Shabbath, even if one was put onto, or poured into, the other before Shabbath.*

substances mixed together before Shabbath

7. *a.* One is permitted to add liquid to two substances of the kinds described in paragraph 1 above which were actually mixed together before Shabbath and to thin the mixture by gentle stirring.

b. 1) One may, therefore, on Shabbath, mix together peanut butter and the oil which has separated out and risen to the top, or even mix another liquid into it, since this loosens the mixture, but

2) one may not mix soft cheese into peanut butter on Shabbath, since the two combine to form an even thicker substance than the peanut butter was to start with.

---

*This is so despite the fact that the principle expressed in the previous paragraph treats two substances poured into each other as having already been kneaded together.

8. In connection with condition *c* contained in paragraph 1 above, a distinction should be made between *two types of mixtures*
    a. a liquid mixture which is thin enough to be poured from one vessel into another and
    b. a mixture which thickens to the point where it does not pour easily.

9. a. The general rule is that it is forbidden to prepare a thick mixture on Shabbath. *main distinction in rules applicable to thick and thin mixtures*
    b. It is forbidden to prepare a thin mixture on Shabbath, unless one is careful to make the following two variations in the usual method adopted.
        1) One should reverse the normal order of putting in the ingredients.
            a) Thus, if, during the rest of the week, one is in the habit of putting the liquid or the substance containing the liquid into the dry substance, one should, on Shabbath, reverse the order and put the dry substance into the liquid or into the substance containing the liquid; however, if one normally follows the latter procedure, one should, on Shabbath, adopt the former.
            b) If one does not have a set order for putting in the ingredients, one should, on Shabbath, put the dry substance in first and then add the liquid.
            c) Whenever preparing a thin mixture by pouring liquid into a dry substance, one should take care to pour all the liquid in at once, without stopping in the middle, in order to ensure that the mixture is indeed thin right from the start.
        2) One should stir the mixture in a different way.
            a) Thus, if possible, one should stir with one's finger or by agitating the vessel containing the mixture.
            b) Where an instrument, such as a spoon or a fork, must be used, one should, instead of stirring in the normal manner, draw the instrument through the mixture with alternate strokes, one back or forth and another from side to side, and this may be

done several times, although it is preferable to remove the instrument from the mixture after each stroke.

thick mixtures partially prepared before Shabbath

10. Where a thick mixture would not keep if prepared before Shabbath, so that it is necessary to make it on Shabbath, one should adopt the following procedure.

 a. Sufficient liquid should be stirred into the dry substance, before Shabbath, to saturate the whole of it.

 b. Additional liquid may then be mixed in on Shabbath, so long as

  1) this does not result in the thickening of the mixture **and**

  2) one is careful to vary the method in the two ways described in the previous paragraph.

making thick mixtures on Shabbath

11. If one needs a thick mixture and either

 a. it is not possible to add some of the liquid to the dry substance before Shabbath **or**

 b. one has forgotten to do so and requires the mixture for a specific purpose, as where one has forgotten to prepare the mixture of nuts, wine, cinnamon and apples (*charoseth*) required for the first night of a Passover which falls on Shabbath, **or**

 c. the food one is preparing must be fresh as, for example, when it is required for a baby,

then one may make it on Shabbath, taking care, however, to vary the methods of putting in the ingredients and of stirring, in accordance with the instructions contained in paragraph 9 above. (For an exception, where making the mixture is altogether prohibited, see paragraph 25 below.)

mixing cream and soft cheese

12. It follows from the rules set out above that it is permissible to mix cream or yogurt with soft cheese, if the result is a thin mixture and one adopts the variations in method previously described.

mixing cheese and honey

13. One may not mix honey and cheese, even if it is intended for immediate consumption.

14. If one wishes to mix lemon juice into soft, white cheese or *mixing* mashed bananas for a baby, one may do so, but one should *lemon juice* observe the following rules. *into cheese or bananas*

    a. The bananas should be mashed in the manner specified in Chapter 6, paragraph 8.

    b. When the juice has to be squeezed out, it should be squeezed onto the cheese or bananas by hand (and not with a specially designed lemon squeezer).

    c. The method of stirring should be varied, as in paragraph 9 above.

    d. When one is using juice which was squeezed out before Shabbath, the order of inserting the ingredients should be reversed, as in paragraph 9 above.

15. *a.* In the circumstances mentioned in paragraph 11 above, *mixing* and subject to the conditions set out there, one may mix *biscuit and* biscuit crumbs with soft, white cheese, should this *soft cheese* become necessary.

    b. If the biscuits need to be crumbled first, one should comply with the rules stated in Chapter 6, paragraph 11.

    c. As long as one varies the methods of mixing and inserting ingredients, as above, one can add fruit juice or any other liquid to the mixture of biscuit and cheese. (See also paragraph 14 above.)

16. *a.* The prohibition against kneading does not apply at all to *mixing sugar* the stirring of sugar or thin, liquidy jam into yogurt or *or jam with* cream, since this produces an even thinner mixture than *cream or* one started with. *cheese*

    b. Mixing sugar or jam, even if it is thin and liquidy, into soft cheese is forbidden, however, except under the conditions and in the circumstances mentioned in paragraph 11 above, since the resultant mixture may well be thicker than the original cheese.

17. Butter or margarine may not be mixed with cocoa powder, *mixing* even for immediate consumption, as this results in a thick *butter and* mixture. *cocoa*

milk powder 18. *a.* If one wishes to prepare milk from ordinary milk powder or from milk powder specially made for infants, and the powder does not dissolve immediately, one of two methods should be adopted, depending on the circumstances.

 1) Where one is accustomed during the week to make the initial concentrated solution by pouring the water into the powder, then, on Shabbath, one should proceed as follows.
   a) Some hot water should be emptied out of the urn or kettle (even if it is still standing on the fire), into a dry cup.
   b) One should roughly estimate the amount of powder required, without measuring it out, although, when preparing milk for an infant, it is permissible to measure it out if necessary.
   c) The powder should be put into the water in the cup and stirred in the manner described in paragraph 9 above.

 2) Where one is accustomed during the week to put the powder into the water, then, on Shabbath, one should proceed in the reverse order.
   a) The amount of powder required should be measured out or roughly estimated, as appropriate, and put into an empty cup.
   b) Water should be emptied from the urn or kettle into another, dry cup, which is a *k°li sheini*. (See Chapter 1, paragraph 2.)
   c) The cup of water should be emptied into the cup of powder and stirred in the manner described in paragraph 9 above.

 b. 1) Particles of powder which become clotted together and do not dissolve while the mixture is being stirred should not be removed from the solution on their own, due to the prohibition against selection. (Compare Chapter 7, paragraph 5.)

2) One may either
  a) break up the clots by pressing them against the side of the cup or
  b) remove the clots together with a little milk.

c. To dilute the concentrated solution of milk powder and water, one should pour the required amount of additional water into it from a k^{e}li sheini and mix as necessary.

19. a. 1) Liquid may be poured onto food which has become soft in cooking and may then be mixed with it, as explained in the example given below. *food softened by cooking*

   2) This is a perfectly permissible way of preparing food and does not contravene the prohibition against kneading.

   b. Consequently, potatoes that have become at least a little squashed in cooking and are easy to crush
   1) may be mashed, even with the prongs of a fork,
   2) may have gravy poured over them, even from a k^{e}li rishon (as to which see Chapter 1, paragraph 2), and
   3) may then be mixed together with the gravy.

20. a. Cinnamon may be mixed into a plate of porridge, semolina or rice. *mixing cinnamon or raisins with rice*

   b. One may, similarly, mix in some raisins in order to improve the flavor.

21. a. If the liquid has evaporated from food which is standing on a covered fire (as described in Chapter 1, paragraph 18), one may gently pour water into it from a k^{e}li rishon which is also standing on the covered fire. *adding water to dried-up food*

   b. Even though the water and the food will mix together, the prohibition against kneading is not transgressed.

   c. This particular case is treated in somewhat greater detail in Chapter 1, paragraph 16.

22. a. 1) Baked food may be dipped into liquid, since this does not knead the food, but makes it become soft and disintegrate. *dipping cake, cookies or bread into liquid*

[87]

2) If the liquid is warm, the food should not be dipped into it unless it is in a *k^eli sh^elishi*. (See Chapter 1, paragraphs 2 and 59.)

b. One may, thus, dip bread into soup or gravy and then eat it or suck the liquid out of it. (See, however, Chapter 5, paragraph 9.)

c. Nevertheless, it is forbidden to press or knead together bread which has become soft and has disintegrated in liquid, in order to make it into one piece again.

chopped eggs and onions

23. When preparing chopped eggs and onions on Shabbath, one should do so in the following manner.

a. The shell should be removed from the hard-boiled eggs immediately before the meal at which they are to be eaten. (See Chapter 3, paragraph 31.)

b. The eggs may be mashed with the prongs of a fork. (See Chapter 6, paragraph 14.)

c. The onions should be peeled and cut up immediately before the meal at which they are to be eaten. (See Chapter 3, paragraph 31 and Chapter 6, paragraph 6.)

d. The onions should not be cut into very small pieces. (See Chapter 6, paragraph 6.)

e. The eggs and onions may then be mixed together.

f. 1) It is an accepted practice to add oil and mix it into the eggs and onions, without bothering to make the variations referred to in paragraph 9 above.

2) Nonetheless, it is preferable to make those variations and to change both the order of putting in the ingredients and the manner of stirring.

g. If boiled potatoes are to be added, the usual way of mashing them should be changed, for example by using the handle of a fork, unless they have been a little squashed in cooking and are easy to mash, in which case they may be mashed by the normal method, for instance with the prongs of a fork. (See Chapter 6, paragraphs 8 and 10.)

h. 1) Should a fragment of eggshell fall into the eggs and

onions, it should not be removed by itself due to the prohibition against selection.

2) a) The best course is to remove the eggs and onions, leaving the shell in the dish.

b) Failing this, the shell should be removed together with a little of the food.

24. a. Soluble powders may be dissolved in water and the prohibition against kneading is not involved, so long as the end product is a liquid.

instant powders for making liquids

b. Powders which have been through a process of boiling during the course of manufacture, such as instant coffee, sugar and refined salt, may be put into water even if it is in a kᵉli sheini. (See Chapter 1, paragraphs 2 and 55.)

c. However, unrefined rock-salt and cocoa powder of the kind normally in use should not be put into a kᵉli sheini, but only into a kᵉli shᵉlishi, since they have not been through a boiling process at any stage. (See Chapter 1, paragraphs 2, 53 and 54.)

25. a. Instant powders which turn into ready-to-eat, solid food, and not into a liquid, when mixed with water, should not have liquid poured into them, nor should they be poured into a liquid, as this falls within the definition of kneading.

instant powders for producing solid foods

b. Examples are powders for making instant, precooked foods, such as puddings, rice and mashed potatoes.

c. The use of these powders is not permitted, even to make a mixture with a thin consistency.

26. a. Some powders or foods, when mixed with liquid and stirred, at first form into a thick mixture and only become thinner with continued stirring.

thick mixtures which become thin

b. Liquid should not be added to such powders or foods, even if one's intention is to continue stirring until one has a thin mixture.

c. See also paragraph 11 above.

Chapter 9

Opening Cans, Bottles and Other Containers on Shabbath and Yom Tov

preferable course

1. *a.* It will be seen below that the opening of containers on Shabbath and Yom Tov is affected by a variety of rules, which are far from easy to apply in practice.

   b. Consequently, the preferable and proper course is to open sealed containers before Shabbath or Yom Tov commences.

   c. This applies to sealed boxes, to cans of preserves and the like, to bottles with re-usable tops that break open when removed for the first time and to all similar, sealed containers.

containers normally re-used

2. *a.* Bags, cans or similar, sealed containers (for example sacks of sugar) which it is customary to re-use after they have been opened and their contents removed may not be opened on Shabbath or Yom Tov, unless they are spoiled before or in the course of being opened (as in paragraph 3*d* below), and their contents emptied into other containers.

   b. The prohibition applies even if the person who wishes to open the container does not intend to re-use it.

   c. The reason for the prohibition is that it is the act of opening the container which converts it into a usable article, whereas previously it merely formed the outer skin or shell of whatever was inside it and was not fit for any other purpose.

containers not emptied on opening but not re-used

3. *a.* It is likewise forbidden, on Shabbath or Yom Tov, except as specified below, to open cartons, bags, cans or other sealed containers

   1) which it is not customary to re-use after they have been opened and their contents removed, but

2) in which it is usual to keep the original contents after they have been opened.

b. The prohibition applies even if one intends to empty out the contents immediately after opening the container.

c. Examples of such containers are
  1) cans of preserves (regarding which see also paragraph 18 below),
  2) cartons containing drink, such as those in which buttermilk or fruit juice is sometimes sold,
  3) plastic bags of milk,
  4) paper bags which are gummed shut, for instance bags of sugar and bags in which bread is packed to preserve its freshness,
  5) plastic bags whose openings have been glued shut or sealed by a process involving the application of pressure and
  6) packets of matzoth.

d. 1) It is permissible to open a can, bag, packet or other container if, before or while opening it, one perforates or tears it at the side or underneath in such a way that it will no longer be fit to be used as a container.
  2) a) Cans of vegetables may be perforated in this manner, even if the liquid inside, which one would in any case throw away, will flow out through the hole.
     b) This does not involve the prohibition against selection, since it is an unintended and incidental result of perforating the can.
     c) One should not, however, pour the liquid out of the opened can, but should remove the food, leaving the liquid inside.
  3) One may open a can if one cuts only half-way around the lid, which one then bends, in order to remove the contents immediately.

e. Some authorities permit the opening of cans, bags, and paper packets which are not normally re-used, even without spoiling them, as long as

1) one does not in fact intend to re-use them after removing their contents **and**

2) one does not specifically intend to make a particularly neat opening for more convenient use.

containers emptied immediately and thrown away

4. *a.* Packets which are usually emptied of their contents and thrown away immediately upon being opened, such as miniature packets of sugar of the type commonly used in hotels, may be opened on Shabbath and Yom Tov.

   b. One should be careful, in opening such packets, not to cut or tear through lettering or pictures, as mentioned in paragraph 12 below.

   c. It is, however, allowed to cut them open along a line specially marked for that purpose, if indeed they are thrown away once opened.

holes in containers

5. *a.* It is forbidden to take special care to make a perforation of a particular shape or size in a can, carton or similar, sealed container, in order to facilitate the removal of the contents through the hole.

   b. This rule should be observed, for example, when opening canisters of oil and cartons or bags of granulated sugar.

perforating containers in marked positions

6. *a.* The prohibition contained in paragraph 5 above applies also if one wishes to perforate a container in positions marked for that purpose.

   b. This is frequently relevant in the case of containers of baby powder and scouring powder. (For limitations on the use of scouring powder on Shabbath and Yom Tov see Chapter 12, paragraph 9.)

slicing spout off plastic bottle

7. *a.* Similarly, one may not slice the top off the sealed spout of a plastic bottle.

   b. It is common for liquid cleaners to be marketed in containers of this type, and they should, accordingly, be opened by perforating or tearing them at the side or underneath.

[92]

8. *a.* Cartons of cut, folded toilet paper should not be opened by cutting along the special marking or tearing along a perforation, as is usually done in order to make a convenient slot to facilitate the removal of the paper, sheet by sheet. *cartons of toilet paper*

   b. The carton should be ripped open and all of the paper removed.

9. Plastic or paper bags which have been stapled shut may be opened by extracting the staples. *stapled bags*

10. Both *boxes sealed with gummed paper*

    a. cardboard boxes whose lids are stuck down with gummed paper or tape and

    b. boxes wrapped in paper which is stuck down with gum may be opened, provided the conditions specified in paragraph 12 below are fulfilled.

11. Subject to careful observance of the conditions contained in paragraph 12 below, one may tear open seals of the following kinds: *paper seals*

    a. the paper seal covering the top of a bottle;

    b. the paper wrapping around chocolate;

    c. the internal seal under the lid of a box or jar of instant coffee* (whether made of paper or other material);

---

*It should be noted in passing that there is a rule whereby, with certain exceptions, vessels made by or purchased from a non-Jew must be immersed in a *mikveh* (a pool of water conforming to strict religious requirements) before they are used. Thus:

a. a container

   1) which is made by or bought from a non-Jew, as is usually the case outside Israel,

   2) which, if sealed, is sealed by means of a lid or top which can be removed, without permanently altering its shape, and replaced, as can the lids of boxes or jars normally used for instant coffee or milk powder, **and**

   3) which one wishes to re-use for food

should be immersed before being re-used in this way, whereas

d. the plastic or metal-foil top of a yogurt or sour-milk container.

*conditions
for opening
wrappings
and seals*

12. Even when it is permissible to open seals and wrappings, whether made of paper or some other material, the following conditions should be observed.

    a. 1) The seal or wrapping should be torn open in such a way that it is spoiled, and it goes without saying that one must not intentionally tear it in a manner which leaves even a part of it fit for any use (as where one tears carefully along the edge of prize tokens printed on a wrapping).

        2) This condition is equally applicable whether one is

          a) tearing the wrapping or seal itself or

          b) separating two pieces of paper or cardboard which are stuck together.

    b. One must not tear through lettering or pictures.

*bags sealed
by pliable
strips*

13. *a.* It is forbidden

        1) to seal a bag by putting a pliable metal or plastic strip around its opening and twining the ends together or

        2) to open a bag by untwining such a strip.

    b. If it is impossible to remove the strip without breaking it, for example where it is secured very tightly, one may snap it or even cut it through with a knife, so long as one does so in a manner which spoils it for further use.

*bags or
parcels tied
with string*

14. Similarly, if one wishes to open a bag, box or parcel tied with string and it is impossible to remove the string without breaking it, for example where it is tied very tightly, one may snap it or even cut it through with a knife, so long as one does so in a manner which spoils it for further use.

---

b. cans containing food, even if made outside Israel, need not be immersed, since they are converted into vessels only in the course of being opened for the first time.

Vessels should not be immersed in a *mikveh* on Shabbath or Yom Tov. (See Chapter 12, paragraph 29.)

15. Likewise, the cord on which dried figs or other fruits or vege- *strings of figs* tables have been strung may be broken or even cut with a knife, so long as this is done in a manner which spoils it for further use.

16. *a.* One may not *knots in*
    1) tie the top of a plastic bag in a knot, or *plastic bags*
    2) untie such a knot.
    (See Chapter 15, paragraphs 49 and 51.)
    b. A bag tied in this way may be torn open if the knot is left intact.

17. *a.* 1) One is not allowed to remove the cap of a bottle, if that *bottle caps*
       very act converts it into a usable top which can then be *which may*
       replaced and removed at will (whether or not that is *not be*
       one's intention). *removed*
    2) a) This prohibition applies to caps whose lower part breaks off and remains as a ring around the neck of the bottle when they are unscewed for the first time.
       b) It is probably also applicable to caps whose lower part cracks and widens to release their clasp on the neck of the bottle when they are unscrewed for the first time.
    b. 1) Bottle tops of this kind may be perforated with the aid of a hammer or a nail, provided this can be done without disfiguring lettering or pictures printed on them. (See paragraph 12*b* above.)
    2) A top in which one has made a hole large enough to render it unfit for further use may subsequently be removed.

18. *a.* There are products, such as oatmeal, which are *can lids* sometimes marketed in cans whose lids are joined to the *sealed by* can and sealed on by means of a metal or other strip. *metal strips*
    b. It is not permitted to open such a can by pulling off this strip, because in doing so, one separates the top from the

rest of the can, making the one a usable lid and the other a usable container.

perforated rubber nipples and salt shakers

19. *a.* One may neither make nor enlarge a perforation in the rubber nipple of a baby's bottle or in the top of a salt shaker.

b. However, material blocking an existing perforation may be removed.

crown-caps and corks

20. *a.* It is permissible to open a bottle sealed with a crown-cap or a cork.

b. This may be done even with the aid of a specially designed instrument, such as a bottle-opener or a corkscrew.

c. If the top of the bottle is covered with wax or a similar substance in which letters or shapes are impressed, the letters or shapes should be erased before the commencement of Shabbath. (See paragraph 12*b* above.)

releasing a vacuum

21. One may facilitate the opening of a vacuum-sealed jar of jam or preserves by puncturing the lid.

above rules also apply on Yom Tov

22. *a.* The various rules set out above are equally applicable on both Shabbath and Yom Tov.

b. Therefore, even on Yom Tov, one should not

1) open any sealed can, bag or package, nor
2) perforate any can or other sealed container or its lid, nor
3) slice the top off the sealed spout of a bottle, nor
4) tie or untie any knot, nor
5) seal or unseal a bag by winding or unwinding a metal or plastic strip around its top,

except as permitted in the circumstances described above.

containers opened in a forbidden manner

23. If one realizes that one has opened a can, bag, bottle or other container in a prohibited manner, one is, nevertheless, permitted to use the contents, even on that same Shabbath or Yom Tov.

24. *a.* A bottle may be stood in cold water in order to cool its contents, despite the fact that the label stuck to the bottle may come off in the water.

labels on bottles

b. A label which remains only lightly attached to the bottle after it has been standing in the water may be removed.

25. *a.* One may not tear paper off a roll, whether one

rolls of paper

    1) tears along a perforation or
    2) tears the paper where there are no perforations or
    3) tears the paper off with the aid of a specially made serrated edge.

b. Common examples to which this rule applies are rolls of wrapping paper or paper towels and toilet paper rolls.

26. *a.* The stopper of a thermos (vacuum flask) or bottle may be wrapped in a piece of cloth on Shabbath or Yom Tov, in order to make the seal more airtight, on condition that the thermos is not filled to the top with liquid.

thermos stoppers

b. One should not use a stopper wrapped in this way to seal a thermos filled to the top with liquid, nor should one remove it from such a thermos, since, in doing so, one will squeeze out some of the liquid absorbed in the cloth, which is forbidden.

27. *a.* It is perfectly in order to screw the cup onto or off the top of a thermos.

unscrewing thermoses

b. 1) One must not unscrew or screw together the outer casing of a thermos, since the casing is made to be a permanent part of the thermos and is not intended to be dismantled and re-assembled in the course of everyday use.

    2) The reason for this prohibition is that the thermos becomes a complete article when its casing is screwed on, and performing the final act which completes an article is forbidden on Shabbath and Yom Tov.

[97]

Chapter 10

The Use of Ice and Refrigerators
on Shabbath and Yom Tov

cooling fruit
and bottles
of drink with
ice

1. *a.* Ice may be melted on Shabbath or Yom Tov if the resultant water goes to waste.
   b. Thus,
   1) fruit or bottles of drink may be cooled with ice and
   2) ice may be disposed of in the kitchen sink.

putting ice
cubes into
drinks

2. *a.* It is also permissible to put ice cubes into a cup or jug
   containing water or another drink, so that they should
   cool the drink when they melt.
   b. This is allowed because the water produced by the
   melting ice is at no time recognizable as a separate entity.
   c. While one may even break up large blocks of ice for this
   purpose, it is advisable not to accelerate the melting of
   the ice inside the drink directly by, for example, pressing
   it with one's fingers or a spoon.

putting ice
cubes into an
empty cup

3. *a.* One should not place ice in an empty cup with the object
   of letting it melt and using the water, unless one would
   otherwise be inconvenienced.
   b. This rule applies equally on Shabbath and Yom Tov.
   c. If one has broken the rule, then
   1) it is not forbidden to drink the resultant water or to use
   it for any other purpose, but
   2) it is advisable not to use it if one has other water.

making ice
cubes

4. One should refrain from putting water into the freezer unit of
   a refrigerator in order to make ice cubes unless one feels
   unable to do without them on that day.*

---

*In passing, it is worth noting that
a. containers for making ice cubes or ice cream, if
1) made outside Israel **and**

5. *a.* It is perfectly in order *freezing*
   1) to put food which is not usually eaten in a frozen state *foods not*
      into a freezer and *usually eaten*
   2) to remove and thaw it for use. *in that state*
   b. One may, therefore, put milk, cooked meat (but not raw
      meat, which is *muktzeh*—see Chapter 20), and the like
      into a freezer or remove and thaw them.

6. *a.* One may not prepare ice cream from powder on Shabbath *ice cream*
      unless one adheres to the conditions set out in Chapter 8, *powder*
      paragraph 9.
   b. Ice cream may not be prepared from instant powder
      which, when mixed with water, turns into a ready-to-eat
      solid even before it is placed in the freezer.
   c. On Yom Tov ice cream may be made from powder in the
      normal way.

7. Liquid ice cream mixture which has been prepared in a *freezing*
   permissible manner (in accordance with the provisions in *ice cream*
   paragraph 6 above or where the solution was prepared before
   Shabbath) may be put into the freezer on Shabbath or Yom
   Tov, for use on that day, since even melted ice cream is
   generally thought of as a food, rather than as a drink, so that
   the freezing is not considered to bring into existence
   something new which did not exist before.

8. One is allowed to melt ice cream, if one does not wish to eat it *melting*
   while it is frozen, so long as one does not place it where it *ice cream*
   could reach a temperature of 45 degrees centigrade (113
   degrees Fahrenheit).

---

2) manufactured from metal or glass,
   need to be immersed, before use, in a *mikveh* (a pool of water
   conforming to strict religious conditions).
b. This immersion should not be performed on Shabbath or Yom Tov.
c. Immediately before performing the immersion, the appropriate
   blessing should be recited.

putting food
into a
refrigerator

9. *a.* It is permissible
1) to put food which has been left over after a meal back into the refrigerator and even
2) to put into a refrigerator food which has not previously been there.

b. 1) It is forbidden to pick meat out of a thick stew containing a mixture of other foods, such as potatoes and beans, in order to put it into the refrigerator so that it will not spoil.

2) This would contravene the prohibition against selection on Shabbath, as stated in Chapter 3, paragraphs 71 and 72.

3) One should do this neither on Shabbath nor on Yom Tov, since while, in principle, selection is permitted in most cases on Yom Tov, this is not so if what is being selected is not intended for use until after that day of Yom Tov.

defrosting for
later use

10. One should not take frozen food out of the refrigerator to defrost in time for use after Shabbath or Yom Tov or on the following day of Yom Tov.

emptying the
defrosting
tray

11. *a.* The defrosting tray of a refrigerator, or any other receptacle designed to collect the water which forms when the refrigerator defrosts, may be
1) removed and emptied on Shabbath or Yom Tov and
2) subsequently replaced.

b. Nevertheless, if practicable, it is better to pull the tray out only partially and scoop the water out with a cup or spoon.

c. An even better method is to use a tray incorporating a tap, through which the surplus water can be drained off.

d. If one has not directly poured the water away, but has emptied the tray into another container, one may pour the water away from that other container.

opening
domestic
refrigerators

12. *a.* There are differing opinions regarding the opening of an electric refrigerator.

b. If one wishes to comply with all of the restrictions expressed in these differing opinions, one should

   1) connect the refrigerator to a time-switch, which will turn the refrigerator off at pre-arranged hours, **and**

   2) open the refrigerator only during those hours.

c. In the absence of a time-switch,

   1) there are some authorities who state that one should be careful to open the refrigerator only when the motor is in operation, while

   2) others permit it to be opened at all times, that is to say even when the motor is not operating.

d. See paragraphs 14, 15 and 16 below regarding electric bulbs inside refrigerators.

13. The rules covering the use of electric refrigerators on Shabbath and Yom Tov and the differing opinions referred to in the preceding paragraph are equally applicable to electric water coolers, since they operate on the same principle.

electric water coolers

14. *a.* 1) One should remember, before the commencement of Shabbath or Yom Tov, to remove or disconnect the light bulb which is fitted inside most electric refrigerators and switches on automatically whenever the door is opened.

   2) Similarly, one should not forget to turn off the ventilator which is fitted inside some modern refrigerators and operates only as long as the door remains closed.

switching off internal lights and ventilators

b. If one has forgotten to remove or disconnect the internal light, one should, where the possibility exists, prevent the bulb from being turned on when the door is opened, by carefully inserting the blade of a knife through the hinge side of the door while it is still closed and holding the switch in a depressed position.

c. Where no such possibility exists and one cannot manage without the food inside the refrigerator, then

   1) one may have the plug connecting the refrigerator to

the electricity supply removed from the socket by a
boy under the age of thirteen or a girl under the age of
twelve, while the refrigerator is closed and its motor is
not in operation.

2) Should no such child be available, one may remove the
plug oneself, provided that
a) one does so in a manner which is different from
that which one would usually employ during the
rest of the week **and**
b) the plug is one which it is usual to remove and re-
insert on a weekday.

3) At all events, one should not reconnect the refrigerator to the electricity supply, in case the re-insertion of
the plug in the socket immediately restarts the motor
(despite the fact that this may not happen, as the
temperature may not have risen above that at which
the thermostat prevents the motor's activation).

4) See Chapter 31, paragraph 1 for the extent to which
one may avail oneself of the assistance of a non-Jew to
remove food from a refrigerator in the circumstances
discussed in this paragraph.

d. In the following two cases, neither of the methods
mentioned in *c*1 and *c*2 above may be used and, unless
the possibility referred to in *b* above exists, there is no
way of removing food from the refrigerator except by
making use of the services of a non-Jew, within the limits
laid down in Chapter 31, paragraph 1:

1) if one has forgotten to remove or disconnect the
internal light and the refrigerator is of a type whose
motor runs without any interruption, even when it is
closed and the desired temperature has been reached
(or if it is fitted with a continuously operating trans-
former from which it cannot be disconnected);

2) if one has forgotten before Shabbath or Yom Tov to
switch off an internal ventilator which operates con-
tinually, as long as the door of the refrigerator is
closed.

15. Should one be in doubt as to whether one did or did not remove or disconnect the internal light of a refrigerator before the beginning of Shabbath or Yom Tov, there is room for permitting the refrigerator to be opened, although some authorities take a stricter view.

    doubt whether light is off inside refrigerator

16. If, upon opening an electric refrigerator on Shabbath or Yom Tov, one finds that the internal light has automatically been switched on,

    internal light found on upon opening refrigerator

    a. this does not make it forbidden to eat the food inside, but
    b. one should consult a qualified rabbinical authority about what to do with regard to closing the door of the refrigerator again.

Chapter 11

Various Laws Relating to the Preparation of Food on Shabbath and Yom Tov

SALTING AND RINSING FOOD

salting foods commonly preserved with salt

1. *a.* Foods which are commonly pickled or preserved by salting may not be salted on Shabbath, except in one of the following two ways.

   1) One may separately dip each piece in salt and eat it right away.

   2) One may even salt many pieces together, but, in that case, one should immediately add vinegar or oil, which weaken the strength of the salt.

   b. Examples of such foods are onions and cucumbers.

   c. These foods should not be salted, except in one of the above ways, even if one's intention is to eat them right after salting.

   d. While food may be salted in the usual manner on Yom Tov, it is preferable, where possible, to restrict oneself to the above two methods, as on Shabbath.

salting foods not commonly preserved with salt

2. *a.* Foods which are not commonly pickled or preserved by salting, but whose flavor is improved by salt, may be salted in the normal way, provided that they are to be used before the end of Shabbath, although it is more advisable to salt them immediately before the meal at which they are intended to be eaten.

   b. Examples of such foods are eggs and tomatoes.

pickling

3. *a.* 1) It is forbidden to pickle cucumbers, green tomatoes and the like, whether on Shabbath or Yom Tov.

   2) Pickling is prohibited whether it consists of putting the vegetables into vinegar or salt-water.

   b. Salted fish may be put into vinegar to give it a better taste, so long as the intention is to eat it before the end of Shabbath or that day of Yom Tov.

4. *a.* Salted fish may be rinsed or soaked in cold water on Shabbath, in order to remove the salt, if one intends to eat it on that same Shabbath. *washing salted fish*

 b. One may not, as explained in Chapter 1, paragraph 57,
  1) pour hot water over it, even from a kᵉli sheini, or
  2) soak it in hot water, even in a kᵉli shᵉlishi.

 c. On Yom Tov, there is no restriction on rinsing or soaking salted fish even in hot water.

 d. Regarding the washing of fruit see Chapter 3, paragraph 21 and Chapter 4, paragraph 9.

5. *a.* One is not allowed to salt raw meat on Shabbath in order to draw the blood out of it and, thus, make it fit to eat in accordance with Jewish religious law. *salting, rinsing and soaking raw meat*

 b. Likewise, the meat should not be rinsed or soaked on Shabbath in order to prepare it for salting after Shabbath.

 c. 1) However, if
  a) the third day after the slaughter of an animal (including the day of slaughter) falls on Shabbath **and**
  b) one has forgotten to salt or rinse its meat before Shabbath,
  one may have it rinsed and soaked, on Shabbath, by a non-Jew. (See Chapter 31, paragraph 5.)
  2) Where there is no non-Jew available, the rinsing and soaking may be done by a Jew.
  3) The reason for this is that, if the meat were not salted or rinsed before the end of the third day, one would be forbidden to prepare it for eating by cooking it in a pot, as one would normally do.
  4) For the purpose of this rinsing or soaking, the meat may be moved, despite the fact that, as mentioned in Chapter 20, paragraph 28, raw meat is *muktzeh*.
  5) a) Where the meat is lying in a pot, dish or other

[105]

vessel, it is preferable to rinse and soak it by washing one's hands over it until it is covered in water.

b) The water may be poured out afterwards.

d. It is permissible to salt, rinse and soak meat on Yom Tov, if one intends to eat it on the same day.

diluting
vinegar

6. The strength of vinegar may be weakened by the addition of water.

LETTERING AND DESIGNS ON FOOD

icing on
cakes

7. *a.* One may eat cakes decorated with lettering or designs made out of other foodstuffs, such as

1) icing sugar, chocolate cream or any similar spread,
2) pieces of fruit or
3) very small, colored candies (sweets),

even though, by eating them, one spoils the lettering or the designs.

b. However, the lettering or designs must not be cut before being eaten.

c. If the cake was cut before Shabbath, a slice may be removed on Shabbath, even if this results in the breaking up of a previously complete letter or design.

food
embossed or
imprinted
with letters
or made in
the shape of
letters

8. *a.* 1) Where the lettering is made of the same material as the food on which it appears, the food may be cut or broken even in the place where the letters are.

2) Common examples of foods which are often lettered in this way are bread, cookies (biscuits) and chocolate.

3) It does not matter whether the letters are embossed or impressed.

b. Similarly, one may cut or break cakes or cookies made in the shape of letters or designs.

labels stuck
on bread

9. *a.* 1) In some countries, it is customary to stick labels bearing the name of the bakery or other information onto loaves of bread or cakes.

2) Such labels should be removed in their entirety —
together with a little of the bread or cake — without
cutting them, so as not to damage the lettering.

b. 1) Any labels attached to the two loaves which are eaten
with each Shabbath meal should not be removed until
after the first loaf has been cut.

2) This is so that the loaves will still be whole when the
blessing is said over them.

10. a. 1) Care must be taken, when cutting salami which has a *salami, eggs*
brand name printed on its skin, not to cut or tear the *and oranges*
lettering.

2) Preferably, the salami should be peeled or sliced
before Shabbath or Yom Tov.

b. In the same way, when removing the shell from an egg,
one should be careful not to break through any letters or
designs which may be stamped on it.

c. This rule is equally applicable to oranges or any other
food stamped or marked with letters or numbers, such as
the price of the product.

11. a. One should not join together or shape food into a specific *smoothing or*
form for decorative purposes, as this is one of the *shaping food*
activities forbidden under the general heading of
"Building."

b. For this reason, when preparing eggs and onions (see
Chapter 8, paragraph 23), one should take care not to
smooth them after putting them on the plate.

12. a. Instruments designed for cutting fruits or vegetables, *cutting*
such as melon, beets or potatoes, into special shapes *shapes out of*
should not be used. *food*

b. Butter, margarine and the like should not be formed into
a decorative design.

13. a. When baking on Yom Tov, *decorative*
1) one should not form the dough into letters or any other *baking*
special shape,

[107]

2) nor should one draw letters or designs on cakes with a spread of any kind or by making an arrangement with confectionery.

b. See also paragraph 7 above and paragraph 14 below.

food in tubes **14.** *a.* Food may be squeezed out of a tube, so long as one is not interested in the special shape which comes out of the tube, as one is when making decorations with whipped cream.

b. It goes without saying that one is forbidden to squeeze icing or any other spread onto a cake, in the shape of letters or in a particular design.

c. See also paragraph 7 above.

cutting food **15.** *a.* The prohibitions against cutting and marking with a line preparatory to cutting are not applicable to food, if the cutting or marking is done

1) for the purpose of eating **or**
2) to serve a person's bodily requirements (as illustrated below).

b. It is, therefore, permissible
1) to mark lines on a cake with a knife, to facilitate cutting it into even slices,
2) to cut lines into the skin of an orange, so as to be able to peel it more easily, or
3) to cut any food into equal portions (subject to the restrictions set out in paragraph 7 above).

c. One is allowed, in the same circumstances, to cut or trim animal fodder.

d. Thus, one may trim a piece of straw (animal fodder) to use as a toothpick (a bodily requirement). (See also Chapter 14, paragraph 34).

SEPARATION OF TERUMOTH, MA'ASROTH AND CHALLA
ON SHABBATH AND YOM TOV

general **16.** *a.* 1) As a general rule, it is forbidden, both on Shabbath
prohibition and Yom Tov,

a) to separate *tᵉrumoth* or *ma'asroth,*

  b) to remove the sanctity from *ma'aser sheini* or from fruit which grows on a tree in its fourth year or

  c) to take *challa*, if the dough was kneaded before the commencement of the day (that is to say before the evening).

 2) There are two reasons for this.

  a) These activities bear a resemblance to the dedication of food for Temple purposes, which was forbidden.

  b) One should not perform the final act which makes fit for use something which was previously unfit.

 3) Food which, due to this injunction, cannot be made fit to eat on Shabbath or Yom Tov is *muktzeh* and should not be moved. (See Chapter 20.)

 4) Regarding the taking of *challa* outside the boundaries of what Jewish religious law considers the Land of Israel, see Chapter 31, paragraph 41.

b. If certain pre-conditions are fulfilled, as explained in paragraphs 18 to 27 below, *t*^e*rumoth, ma'asroth,* and *challa* may be removed on Shabbath and Yom Tov.

c. 1) *Challa* may be taken on Yom Tov without any pre-conditions, if the obligation to do so arises on Yom Tov. *taking challa on Yom Tov*

 2) This occurs not only

  a) if an appropriate quantity of dough is kneaded on Yom Tov, but also

  b) if separate doughs, loaves or cakes which together, but not individually, are large enough to require *challa* to be taken from them are, on Yom Tov, for the first time all put in the same container or placed on a cloth which is then folded over to cover them (even if they were kneaded and baked before Yom Tov).

17. If a person has separated *t*^e*rumoth, ma'asroth* or *challa* on Shabbath or Yom Tov in breach of the above prohibitions, then, *infringement of prohibitions*

 a. if he has done so without realizing that what he was doing

was forbidden, he or anyone else may eat the food which
remains, even on the same day, but,

b. if he has done so deliberately, neither he nor anyone else
may eat the remaining food until after Shabbath or Yom
Tov.

*where
imprac-
ticable to
separate
before
Shabbath or
Yom Tov*

18. a. Sometimes, circumstances are such that one is unable to
separate *terumoth* and *ma'asroth* before Shabbath or
Yom Tov, or it is impracticable to do so, as where

1) one is afraid that fruit will go bad if a piece is cut off
for this purpose before Shabbath or Yom Tov, as
would, for example, be the case with a melon, or

2) *terumoth* and *ma'asroth* have not been separated from
the ingredients of the Shabbath loaves, and one
cannot cut a piece off before Shabbath, because two
loaves must be kept whole for each Shabbath meal.

b. In such circumstances, one may, before Shabbath or Yom
Tov, make a prior stipulation which will enable one to
separate *terumoth* and *ma'asroth* on the Shabbath or
Yom Tov.

c. One should make the stipulation in one of the forms
specified in paragraphs 20 to 22 below and one should, in
addition, express one's intention that whatever will be
separated for the purpose on Shabbath or Yom Tov
should become *terumoth* or *ma'asroth* at the moment of
separation.

d. The contents of this paragraph are equally applicable,
with appropriate amendments, to the taking of *challa**
inside the boundaries of what Jewish religious law
considers the Land of Israel, but reference should be
made to Chapter 31, paragraph 41 for the position with
regard to the taking of *challa* elsewhere.

---

*The preferred course when taking *challa* from a loaf one has left whole
for the Shabbath meal is to separate it immediately before reciting the
blessing over the bread.

19. *a.* The blessings said on taking *challa* or *t^erumoth* and
ma'asroth and on redeeming *ma'aser sheini* in the case of
food from which one is certain they have not previously
been taken should be recited when making the
separation, on the Shabbath or Yom Tov.

recital of blessings and declarations on Shabbath and Yom Tov

b. At the time of making the separation on Shabbath or
Yom Tov, one should recite the same declaration as on a
normal weekday, and if it is *challa* which one is taking (in
accordance with paragraph 18*d* above), one should ex-
plicitly designate it as *challa*.

c. *T^erumoth*, *ma'asroth* and *challa* which have been separated on Shabbath or Yom Tov

1) may be moved in the course of putting them aside,
but,

2) once they have been put down, they may not be moved
again, owing to the prohibitions regarding *muktzeh*.
(See Chapter 20.)

d. *Challa* may of course not be burned on Shabbath, nor on
Yom Tov.

20. The stipulation to be recited before Shabbath or Yom Tov
for the purpose of being able to separate *t^erumoth* and
ma'asroth on Shabbath or Yom Tov is similar in form to the
declaration used for separating *t^erumoth* and *ma'asroth* and
redeeming *ma'aser sheini* on a weekday, except that the
future tense is used throughout, since, instead of referring to
the food which has been separated, one refers to the food
which will be separated.*

text of stipulation for t^erumoth and ma'asroth

---

* *a.* The following Hebrew form of stipulation may be recited:

"הָעוֹדֵף עַל אֶחָד מִמֵּאָה מִכָּל מַה שֶׁאֲנִי עָתִיד לְהַפְרִישׁ מָחָר לְתַקֵּן בּוֹ אֶת הַטֶּבֶל, יְהֵא
תְּרוּמָה גְדוֹלָה בְּצַד צָפוֹן, כָּל מִין עַל מִינוֹ. אוֹתוֹ אֶחָד מִמֵּאָה הַנִּשְׁאָר וְעוֹד תִּשְׁעָה חֲלָקִים
כָּמוֹהוּ בְּצַד צְפוֹנָם שֶׁל הַפֵּרוֹת, כָּל מִין עַל מִינוֹ, יִהְיוּ מַעֲשֵׂר רִאשׁוֹן. אוֹתוֹ אֶחָד מִמֵּאָה
שֶׁהִתְנֵיתִי שֶׁיְּהֵא מַעֲשֵׂר רִאשׁוֹן, יְהֵא תְּרוּמַת מַעֲשֵׂר, כָּל מִין עַל מִינוֹ, וּמַעֲשֵׂר שֵׁנִי יְהֵא
בִּדְרוֹמָם שֶׁל הַפֵּרוֹת, כָּל מִין עַל מִינוֹ, הוּא וְחֻמְשׁוֹ, עַל פְּרוּטָה שֶׁבְּמַטְבֵּעַ
שֶׁיִּחַדְתִּיהָ לְחִלּוּל מַעֲשֵׂר שֵׁנִי."

b. 1) One must not make the stipulation unless one has set aside a coin
for the purpose of redeeming *ma'aser sheini*.

[111]

<table>
<tr><td>

*text of
stipulation
for challa*

</td><td>

21. The stipulation to be recited before Shabbath or Yom Tov
for the purpose of being able to take *challa* on Shabbath or
Yom Tov is in the following form: "That which I shall
separate tomorrow shall be *challa*."*

</td></tr>
<tr><td>

*text of
stipulation
for tᵉrumoth,
ma'asroth
and challa*

</td><td>

22. The stipulation to be recited before Shabbath or Yom Tov
for the purpose of being able to remove *tᵉrumoth* and
ma'asroth, as well as *challa*, on Shabbath or Yom Tov is in
the form mentioned in paragraph 20 above, with the
insertion, however, of the words, "That which I shall
separate for *challa* shall be *challa*."**

</td></tr>
<tr><td>

*shortened
form of
stipulation*

</td><td>

23. The form of the stipulation may be shortened to the
following: "Whatever I shall separate tomorrow shall become
tᵉrumoth, *ma'asroth* and *challa* and the redemption of

</td></tr>
</table>

---

2) If one is unsure how to set aside a coin or, indeed, concerning any
other aspect of separating *tᵉrumoth*, *ma'asroth* or *challa*, one
should consult a qualified rabbinical authority.

c. When separating *tᵉrumoth* and *ma'asroth* from products of the
third or sixth year after the septennial Sabbatical year, one
should substitute for the final part of the stipulation, beginning,
"וּמַעֲשֵׂר שֵׁנִי ...," the words, "כָּל מִין עַל מִינוֹ," "וּמַעֲשַׂר עָנִי בְּצַד דְּרוֹמוֹ, כָּל מִין עַל מִינוֹ ...".

*In Hebrew, "מַה שֶּׁאֲנִי עָתִיד לְהַפְרִישׁ מָחָר, יְהֵא חַלָּה."

**a. The complete stipulation, in Hebrew, should be in the following
form:

"הָעוֹדֵף עַל אֶחָד מִמֵּאָה מִכָּל מַה שֶּׁאֲנִי עָתִיד לְהַפְרִישׁ מָחָר לְתַקֵּן בּוֹ אֶת הַטֶּבֶל, יְהֵא
תְּרוּמָה גְּדוֹלָה בְּצַד צָפוֹן, כָּל מִין עַל מִינוֹ. אוֹתוֹ אֶחָד מִמֵּאָה הַנִּשְׁאָר וְעוֹד תִּשְׁעָה חֲלָקִים
כָּמוֹהוּ בְּצַד צְפוֹנוֹ שֶׁל הַלֶּחֶם (אוֹ הָעִוּגָה), כָּל מִין עַל מִינוֹ, יִהְיוּ מַעֲשֵׂר רִאשׁוֹן. אוֹתוֹ אֶחָד
מִמֵּאָה שֶׁהִתְנֵיתִי שֶׁיְּהֵא מַעֲשֵׂר רִאשׁוֹן, יְהֵא תְּרוּמַת מַעֲשֵׂר, כָּל מִין עַל מִינוֹ. וְעוֹד, מַה
שֶּׁאֲנִי עָתִיד לְהַפְרִישׁ לְשֵׁם חַלָּה, יְהֵא חַלָּה. וּמַעֲשֵׂר שֵׁנִי יְהֵא בְּדְרוֹמוֹ, כָּל מִין עַל מִינוֹ,
וִיהֵא מְחֻלָּל, הוּא וְחֻמְשׁוֹ, עַל פְּרוּטָה שֶׁבְּמַטְבֵּעַ שֶׁיִּחַדְתִּיהָ לְחִלּוּל מַעֲשֵׂר שֵׁנִי."

b. See Note *b* to paragraph 20 above.

c. When separating *tᵉrumoth* and *ma'asroth* from products of the
third or sixth year after the septennial Sabbatical year, one
should substitute for the final part of the stipulation, beginning,
"וּמַעֲשֵׂר שֵׁנִי ...," the words, "כָּל מִין עַל מִינוֹ," "וּמַעֲשַׂר עָנִי בְּצַד דְּרוֹמוֹ.".

ma'aser sheini shall take effect, in accordance with the requirements of Jewish religious law."*

24. *a.* According to some authorities there are two other methods of separating *t^erumoth, ma'asroth* and *challa* and redeeming *ma'aser sheini* on Shabbath and Yom Tov.

other methods of taking t^erumoth, ma'asroth and challa on Shabbath and Yom Tov

    b. Since, for practical purposes, the method outlined in paragraphs 18 to 23 above is sufficient, it has not been considered necessary to expand on the other two methods, particulars of which are to be found in the parallel paragraph of the second Hebrew edition of this book.

25. *a.* If one is afraid that one may forget to remove *t^erumoth, ma'asroth* or *challa* from something before Shabbath or Yom Tov, one may, as a precautionary measure, make the stipulations referred to in paragraphs 18 to 23 above on the day preceding each Shabbath or Yom Tov.

precautionary stipulations

    b. One would then be permitted to remove *t^erumoth, ma'asroth* and *challa* on the Shabbath or Yom Tov from anything one had in the house at the time of making the stipulations.

26. *a.* The stipulations referred to in paragraphs 18 to 23 above are only effective with regard to food which is in one's possession at the time when the stipulations are made.

eating away from home

    b. Consequently, they are not of assistance if one is invited to a meal on Shabbath or Yom Tov by a person who one suspects may not have taken *t^erumoth, ma'asroth* or *challa.*

27. *a.* The stipulations referred to in paragraphs 18 to 23 above are only effective with regard to food which one wishes to eat on that Shabbath or Yom Tov.

quantity to which stipulations apply

    b. They do not permit one to remove *t^erumoth, ma'asroth* or

---

*In Hebrew,   "כָּל מַה שֶּׁאֲנִי עָתִיד לְהַפְרִישׁוֹ מָחָר יִהְיֶה לִתְרוּמוֹת וּלְמַעַשְׂרוֹת
וּלְחַלָּה וְיָחוּל הַפִּדְיוֹן כְּדִין."

challa on Shabbath or Yom Tov from food which one wishes to eat on a subsequent weekday.

c. This is so even if one wishes, at the same time and in the one action, to remove *t^erumoth, ma'asroth* or *challa* from food which one wishes to eat both on the Shabbath or Yom Tov and on the subsequent weekdays.

omission to remove challa before Yom Tov

28. *a.* 1) If, before Yom Tov, one has forgotten to take *challa* from what one has baked and has not made any of the stipulations mentioned in paragraphs 21 to 23 above, one may, on Yom Tov,

a) knead a fresh dough, of the same or another variety, of a quantity which requires the removal of *challa,*

b) place it next to what was baked before Yom Tov and then

c) remove from the fresh dough the *challa* which needs to be taken from both.

2) Should one be unable, on Yom Tov, to prepare a fresh dough large enough to require the removal of *challa,* one may make a smaller one, but, in this case,

a) one must be particular to make the fresh dough of the same variety as the old, **and,**

b) before taking *challa* from it, it should be baked, and put with that which was baked before Yom Tov into one container, or onto a cloth which should then be folded over to cover them both.

3) Whichever of the above two courses is adopted, the fresh dough should be prepared or baked, as the case may be, with the intention of eating at least part of it on the same day.

4) See paragraph 19*c* and *d* above for what one may and may not do with *challa* once it has been removed.

5) Quantities of flour should be estimated and not measured. (See paragraph 30 below.)

b. See Chapter 31, paragraph 41 regarding the taking of *challa* outside the boundaries of what Jewish religious law considers the Land of Israel.

29. *a.* Although weighing and measuring is generally forbidden *measuring* on Shabbath and Yom Tov, one is allowed to weigh or *baby food* measure baby food, if one has to know how much the baby eats.

b. However, if possible, one should try to estimate the quantity rather than measure it exactly.

c. This is preferable, since making a rough estimate is permitted even when preparing food for an adult.

d. See also the following paragraph concerning the measuring of food.

30. *a.* 1) When preparing food on Yom Tov, one may use a *measuring* marked measuring cup, in order to ascertain the *ingredients* quantities of the various spices and flavorings one is *of food on* using, provided that *Yom Tov*

    a) the taste of the food would be adversely affected if one were to use inexact quantities **and**

    b) one would normally measure the ingredients if preparing the food on another day.

  2) Nevertheless, one should not use scales to weigh the ingredients.

b. 1) Flour and other commodities which can be added in approximate quantities, without adversely affecting the taste of the food, should not be measured on Yom Tov.

  2) One should not measure flour even in order to make certain that one is kneading a dough of a quantity sufficient to require the removal of *challa*.

  3) In these cases, the amount of the flour or other ingredients should be estimated.

31. *a.* The whipping of eggs or cream is forbidden on Shabbath, *whipping* but permitted on Yom Tov. *eggs or cream*

b. See also the following paragraph.

32. *a.* On Yom Tov it is permissible to make mayonnaise, *mayonnaise* whether thin or thick in consistency, and, in so doing,

1) one may use a hand-operated mixer (but not an electric mixer) and

2) one may separate the yolk of an egg from the white.

b. On Shabbath

   1) one may not prepare a stiff mayonnaise and,

   2) even if the mayonnaise is thin in consistency, it is preferable to make it before Shabbath.

spreading jam, etc. on bread

33. a. Butter, jam, honey, chocolate spread and any other spread may be smoothed onto a slice of bread.

b. The same applies to fruit preserves.

c. For the spreading of raw fruit, such as banana and avocado, see Chapter 6, paragraph 7.

d. See also paragraph 14 above.

e. 1) The spreading of foodstuffs for a purpose other than eating is prohibited.

   2) Thus, margarine or butter should not be smeared onto chapped lips or a burn.

   3) See further Chapter 35, paragraph 20.

greasing baking tins

34. Baking tins may be greased with margarine and the like on Yom Tov, to prevent the dough from burning or sticking to the tin.

soda-water

35. a. It is permitted to prepare soda-water in a syphon, even on Shabbath.

b. See Chapter 34, paragraph 4 for the preparation and drinking of a bicarbonate of soda solution on Shabbath for medicinal purposes.

removing thread from stuffed food

36. a. If one wishes to eat food which has been sewn or tied up, such as stuffed neck or stuffed chicken, one may cut the thread with a knife or a pair of scissors. (See also Chapter 9, paragraphs 14 and 15.)

b. The removal of the thread from the food is

   1) forbidden on Shabbath (due to the prohibition against selection discussed in Chapter 3) but

   2) permissible on Yom Tov.

37. *a.* On Yom Tov, one is also allowed to sew up stuffed food, so long as *(sewing up stuffed food)*
   1) the thread was cut from the reel **and**
   2) the needle was threaded
   before Yom Tov.

    b. The end of the thread may be cut off after the sewing has been completed, but it is better to burn it off, if possible.

38. *a.* 1) No prohibition is infringed, either on Shabbath or Yom Tov, if food is incidentally colored in the course of being prepared or having its flavor improved, provided that the coloring of the food is not one's purpose. *(coloring food)*
   2) One may accordingly add tea essence, red wine, orange squash, instant coffee or raspberry juice to water, subject on Shabbath to the rules set out in Chapter 1, paragraphs 14, 15 and 55.

    b. One should refrain from putting coloring into food with the sole intention of changing its color, even if the coloring itself consists of food.

    c. 1) Clearly then, it is forbidden to add coloring to food or drink which one has no intention of eating or drinking, in order to improve its appearance for ornamental purposes.
   2) See also Chapter 33, paragraph 19.

    d. 1) Even when one's sole intention in adding the coloring is to improve the flavor, it is preferable to add the food to the coloring rather than the other way around, but, if it is Shabbath, only so long as this is permissible in accordance with the rules set out in Chapter 1, paragraphs 47 and 56.
   2) Thus, if those rules allow, it is better to make tea by putting the essence into the cup first and pouring the water in afterwards.

39. *a.* There is no prohibition, either on Shabbath or on Yom Tov, against the scenting of food, if the addition of the scent increases its appeal to the palate. *(scenting food)*

b. All kinds of spices and herbs may accordingly be added to food.

folding table- **40.** a. Paper table-napkins must not be folded into special
napkins shapes, as is often done when laying a table for guests, but
b. they may be folded in half or into quarters for the sake of neatness.
c. A cloth table-napkin which has unfolded should not be refolded into its original folds, except as explained in Chapter 15, paragraph 44.

plates with **41.** a. A child's feeding plate may be attached to the table by
suction pads means of a rubber or plastic vacuum pad in its base, in
in their bases order to prevent the child from spilling the food while eating.
b. See Chapter 1, paragraph 50 for the heating of food in this kind of plate on Shabbath.

Chapter 12

Washing Dishes and Cleaning the Table on Shabbath and Yom Tov

WASHING DISHES

1. *a.* One is not allowed to wash dirty dishes or cutlery, either *when* on Shabbath or Yom Tov, unless there is a possibility *permitted* that one will need them again on the same day; however,
   1) one does not have to work out the precise number of pieces of crockery or cutlery of each kind which will still be required for the rest of the day and
   2) one may even wash several pieces of the same kind, despite the fact that one only needs one of them.

   b. Thus,
   1) dishes may be washed even in the evening after the first Shabbath meal, in preparation for another Shabbath meal on the following morning or afternoon, but,
   2) after the last meal on Shabbath or Yom Tov afternoon, one should not wash the dishes until nightfall, even if one intends to use them on the Yom Tov which occurs on the following day; however,
   3) cups and saucers, teaspoons, fruit plates and other utensils which it is customary to use also between meals and which one may, therefore, require even after the last meal, may be washed at any time, except if it is clear that they will no longer be used until nightfall.

2. *a.* If one is afraid that flies, ants or other insects will be *insects* attracted by unwashed dishes, one may stand them in *attracted by* water, even if one has no intention of using them that day. *dirty dishes*
   b. The same applies to silver dishes or cutlery which may be spoiled by the remains of food left on them.

3. *a.* Where there is a possibility that the remains of food will *leftovers* dry onto the sides or bottom of a pot so that it will be *stuck to pots*

more difficult to clean after Shabbath or Yom Tov, the pot may be stood in water on Shabbath or Yom Tov.

b. The reason for this is that standing the pot in water is a semi-automatic act, merely preserving the pot in its existing moist state.

c. If, however, the leftovers have already dried up and become stuck to the pot, one must not stand it in water on Shabbath or Yom Tov, since, in this case, one would be doing so with the specific object in mind of making it easier to clean afterwards than it is now. (See Chapter 28, paragraph 81.)

heating water for washing dishes on Yom Tov

4. a. It is better to refrain from heating up water on Yom Tov for the purpose of washing dishes which became dirty before Yom Tov. (On Shabbath the heating up of water is nearly always forbidden by the rules in Chapter 1.)

b. Water may be heated on Yom Tov for the purpose of washing dishes which have become dirty on Yom Tov, provided they are required for use on the same day.

c. Nevertheless, if water could have been heated before Yom Tov, it is desirable to refrain from heating it on Yom Tov, even for dishes which become dirty that day.

d. It is also desirable that any water which will be required for sterilizing a baby's bottle before each feeding be heated prior to the commencement of Yom Tov.

e. Water may be extracted from an electric boiler on Yom Tov, as explained in Chapter 2, paragraph 7.

f. For the use of dishwashers see paragraph 35 below.

cleaning materials not boiled in manufacture

5. a. The use one is permitted to make of soaps, wash powders and other dish-cleaning materials depends on whether or not they have been boiled in the process of manufacture.

b. Most cleaning materials, other than soap, are not boiled and are consequently subject to the rules set out in this paragraph.

c. 1) On Shabbath,
   a) they may be dissolved in cold water, but
   b) they may not be dissolved in hot water, even in a

k^eli *sheini* (as defined in Chapter 1, paragraph 2), and

    c) hot water should not be poured from a k^eli *rishon* (as defined in Chapter 1, paragraph 2) onto the solution produced by dissolving these materials.

2) On Yom Tov,

    a) they may be dissolved, even in hot water, in a k^eli *sheini*, but

    b) it is desirable to refrain from dissolving them in a k^eli *rishon*, whether or not it is standing on the fire, although

    c) one may be more lenient in permitting hot water to be poured into a solution of these materials, even from a k^eli *rishon*.

6. *a.* On Shabbath,   *soap*

    1) a) one should refrain from pouring hot water from a k^eli *rishon* onto soap in order to dissolve it, but

       b) one may put the soap (which is boiled during the course of manufacture) into hot water in a k^eli *sheini*.

    2) a) Liquid soap too may be put into hot water in a k^eli *sheini*, but

       b) hot water should not be poured onto liquid soap from a k^eli *rishon*.

  b. On Yom Tov, bars of soap and liquid soap, which are boiled in manufacture, may be put even into a k^eli *rishon* standing on the fire.

  c. See also paragraph 14*b*2 below and Chapter 14, paragraph 16.

7. It is the practice to wash dishes with cleaning materials even if they produce a lather, since this is not in itself an infringement of any prohibition.   *lather-producing cleaning materials*

8. *a.* On Shabbath,

    1) it is forbidden to pour hot water over greasy dishes, thereby dissolving the fat which is stuck to them, but   *greasy dishes*

2) they may be put into hot water in a *k^eli sheini*, where the fat will dissolve of its own accord.

b. On Yom Tov, both methods are permissible.

scouring
powder

9. a. On Shabbath,

1) one must not wash dishes with scouring powder mixed with water, since this contravenes the prohibition against kneading, but

2) one is allowed to clean them with dry scouring powder, even if one's hands are wet,* as this is not the normal manner of kneading.

b. On Yom Tov, scouring powder may be used with water.

c. See also paragraph 11 below.

pot scourers

10. a. Steel wool may not be used to wash kitchen utensils, either on Shabbath or on Yom Tov.

b. On the other hand, the use of synthetic pot scourers is permitted, so long as they are not absorbent and the fibers from which they are made are not so close together that they are capable of retaining water.

c. The use of synthetic materials which are absorbent is forbidden. (See paragraph 11 below.)

wet cloths
and sponges

11. a. On both Shabbath and Yom Tov, it is prohibited

1) to wet a sponge or cloth or

2) to wash dishes with a wet sponge or a wet cloth.

b. One should not use a sponge or cloth to wash dishes even beneath the surface of the water in a bowl or sink.

flax-like dish
cleaners

12. Neither natural loofahs nor artificial dish cleaners made in the form of flax-like strands may be used on Shabbath and Yom Tov when they are wet, since the rules set out in paragraph 11 above with regard to sponges and cloths are also applicable to them.

---

*Nevertheless, if the scouring powder will dissolve, it is advisable not to use it.

13. *a.* Dishes may be washed with specially designed rubber-bladed scrapers (squeegees).

    b. Rubber or plastic gloves may be worn while one is washing the dishes.

squeegees and rubber gloves

14. *a.* One may wash dishes with a liquid-soap container fitted at the top with a brush the bristles of which are made of synthetic material and are not close enough together to hold water.

    b. 1) One is allowed to wash dishes with dish-washing paste (but without the aid of a cloth or sponge).

    2) Bars of soap may not be used in any circumstances, unless they have been dissolved. (See, however, paragraph 6 above.)

liquid-soap containers with fitted brushes

dish-washing paste and bars of soap

15. *a.* Baby bottles may be cleaned inside with a dry soft-bristled brush.

    b. If 1) one wishes to use a wet brush **or**
        2) the inside of the bottle is wet,
    it is better to use a brush whose bristles are synthetic and are not close enough together to hold water.

brushes

16. *a.* It is permissible to plug up a sink with a stopper in order to prevent the water from draining out when one is washing the dishes.

    b. 1) One may, likewise, put a perforated cover over the sink drain.

    2) The fact that this will result in the filtering out of the larger pieces of refuse does not contravene the prohibition against selection, since one's intention is solely to prevent the pipe from becoming blocked, whereas the essence of making a selection is that one wishes, at some time, to use what is selected or what is left or both.

    c. One is also allowed to pour the water into the sink through a perforated receptacle, to avoid the spreading of refuse all over the sink.

pouring away dishwater

d. The refuse which accumulates in this receptacle may be emptied into the waste bin.

e. Regarding the emptying of the waste bin see Chapter 22, paragraph 45.

unblocking **17.** A domestic rubber plunger (but not the larger variety used
a sink by professional plumbers) may be employed to unblock a clogged sink, if there is an important need for it.

sink draining **18.** a. If the pipe leading from a sink or basin is so positioned
onto sown that water flows along it until it is discharged over sown
ground ground, one is, nonetheless, permitted on Shabbath

1) to wash one's hands into the sink or basin and

2) to pour water into it

without having to worry about the watering of the seeds which will be indirectly brought about thereby, so long as this consequence is unintended.

b. It is, of course, forbidden to pour water directly onto seeds or onto a sown or planted area, even if one has no intention of watering a plant.

water meters **19.** One may turn on a water tap, even if the water will pass through a meter which measures the amount of water used.

extermi- **20.** In regard to ants and other insects which one finds, for
nating insects example, on the kitchen floor, in the sink or on the dishes,

a. one should not wash them away in a manner that will cause them to die,

b. nor put down poison with the object of exterminating them,

c. nor deliberately tread on them, even in the process of walking.

DRYING, SORTING AND POLISHING
CUTLERY, DISHES AND OTHER VESSELS
AND MAKING THEM FIT FOR USE

21. *a.* Wet dishes or cutlery may be dried with a dish towel *drying dishes*
specially made for that purpose.

b. Many dishes may be wiped with the same dish towel and
one need not be afraid that it will become so wet that one
will come to squeeze it out (in contravention of the rules
set out in Chapter 15, paragraph 2), since, if it becomes
too wet, one will in any case take a fresh one.

c. Nonetheless, narrow vessels, such as thermoses (vacuum
flasks), which still contain water should not be wiped dry,
as one would inevitably come to squeeze out the towel
when pushing it into the narrow opening.

22. A towel which has become wet in use *drying wet*
a. must not be hung up to dry, but *towels*

b. may be returned to its proper place, even if it will dry
there, so long as this is not next to an oven, a stove or a
heater.

23. *a.* Cutlery or dishes of various similar kinds, which are *sorting*
jumbled together, must not be sorted, except for imme- *cutlery and*
diate use. *dishes*

b. The prohibition against making a selection applies even if
1) one's intention in sorting them is to wash each kind
separately **or**
2) to wash only one variety **or**
3) one removes each variety from the batch separately
and dries it.

c. It is, however, permitted to put each utensil in its allotted
place immediately after it has been separately washed or
dried.

d. See also Chapter 3, paragraphs 78 and 80.

24. *a.* It is forbidden to polish silverware or copperware on *polishing*
Shabbath and Yom Tov.

b. Owing to the fact that what is prohibited is the very act of polishing, it is forbidden not only
  1) where one would use an ordinary cloth dipped in liquid polish, but also
  2) where one wishes to use a special polishing cloth without the addition of any liquid.
c. Nevertheless, one is allowed to dry glassware thoroughly even if one rubs it with the towel until it shines.

sharpening
knives

25. On both Shabbath and Yom Tov,
  a. one is not allowed to sharpen a knife, in any way whatsoever, and
  b. one is not allowed to remove rust which has accumulated on the sides of the blade.

bent cutlery

26. Bent fork prongs or knife blades may not be straightened on Shabbath or Yom Tov.

thermoses

27. a. A thermos (vacuum flask) should not be dismantled or assembled, but
  b. there is nothing wrong with screwing on or off the top which serves as its cup.

vessels unfit
for use for
religious
reasons

28. a. 1) There are two main methods of treating vessels that have become unfit for use through contact with food which a Jew is not permitted to eat, namely
      a) immersing them in boiling water **or**
      b) heating them to a high temperature in a flame.
   2) Both methods must be carried out in strict accordance with the detailed requirements of the religious law applicable to each case.
   3) Subject to what is stated below, both of these methods are forbidden on Yom Tov (and, it goes without saying, on Shabbath), even if one wishes to use the vessel on the same day.
   4) Similarly, a knife which has become prohibited for use due to the adhesion of some food that may not be eaten must not be scraped on Shabbath or Yom Tov to

remove the forbidden food, since making a previously unfit utensil fit for use is in itself not permitted.

b. Notwithstanding the above, if the following four conditions are all fulfilled, an unfit vessel of a kind which, according to religious law, can be made fit for use by immersion in boiling water may be so immersed on Yom Tov:

1) The vessel became unfit for use on Yom Tov.

2) The vessel is required for use on that day.

3) Either

   a) one has water ready which was boiled for drinking or for putting into food on Yom Tov **or**

   b) at least some of the water one is boiling up for the immersion of the vessel will be used for drinking or for putting into food.

4) The volume of the water mentioned in the previous condition is at least sixty times that of the vessel to be immersed (and all the other requirements imposed by religious law when vessels are made fit for use by immersion in boiling water are satisfied).

29. a. Jewish religious law prescribes that metal and glass vessels and implements used for food, which have been made by or acquired from a non-Jew, must, with certain exceptions, be immersed in a *mikveh* (a pool of water conforming with set conditions). *vessels acquired from a non-Jew*

b. Such an immersion must not be made on Shabbath or Yom Tov.

CLEANING THE TABLE OR A TABLECLOTH AND THE USE OF
DISHWASHERS ON SHABBATH OR YOM TOV

30. a. From Chapter 17, it will be seen that, in general, it is forbidden to transfer something on Shabbath from what can very loosely be termed "enclosed property" to what can equally loosely be described as "a public thoroughfare" or "an open area," unless one has made what is known as an *eiruv chatzeiroth*. *shaking cloths out of a window*

b. Where no *eiruv chatzeiroth* has been made, a tablecloth must not be shaken out of the window on Shabbath, if the crumbs would fall from "enclosed property" into "a public thoroughfare" or "an open area," or, to be more precise, from *rᵉshuth ha-yachid* into *rᵉshuth ha-rabbim* or *carmᵉlith*, as these expressions are defined in Chapter 17.

folding cloths **31.** Regarding the folding of a tablecloth on Shabbath and Yom Tov, see Chapter 15, paragraph 44.

bones, peels, etc. not fit for any use **32.** a. One may sweep bones, peels and the like off the table with a cloth or a knife, despite the fact that they are not fit for consumption even by animals, provided that one needs the table to be clean.

b. Subject to the same proviso, one may remove the cloth on which they are lying and shake it out (but see paragraph 30 above).

c. However, if one finds the litter of bones or peels on the table offensive, one may remove them
1) even with one's hands and
2) even if one does not actually need to use the clean table.

(See also Chapter 22, paragraph 42.)

bones, peels, etc. fit for animal consumption **33.** a. On Shabbath, one is permitted, even directly with one's hands, to move bones, peels, and the like which are fit for animal consumption.

b. Nevertheless, on Yom Tov, if the bones came apart from the meat or the peel was removed from the fruit on that same day, one should deal with them in the way described in paragraph 32 above, since, on Yom Tov, it is forbidden to move them directly, as will be explained in Chapter 21, paragraph 2.

clearing dishes **34.** a. Dishes or cutlery may not be sorted, for example when clearing them from the table, even if one's object is merely to stack them in such a way that room will be saved on the drain-board or that they will not fall.

b. See also paragraph 23 above and Chapter 3, paragraphs 78 and 80.

35. *a.* On Shabbath, it is prohibited to use a domestic dish-   *dishwashers*
washer, even if it will be turned on by a time-switch
which was set before Shabbath.

b. On Yom Tov, one may use a dishwasher, as long as
  1) the dishes will be needed again that day (as mentioned
     in paragraph 1 above) and
  2) the machine will be turned on by a time-switch set
     before Yom Tov so that one does no act directly to
     switch the machine on or off or to regulate its oper-
     ation.

c. See Chapter 30, paragraph 23 for the use of a dishwasher
by a non-Jew who is washing dishes for a Jew.

d. A person who, throughout the week, is accustomed to put
the dirty dishes straight from the table into the dishwasher, where they are left until they are washed (on a
weekday of course), may also do so on Shabbath and Yom
Tov, but
  1) he must be careful not to sort the various dishes and
     other utensils, even if his intention is to be able more
     easily to put each object into its proper place in the
     machine (although putting each object, as it comes to
     hand, into its proper place is permitted) and
  2) if the normal place for the dishes, after their use, is not
     inside the machine, it is not allowed to put them in on
     Shabbath or Yom Tov so that they will be ready for
     washing in the evening.

36. *a.* Dishes, cutlery and leftovers may be cleared off the table,   *clearing the*
even after the last meal of Shabbath or Yom Tov,   *table after*
  1) so that the room should look clean and tidy **or**   *the last meal*
  2) to avoid attracting insects.

b. It is, however, forbidden to clear dishes, cutlery or leftovers off the table
  1) during the last few minutes of Shabbath or Yom Tov,

if one no longer needs to be in the room until after Shabbath or Yom Tov, or

2) even in the middle of the day, if one has decided not to use the room until after Shabbath or Yom Tov is over.

removing spilled liquid from a cloth with a spoon or a knife

37. Water or other liquid which has spilled on the tablecloth may, when necessary, be moved off gently and without the application of any pressure into a cup or plate, with the assistance of a spoon or a knife, even if the cloth is made of an absorbent material, but

a. one must be extremely careful not to squeeze the table-cloth in the course of moving the liquid off and,

b. where the liquid is colored, as in the case of red wine, one should beware not to move it onto a part of the cloth which has not yet been stained, since this contravenes the prohibition against dyeing.

soaking up spilled liquids

38. a. Small quantities of water spilled on a table, whether or not covered with a tablecloth, may, subject to the restrictions mentioned in sub-paragraph c below, be soaked up with a wiping-up cloth specially intended for such use (and only with such a cloth).

b. Small quantities of other liquids spilled on a table, whether or not covered with a tablecloth, may, subject to the restrictions mentioned in sub-paragraph c below, be soaked up with any cloth, since the liquid is not normally squeezed out for use but is disposed of.

c. At all events,

1) one must be careful not to squeeze the cloth and

2) one should not soak up the liquid with the intention of using it, even after Shabbath or Yom Tov.

terylene cloths

39. The rules set out in paragraphs 37 and 38 above apply also to liquids spilled on tablecloths made of terylene or any other synthetic fabric which is capable of absorbing liquid in its fibers or retaining it between them.

cleaning hard surfaces

40. A bare table-top, a kitchen drain-board or any other hard surface which has become dirty may be cleaned (if it is still needed on the same day or one is afraid it will attract insects), subject to the following provisos:

a. 1) An ordinary cloth may be used provided that both the cloth and the surface are dry, and the remains of food stuck to the surface being cleaned may even be rubbed off with it.

2) An ordinary cloth must not be used if the surface to be cleaned is wet or if the cloth is wet or even only a little damp, as liquid absorbed in the cloth is bound to be squeezed out, at least slightly, in use.

b. 1) A cloth or scourer made of non-absorbent, synthetic material whose fibers are not close enough together to hold water may be used, as may a specially designed rubber-bladed scraper (squeegee), even if they or the surface being cleaned or both are wet.

2) In the course of cleaning, one may
   a) pour water onto the surface being cleaned and
   b) rub the dirt off with such a synthetic cloth or scourer or rubber-bladed scraper or with one's hand.

41. The rules with regard to the cleaning of sheets of purely synthetic non-woven material, such as plastic tablecloths or oilcloths, not sewn with any natural thread, are as follows: *plastic tablecloths*

a. If the surface to be cleaned is dry, it is treated in the same way as a hard surface. (See paragraph 40 above.)

b. If it is wet, one may clean it with a non-absorbent, synthetic cloth or scourer or a rubber-bladed scraper, as in the case of a hard surface, but

1) one should do so only lightly, and one must not rub the soiled spot with the synthetic cloth or scourer or with the scraper or even with one's hand,

2) stains on a wet plastic tablecloth or on a wet oilcloth may not be removed by rubbing the two sides of the cloth together and

3) a wet plastic tablecloth or oilcloth must not be cleaned with an ordinary cloth, not even with a dry one.

     c. 1) A plastic tablecloth or an oilcloth which is not sewn, trimmed or backed with natural thread or fiber may be soaked in water so that food stuck to it will come off.

     2) Water may be run or sprayed over the plastic tablecloth or oilcloth for the same purpose, and the remains of food gently removed by hand (without rubbing).

     3) It may also be hung up to dry after soaking or spraying (but not near an oven or heater).

plastic cloths **42.** One must not intentionally wet the edge of a plastic table-
with natural cloth or oilcloth sewn, trimmed or backed with natural
trimming or thread or fiber, nor should one spray it or soak it in water,
backing since the natural thread or fiber will inevitably become wet
too.

Chapter 13

Laws Relating to Fire on Shabbath and Yom Tov

PROHIBITION AGAINST LIGHTING OR EXTINGUISHING
A FIRE ON SHABBATH

1. *a.* On Shabbath, it is forbidden to light or extinguish a fire, by any means whatsoever.
   b. The prohibition also extends to
   1) switching electricity on or off,
   2) burning with a magnifying glass,
   3) igniting with a flame taken from a fire which is already burning and
   4) raising or lowering a flame.
   c. If a fire has been lit on Shabbath in breach of this prohibition, one may not derive any benefit from it on Shabbath.
   d. See paragraphs 23 to 31 below for the use of a time-switch to turn electricity on and off.

scope of prohibition on Shabbath

PROHIBITION AGAINST LIGHTING A FIRE
ON YOM TOV

2. *a.* On Yom Tov, it is forbidden to light a "new" fire by any means whatsoever.
   b. The prohibition includes
   1) striking a match,
   2) operating a lighter,
   3) burning with a magnifying glass,
   4) switching on electricity and
   5) any other method of lighting a fire, except by means of a flame taken from a fire which is already burning.
   c. If a fire has been lit on Yom Tov in breach of this prohibition, one may, nonetheless, use it (in a permitted manner) on Yom Tov.

scope of prohibition on Yom Tov

d. See paragraphs 8 to 15 below for the prohibition against extinguishing a fire on Yom Tov.

permitted methods of lighting fire on Yom Tov

3. a. 1) It is permitted, on Yom Tov, subject to the reservations in paragraphs 4 and 5 below, to light a fire with a flame taken from a fire which is already burning.

    2) This may be done, for example,

       a) by lighting a match, whether new or used, from a burning flame and then using it to light a fire elsewhere,

       b) by lighting the match from a burning cigarette,

       c) by holding the match not in but above a flame until it ignites,

       d) by touching the match to a live electric element, or

       e) by turning on the knob (tap) of a gas burner which will be ignited by a pilot light (but see paragraph 9 below).

b. 1) It is also permitted, on Yom Tov, subject to the reservations in paragraphs 4 and 5 below, to make a flame larger, by increasing the supply of gas, oil or other inflammable material, or, for instance, by elevating the wick of a paraffin heater or lamp. (See also paragraph 17 below.)

    2) One may not, however, raise the temperature of an electric hot-plate, stove or heater or of any other electrical appliance, since this is usually effected by the extinguishing of one electric element and the turning on of another in its place, or by the switching on of an additional element. (See also Chapter 1, paragraph 27.)

when fire may be lit on Yom Tov

4. a. Lighting a fire with a flame taken from a fire which is already burning, or making a flame larger, is permitted on Yom Tov only if it is done for the purposes of cooking, heating, lighting or smoking.

b. Regarding smoking see further in paragraph 7 below.

c. When lighting a flame is permitted on Yom Tov, it may be for immediate use or for use later on the same day of

Yom Tov, as when a long-burning candle is lit in the evening so that a flame can be taken from it on the next morning for the purpose of cooking.

5. *a.* Lighting a fire or making it larger is not permitted on Yom Tov by any method, unless it is done either
   1) for the purpose of Yom Tov itself, as where candles which one does not need for their light are lit in honor of Yom Tov, or
   2) for the use of a person on Yom Tov.

   b. It is therefore forbidden on Yom Tov
   1) to burn *chametz* which one has found on Pesach or
   2) to burn *challa*, even if it has been separated on Yom Tov (as explained in Chapter 11, paragraphs 16 to 28).

when fire may not be lit on Yom Tov

6. *a.* However, one may, on Yom Tov (in a permitted manner of course),
   1) light candles in the synagogue (even during daylight) so that they burn during the service or while memorial prayers for the dead are being recited, or
   2) light candles in honor of a mitzva, for example when a circumcision is to be performed.

   b. 1) Memorial candles which one lights at home should be kindled before the commencement of Yom Tov.
   2) If one has not done so, or if it was impossible to do so, as where the previous day was also Yom Tov,
      a) the preferable course is to light the candle in the synagogue—whose dignity is enhanced with each additional light—but,
      b) if one does light it at home, one should at least light it in the dining room (perhaps next to the lights one has kindled in honor of Yom Tov) where it could be of some use.
   3) Where one has no other choice, one may rely on the view that the memorial candle may be lit on Yom Tov anywhere at home.
   4) The lighting must always be done in a permitted manner.

memorial lights on Yom Tov

*smoking on
Yom Tov*

7. *a.* A person who is in the habit of smoking may also smoke on Yom Tov,* although there are some authorities who forbid it and some who even prohibit moving cigarettes because of the rules of *muktzeh* (discussed in Chapter 20).

b. A person who does not derive any direct enjoyment from the act of smoking is not permitted to smoke on Yom Tov.

EXTINGUISHING A FIRE AND
LOWERING A FLAME ON YOM TOV

*extinguish-
ing forbidden*

8. *a.* It is, in general, forbidden to extinguish fire on Yom Tov, whatever the means.

b. Consequently, one should not
   1) turn off an electric light or appliance,
   2) throw down a burning match,
   3) tap a burning cigarette, so as to shake off the ash which has collected at its tip,**
   4) cover the bowl of a lit pipe,
   5) tread on a burning cigarette end or
   6) release the air from a burning primus stove, thereby indirectly causing the flame to go out.

c. Burning matches should be carefully put down and left to go out of their own accord.

*prohibition
against lower-
ing a flame*

9. *a.* Lowering a flame is included within the definition of

---

*a. It is better to open packets of cigarettes before Yom Tov. (See Chapter 9, paragraph 1.)

 b. If one opens them on Yom Tov, one should tear the wrapping completely, taking care, however, not to tear the lettering or design. (See Chapter 9, paragraph 12.)

 c. It is advisable, before Yom Tov, to delete letters printed on cigarettes which one intends to smoke on Yom Tov, by scribbling over them with a pen.

 d. See paragraph 45 for cigar smoking.

**Ash which has formed from a cigarette on Yom Tov is *muktzeh* and should, accordingly, not be moved, except in the circumstances set out in Chapter 22, paragraph 42.

extinguishing; so it too is, in general, forbidden on Yom Tov.

b. Consequently,

1) when adding fuel to a burning paraffin stove or lamp, one should not totally remove the wick from the remaining paraffin, but should leave the end of it still immersed,* and,

2) before lighting a gas burner or a paraffin lamp or stove, it is advisable to ensure that it is turned on low, as it will be forbidden (except in the circumstances mentioned below) to lower the flame, should it transpire that it is too high.

c. The flame of a paraffin lamp may be turned lower if it is so high that one fears the glass will be blackened or split, to the detriment of the light being produced.

10. a. One may, on Yom Tov, lower the flame of a gas, paraffin or primus stove, if all of the following requirements are satisfied:

lowering a flame to prevent food from spoiling

1) the flame is so high that one is afraid the food will burn and spoil or the water will evaporate,**

2) one has only the one flame and cannot light another which is smaller **and**

3) one does not wish to remove the pot altogether from the flame, because one wants the food kept warm.

b. One may not lower the flame

1) to prevent the food from acquiring a slightly charred appearance or

2) to avoid the pot's being blackened and certainly not

3) in order to stop money being wasted.

c. It is prohibited to lower the temperature of an electric

---

*Paraffin should not be added to a primus which is running short of fuel, until the flame has gone out by itself.

**A flame may be turned higher, on Yom Tov, for cooking purposes, even if one will afterwards have to turn it lower again in order to prevent the food from burning, water from evaporating or a pressure-cooker from exploding.

hot-plate, stove or heater or of any other electrical appliance, even with the object of preventing food on it from burning, since this is usually effected by the extinguishing of an electric element and, sometimes, the lighting of another in its place (in contravention of the prohibition against lighting or extinguishing fire). (See also Chapter 1, paragraph 27.)

replacing spent gas cylinders

11. *a.* It is permitted, on Yom Tov,
    1) to turn off the tap of a spent gas cylinder and
    2) to turn on the tap of a full cylinder which is already connected.
    b. On the other hand, it is best to avoid connecting a fresh cylinder.

limiting the supply of gas in a cylinder

12. It is not permitted, while the gas is burning, to turn off the tap of a gas stove or of a cylinder to which it is connected, but gas can be saved on Yom Tov in the following way, if one has two cylinders, one full and one empty, connected to the stove.
    a. A quantity of gas can be transferred from the full to the empty cylinder, by opening the taps of both (when the gas is not burning).
    b. The tap of the full cylinder should next be turned off.
    c. If one then uses the stove with the tap of the other cylinder turned on, the flame will automatically go out when the limited amount of gas one has transferred is exhausted.

water boiling over onto gas flame

13. *a.* One must not light a gas stove on Yom Tov with the intention that after one has finished the cooking one will put a pot full of water on the flame so that it should boil over and extinguish the fire, since even indirectly causing the extinguishing of a flame is forbidden in these circumstances.
    b. However, should one either have forgotten to turn the gas off before Yom Tov or mistakenly turned it on on Yom

Tov, one may cause it to go out by making a pot of water boil over onto it, but only if

1) leaving the gas on would result in an appreciable loss **and**

2) one intends to use, on Yom Tov, the water which is being heated up.

c. It is of course strictly forbidden to move the pot, with water brimming over its edge, while it is on the flame, as this is tantamount to extinguishing the fire directly.

14. a. One is allowed on Yom Tov to turn off a gas tap, if the flame has for some reason gone out. (For the rule on Shabbath see Chapter 1, paragraph 28.) *turning off gas after flame goes out*

b. One is also permitted on Yom Tov to release the air from a primus which has gone out.

15. a. A water heater which works in such a way that when the hot-water tap is turned on the gas is ignited and when it is turned off the gas is extinguished may not be operated even on Yom Tov, since one is not permitted to extinguish the flame by turning off the water. *gas water heaters*

b. Nonetheless, one may draw water from a heater which has only the pilot light turned on in order just to take the chill off the water, even on Shabbath, so long as one has made certain

1) that the gas tap controlling the large flame is properly turned off **and**

2) that the water cannot reach a temperature of 45 degrees centigrade (113 degrees Fahrenheit).

c. Water which has had the chill taken off in this way must not be used for washing oneself on Shabbath, as will be explained in Chapter 14, paragraph 2, but it may be used for washing cutlery, dishes and the like.

PARAFFIN LAMPS, STOVES AND HEATERS

putting in fuel on Yom Tov

16. *a.* One is allowed, on Yom Tov, to pour fuel into the tank of a paraffin lamp, stove or heater, even if some of it is in excess of the quantity which is required for Yom Tov, subject to compliance with the following conditions:
  1) The fuel must be poured into the tank out of only one, and not two or more, containers.
  2) Even the same container may not be refilled and emptied into the tank again.
  3) If the lamp, stove or heater is burning, one must also ensure that all of the additional fuel is poured in at once, and not in two separate actions (except in the case of a heater whose tank is removed for refilling, as mentioned in paragraph 19 below).
  4) One should not expressly say that one is putting in additional fuel for after Yom Tov.

  b. Compliance with the first three conditions is not essential where the addition of fuel in excess of what is strictly required for Yom Tov also improves the light or heat emitted by the lamp, stove or heater on Yom Tov.

  c. See also paragraph 9 above in connection with the manner of inserting fuel on Yom Tov.

raising the flame

17. One may raise the wick of a paraffin lamp, stove or heater on Yom Tov in order to increase the size of the flame, despite the fact that the bottom of the wick is thereby lifted to a higher level in the paraffin, reducing the amount of available fuel, with the result that the flame will go out sooner.

smoking or defective appliances

18. *a.* If the room is being filled with soot or smoke or if there is a risk of a fire's being caused by a defective paraffin lamp, stove or heater, one may take them out of the room on Shabbath or Yom Tov, even if conditions outside are such that they will be extinguished there, provided that
  1) one is careful not to put the appliance down in a spot where the wind will extinguish it at once **and**
  2) one lifts it gently and carries it with caution, so as not

to increase or decrease the size of the flame during removal.

b. Where there is a danger to life, the limitations on removing or extinguishing the lamp, stove or heater are, of course, not applicable. (See Chapter 41, paragraph 1.)

19. a. The separate, removable tank of a burning paraffin heater may be taken out, on Yom Tov, either *removal of fuel tank*
    1) in order to refill it **or**
    2) because the room is uncomfortably hot and one wishes the heater to go out when the fuel already inside is exhausted,
    but only if the paraffin is not actually in the process of flowing out of the tank, into the burning heater.

b. The reason why this is permitted is that the paraffin in the tank is not considered as already being inside the burning heater.

20. a. The wick of a paraffin lamp or similar appliance may not be cut to straighten it, even on Yom Tov, since making an improvement in the wick itself is forbidden. *trimming the wick*

b. On the other hand, carbon which has formed on the wick may be removed before lighting, as it is no longer considered to be part of the wick.

21. a. The expended wick of an oil lamp which consists of a container full of oil with a wick lying inside it may be removed and replaced on Yom Tov. *oil-lamp wicks*

b. It is forbidden, on Yom Tov,
    1) to make a wick out of absorbent cotton (cotton wool) or similar material,
    2) to remove wisps of absorbent cotton from a new wick, so as to enable it to burn better, or
    3) to cut a wick, in order to shorten it or make it into two.

22. One is not permitted to insert a new wick into a paraffin lamp, stove or heater on Yom Tov, as this falls within the scope of the prohibition against making an implement, *replacing wick of paraffin lamp or stove*

namely the paraffin appliance in question, of which the wick will form an intrinsic portion when in place (unlike the oil-lamp wick, which merely lies freely in the oil).

USE OF A TIMER ON SHABBATH AND YOM TOV

setting a timer

23. A timer (time-switch) connected to an electric circuit may be set, before Shabbath or Yom Tov, to turn the current off and on at the desired times on Shabbath or Yom Tov.

use of alarm clock to cut off current

24. *a.* An ordinary alarm clock which has been attached or placed next to a switch, before Shabbath, in such a way that the revolving of the winder when the alarm rings will turn off the current on Shabbath may be moved after the current has indeed been cut off.

b. What is more, one may depress the release-button or lever or move the clock away from the switch, before the alarm rings, in order to prevent it from cutting off the current, but one must take care not to untie a knot in any string connecting the winder to the switch.

adjusting timer on Shabbath to turn current on or off earlier or later

25. *a.* Whether and in what circumstances a timer may be adjusted on Shabbath depends to a large extent on its design.*

1) There are timers which can be adjusted without interrupting their operation, for instance by means of
   a) a movable dial or
   b) indicators that are moved after being freed from a slot by the application of pressure, and automatically catch in the slot at which they are released.

2) There are others which temporarily cease to operate when being adjusted and can be restarted only by means of a direct, independent action, such as those adjusted by moving an indicator which has first to be

---

*For the winding up of a clock on Shabbath or Yom Tov, see Chapter 28, paragraphs 19 to 21.

unscrewed, thus making it impossible for that indicator to turn the current on or off when it reaches the predetermined point, unless and until it is screwed tight again afterwards.

b. 1) If a timer of the first variety was set before Shabbath to turn the current off or on at a particular time,

     a) one may, on Shabbath, adjust it in such a way that the current will be turned off or on, as the case may be, at a later time, but

     b) not in such a way that it will be turned off or on at an earlier time.

   2) A timer of the second variety may also be adjusted to delay (but not to accelerate) the turning off or on of the current, but only

     a) if there is a pressing need to do so **or**

     b) if it can be done by screwing on another indicator at a marking subsequent to that of the indicator which it is desired to cancel before removing the latter.

26. A timer may also be adjusted on Shabbath

   a. while the electricity is off, in such a way that after it has been turned on it will be switched off again earlier than would otherwise have been the case, **or**

   b. while the electricity is on, in such a way that after it has been turned off it will be switched on again earlier than would otherwise have been the case.

adjusting timer on Shabbath to turn current on or off a second time

27. The rules set out in paragraphs 25 and 26 above are equally applicable on Yom Tov, except that on Yom Tov a time-switch may be adjusted even in circumstances other than those of paragraph 26 in order to turn the electricity on (but not off) earlier than the time set before Yom Tov.

adjusting a timer on Yom Tov

28. a. While the current is disconnected, one may, subject to the qualification which follows, remove a plug from a socket (or turn a switch into the "off" position) on Shabbath or

removing plug while current is turned off

Yom Tov in order to prevent the electricity from coming on when the current is reconnected.

b. Since the plug is *muktzeh*, one should avoid moving it in the normal manner with one's hands and should instead pull it out in a different way, such as with one's wrists or knuckles. (See Chapter 22, paragraph 34.)

c. At a time of great need, it may even be permissible, subject to the above qualification, to insert a plug in a socket (or turn a switch into the "on" position), so that the electricity should come on when the current is reconnected, but one should not do this without first obtaining the approval of a rabbi who is well versed in this sphere of Jewish law.

removing light bulbs while current is turned off

29. a. There are grounds for permitting the removal of a light bulb from a socket on Shabbath while the current is disconnected in order to prevent its being turned on when the current is reconnected, on condition that

1) the bulb is one which is, from time to time, taken out of its socket and put back, or alternated with another bulb, **and**

2) one does not remove the bulb in the normal manner, with one's hands, but in a different way (as in paragraph 28*b* above).

b. At a time of great need, it may even be permissible, in some circumstances, to insert a bulb in a socket (not in the normal manner) so that the light should come on when the current is reconnected, but one should not do this without first obtaining the approval of a rabbi who is well versed in this sphere of Jewish law.

c. The points enumerated in this paragraph are equally applicable to Shabbath and Yom Tov, except that, on Yom Tov, the bulb may be handled in the normal way, while being inserted or removed.

d. There are no grounds, even at a time of great need, for permitting the removal or insertion, either on Shabbath or Yom Tov, of an electric bulb which is normally left in the socket for an extended period.

30. *a.* A timer, even when operating, will not affect the supply of *connecting* electricity, unless it is connected to the circuit. *timer on*

  b. The connection is usually made by means of a switch or *Shabbath* plug.

  c. It may happen that one has set a timer before Shabbath to cut off the current at a particular time, but has forgotten to turn on this switch or insert this plug.

  d. Should this occur, one may, at a time of great need, turn on this switch or insert this plug on Shabbath but **only if**
  1) the timer itself is operating in any event and one is merely making the connection between it and the circuit to enable it to cut off the current, **and**
  2) the time set for the current to be cut off has not yet arrived — otherwise it would be cut off immediately by the act of turning on the switch or inserting the plug.

31. It is forbidden to repair or replace a fuse on Shabbath or Yom *mending or* Tov, even when the current is not connected, since, in doing *replacing a* so, one is, as it were, putting the final touch to the *fuse* completion of the circuit.

MISCELLANEOUS LAWS IN CONNECTION WITH FIRE
ON SHABBATH AND YOM TOV

32. *a.* One may, on Shabbath or Yom Tov, read by the light of *variable-* an electric lamp which can be adjusted to different *strength* strengths, and one need not fear that one will come to *lighting* regulate it on Shabbath or Yom Tov.

  b. Nonetheless, it is advisable to cover the regulator or control button before Shabbath or Yom Tov begins.

33. *a.* 1) One should not open a door or a window close to a *candles* burning candle, either on Shabbath or on Yom Tov, if *standing in a* there is a reasonable likelihood that the flame will be *draught* blown out by a wind from outside, even if there is no such wind at present.

  2) However, where there is no appreciable wind outside, one may, if circumstances make it necessary, as when

[145]

it is very hot in the room, open a door or a window near a burning candle, so long as one does so gently, without causing a draught which is itself likely to blow out the flame.

b. One is permitted to close a door or window close to a burning candle, to prevent the wind from extinguishing the flame, so long as one does so gently.

c. 1) A door or a window may be opened, even if this causes the flame to flicker or change its shape, **but**
2) on Shabbath one is only allowed to do so provided that it does not make the candle burn more quickly.

turning on of ventilator or air conditioning by non-Jew **34.** a. On a very hot summer's day, one is permitted to request a non-Jew to turn on an electric ventilator or the air conditioning.

b. See also Chapter 30, paragraph 11.

regulation of ventilator **35.** a. An electric fan which was turned on
1) before the commencement of Shabbath or Yom Tov or
2) on Shabbath or Yom Tov, by a non-Jew as in paragraph 34 above, or by means of a time-switch,
may not be adjusted by a Jew to a higher or lower speed.

b. One is permitted
1) to swivel it to face a different direction or
2) to move it, if it is portable, for one's own physical convenience or because one needs the place which it occupies, taking care not to disconnect it from the electricity supply.

central heating **36.** Central heating is discussed in detail in Chapter 23, paragraphs 18 to 31, Chapter 30, paragraphs 11 and 53, and Chapter 31, paragraph 6.

disconnecting the telephone **37.** a. If one wishes to avoid being disturbed by the telephone, one should disconnect it or turn the bell off before Shabbath or Yom Tov commences.

b. Where one has not done so, one may pull the plug out of

the socket on Shabbath or Yom Tov to prevent disturbance, but not while the bell is ringing.

38. *a.* It is forbidden to put an empty tray or dish or a newspaper under or next to a dripping candle on Shabbath or Yom Tov to catch the wax, even if one's sole intention is to prevent the tablecloth from being soiled.   *dripping candles*

   b. The reason for the prohibition is that it is not permitted to render an article incapable of its normal use by causing something which is *muktzeh* (the wax) to be put onto it, and thereby making it forbidden to be moved. (See Chapter 22, paragraph 24.)

   c. It is permitted to put a tray, a dish or a newspaper under or next to a candle,

     1) before Shabbath or Yom Tov, even if it is empty, to catch the wax which will drip off on Shabbath or Yom Tov, or,

     2) on Shabbath or Yom Tov, if it has on it an item which one may move on Shabbath or Yom Tov, since in that case one will be allowed to move the tray, dish or newspaper even after wax has dripped onto it.

   d. It is permitted to put a tray or a dish, not containing water, under or next to a candle, either on Shabbath* or on Yom Tov, to catch sparks which it gives off. because they are not considered as having any physical substance and one will be able to move the tray or dish, even after they have dropped in.

39. For the use of electric bells, see Chapter 23, paragraphs 45 and 47 and Chapter 28, paragraph 29.   *electric bells*

40. A portable electric lamp or heater may be moved on Yom Tov, even while it is on, either for the purpose of using it or because one needs the space which it occupies (as explained in Chapter 20, paragraphs 7 to 10), provided one is careful not to disconnect it from the electricity supply.   *portable lamps and heaters*

---

*In so doing, one must not move the burning candle on Shabbath.

lamp shades   **41.** *a.* A lamp shade is subject to the same rules as the lamp to which it is attached, and accordingly it may not be moved on Shabbath.

b. Nevertheless, a shade which is made to direct the light or to cover it up altogether may be adjusted on Shabbath, even if it is made in such a way that it forms part of the lamp.

inserting a candle into a candlestick   **42.** *a.* When preparing a candle for lighting on Yom Tov, one must not heat its base to make it melt and adhere more firmly to the candlestick.

b. It is likewise forbidden to make the base of the candle narrower, to fit the size of the hole in the candlestick.

c. Moreover, there are grounds for the view that it is prohibited to force a candle into a hole which is too narrow for it, so that the excess wax is scraped off.

cleaning out the hole of a candlestick   **43.** *a.* Wax blocking the hole of a candlestick may be extracted on Yom Tov in order to enable one to insert a fresh candle.

b. It is better to refrain from removing the wax by pouring boiling water over it.

c. A knife,* screwdriver or other implement should be employed, and not a stick of wood which has not been designated for any use and which one is therefore not allowed to move at all on Yom Tov. (See Chapter 20, paragraph 25.)

d. Once extracted, the surplus wax may not be moved.

lighting candles near end of day   **44.** *a.* 1) It is permitted to light a candle (in a manner which is allowed) close to the end of the day, on Yom Tov, since one also benefits from its light on Yom Tov, but

2) it is forbidden to do so if one's whole purpose is to use

---

*A knife or other implement used for food should not be used unless the candle contains no substance which one is forbidden, by Jewish religious law, to eat.

the light after the end of the day, in the evening, even
if that evening will also be Yom Tov.
3) Similarly, one is not allowed to put candles in the
candlesticks on Yom Tov so that they will be ready for
lighting in the evening of the second day of Yom Tov.
b. (See also Chapter 28, paragraph 80.)

45. One may not clip the sealed tip off a cigar on Yom Tov, since   *clipping the*
this in effect completes the cigar, making it ready for use.   *end of a cigar*
(See also paragraphs 7 and 8 above.)

Chapter 14

Washing and Otherwise Attending to the Body on Shabbath and Yom Tov

WASHING IN WARM WATER ON SHABBATH

water heated before Shabbath

1. *a.* One is allowed, on Shabbath, to wash one's face, hands and feet or other individual parts of the body, in water which was heated before Shabbath.

   b. One is generally not allowed to wash or shower the whole, or the major part, of one's body in such water, even if one does so bit by bit.*

   c. A person who is used to washing the whole of his body in warm water every day and will suffer extreme discomfort should he not do so, or someone who is ill, may wash the whole of his body, even on Shabbath, in warm water, provided that it was heated before Shabbath.

   d. Anyone washing himself on Shabbath should take care to avoid squeezing water out of his hair.

water a person has heated on Shabbath

2. One may not wash even the smallest part of one's body on Shabbath

   a. in water which was heated on Shabbath in breach of any prohibition **or**

   b. in water which was heated, even in permissible circumstances, as a result of an action performed on Shabbath, for example

      1) where water was heated by a non-Jew for a person who is ill (as explained in Chapter 33, paragraph 2) or

      2) where one has taken the chill off water, by standing it near the fire in a position in which it cannot reach a temperature of 45 degrees centigrade (113 degrees

---

*A married woman may attend the *mikveh* (ritual bath) on Friday night if that is the time for her immersion in accordance with the rules governing the matter.

Fahrenheit) (as explained in Chapter 1, paragraph 13).

3. *a.* Water heated on Shabbath, but not as the result of any act of heating that a person has performed on Shabbath, is treated like water which was heated before Shabbath.

   water heated, but not put on the fire, on Shabbath

   b. The rules set out in paragraph 1 above accordingly apply also to
   1) water which one put on the fire before Shabbath, but which was heated on Shabbath,
   2) water heated on Shabbath in a solar-energy heater* and
   3) cold water which has been mixed on Shabbath with hot water not warmed by any act of heating that a person has performed on Shabbath. (See paragraph 5 below.)

   c. It is permitted to place cold water in the sunshine to warm it and use it for washing part of one's body.

4. For the use of electric and gas boilers and oil and paraffin-fired water heaters on Shabbath see Chapter 1, paragraph 39.

   water heaters

5. *a.* On Shabbath, when pouring hot water from a *keli rishon* (as to which, see Chapter 1, paragraph 2) into cold water, or cold water into a *keli rishon,* one should be careful that the resultant mixture does not have a temperature of 45 degrees centigrade or more.

   mixing hot and cold water

   b. If one wishes to pour the cold water into the hot water in the *keli rishon,* then
   1) one is only permitted to do so when the *keli rishon* is not standing on the fire **and**
   2) one should take care to pour the cold water in all at once and not little by little.

---

*From Chapter 1, paragraph 45 it will be seen that it is advisable to refrain from using water from a solar-energy heater on Shabbath, if this will result in the heating up on Shabbath of cold water which flows in.

c. Where the hot water is either
  1) in a *k^eli sheini* (as to which, see Chapter 1, paragraph 2) or
  2) being poured out of a *k^eli sheini* into the cold water,
  one may mix the two together, even if the resultant mixture will have a temperature of 45 degrees centigrade or more.
d. See also Chapter 1, paragraphs 51 to 53.

therapeutic hot springs

6. It is forbidden, on Shabbath, to bathe for reasons of health in a therapeutic hot spring.

WASHING IN WARM WATER ON YOM TOV

to what extent permitted

7. a. Washing the whole or most of one's body at once in warm water is forbidden on Yom Tov, as it is on Shabbath, even if the water was heated before Yom Tov.
  b. Water which was heated before Yom Tov may be used to wash parts of one's body or even the whole of one's body part by part.
  c. Water may be heated on Yom Tov itself to wash one's face, hands and feet.

bathing babies

8. a. 1) While one may wash the whole of a baby's body (even all at once) in warm water on Yom Tov (taking care not to squeeze out the baby's hair), if
      a) one normally does so every day **or**
      b) a specific need arises,
    2) it is prohibited to warm up water on Yom Tov specially for this purpose.
  b. One may, when about to heat water for drinking or for washing dishes, put an additional quantity of water, sufficient for bathing the baby, into the kettle or urn, before putting it on the fire.
  c. However, if the water to be used for drinking or for washing dishes is already on the fire, one may not pour in additional water to be heated for bathing the baby.

9. For the use of boilers and water heaters of all kinds on Yom *water heaters*
Tov see Chapter 2, paragraph 7.

10. On Yom Tov, as on Shabbath, it is forbidden to bathe for *therapeutic*
reasons of health in a therapeutic hot spring. *hot springs*

WASHING IN COLD WATER ON SHABBATH AND YOM TOV

11. *a.* On Shabbath and Yom Tov, the practice is, generally, not *to what*
to wash the whole of the body, even in cold water, but *extent*
only those parts which are not thickly covered with hair. *permitted*
b. These parts of the body may be washed not only in cold
water, but also in water which has had the chill taken off
before Shabbath, as long as it does not actually feel warm
to the touch.
c. If one is suffering from discomfort, as on a very hot day,
one may take a shower (in water of this kind) in the same
way as on a normal weekday, being careful, nevertheless,
not to squeeze out any hair. (See paragraph 20 below
concerning the drying of hair.)

12. *a.* Swimming is forbidden, both on Shabbath and on Yom *swimming*
Tov.
b. It is also the practice, on Shabbath and Yom Tov, not to
bathe in the sea or in a pool, even without swimming.

MISCELLANEOUS LAWS RELATING TO WASHING ONESELF
ON SHABBATH AND YOM TOV*

13. *a.* Even when washing oneself is permitted, one must not *face cloths,*
use a sponge or a cloth for that purpose. *sponges and*
b. A brush should not be used for washing oneself, unless *brushes*
1) its bristles are made of a synthetic material **and**
2) are not close enough together to hold water **and**
3) the brush is kept specially for washing on Shabbath
and Yom Tov.

---

*The problems which can arise in connection with the use of sinks are
dealt with in Chapter 12, paragraphs 16 to 18.

bath salts

14. When one is allowed on Shabbath or Yom Tov to bathe a person who is unwell*—even if he is not seriously ill—or a baby, one may also add bath salts to the water.

scenting
bath water

15. It is forbidden to scent the bath water (or any other water, for that matter) by the addition of perfumes or similar substances.

soap

16. *a.* One may not wash with a bar of soap on Shabbath or Yom Tov.

b. The use of liquid soap is permitted.

c. It is advisable to have liquid soap ready for use before Shabbath or Yom Tov, but, if one has not prepared or obtained any,

   1) one may prepare liquid soap by allowing a bar of soap or soap powder to dissolve in hot water (even on Shabbath, if one is not using water in a *kᵉli rishon,* as defined in Chapter 1, paragraph 2, nor pouring water onto the soap from a *kᵉli rishon*) and

   2) one may go so far as to speed up the process of dissolution by agitating the cup or bowl containing the soap and water, but

   3) one must not rub or crush the soap in the water with one's hand or with an instrument.

stained
fingers

17. *a.* Stains may be removed from the fingers by rubbing with lemon juice, but

b. not with a piece of lemon itself or with lemon rind, as squeezing the juice out is prohibited.

c. One should also refrain from using paraffin (kerosene) or turpentine for this purpose.

washing a
baby on a
towel

18. *a.* One is allowed to place a baby one is washing onto an absolutely clean towel, regardless of the fact that the towel will become wet.

---

*See paragraph 1 above.

b. One should not wash a baby
   1) on a towel which is not completely clean (since wetting
      a dirty towel washes it, to a certain extent) or
   2) on a cloth which one is particular not to make wet
      (since one may come to squeeze the water out of it).

c. See also paragraph 22 below.

19. a. A napkin may be used for wiping the remnants of food *table-* from one's mouth or hands. (See also paragraph 26 *napkins* below.)

   b. If one's face or hands have become soiled by food which
      gives off color, such as cocoa or strawberries, one should
      try to rinse them before wiping with a napkin or towel, to
      avoid transferring the color to the cloth.

   c. It is perfectly in order to wipe one's mouth or hands with a
      paper napkin, which is disposed of after use, even if this
      incidentally colors the paper.

DRYING ONESELF ON SHABBATH AND YOM TOV

20. a. One may dry one's body, including those parts which are *drying hair*
       covered by hair, with a towel, but

    b. one may not squeeze out the hair otherwise than in the
       process of drying it.

    c. Nonetheless, one may rub wet hair, in order to ease pain
       or discomfort, even if there is a possibility that water may
       be squeezed out of it as a result. (See also paragraph 42
       below.)

21. a. Paper towels or tissues may be used, notwithstanding the *paper towels*
       fact that they are liable to tear in use. *and tissues*

    b. 1) Paper towels must not be torn off a roll, whether or not
          one tears along the perforation.
       2) Tissues which have not been properly separated in
          manufacture must not be pulled apart, even if they
          only remain slightly joined at the corners.

    c. See also paragraph 33 below.

handling wet towels **22.** A towel may be handled even after it has become wet, and one need not be afraid that one will come to squeeze the water out of it.

hanging up towels **23.** *a.* 1) A wet towel must not be hung up to dry, but
2) it may be hung in its usual place, even if it will, incidentally, dry there.
3) A wet towel may not be placed near a heater or on a radiator.
b. It is permissible to dry one's hands on a towel hanging on a line strung between two trees, but one must not take it off the line (as explained in Chapter 26, paragraph 17).

warming wet hands **24.** *a.* It is forbidden
1) to hold wet hands in the heat of an oven or heater, even if its temperature does not reach 45 degrees centigrade (113 degrees Fahrenheit) or
2) to dry one's hands in the stream of hot air emitted from an electric hand-dryer, even if it has been on continuously since before Shabbath or Yom Tov, or is operating by means of a time-switch.
b. There is nothing wrong with holding one's hands in front of a heater after they have been dried.

bringing towel home **25.** A person returning from the *mikveh* (ritual bath) may wrap himself in his towel and so bring it home, even in a place where there is no *eiruv* (as to which see Chapter 17 below).

wiping dirty hands **26.** If one's hands have been dirtied with mud or the like,
a. one must not wipe them clean on a towel or with a handkerchief, which one might come to wash in order to remove the dirt adhering to them; however,
b. one may wipe them on a cloth which one does not mind becoming dirty. (See also paragraph 19 above.)

CARE OF THE BODY ON SHABBATH AND YOM TOV

27. a. Rubbing ointment on a baby is not permitted.

    b. The prohibition extends as well to thick zinc oil.

    c. See also Chapter 37, paragraphs 6 and 7.

    d. Even rubbing butter, margarine or any other edible "cream" on a baby, for example on his lips, is forbidden.

rubbing ointment on a baby

28. a. It is permitted to apply oil of a normal consistency to a baby's body

    1) with one's bare hand or

    2) with a piece of non-absorbent, synthetic fabric (for example, plastic).

    b. One may not apply the oil by putting it on absorbent cotton (cotton wool) or on an absorbent cloth (as the oil will be squeezed out during the application), and one ought not to do so even if the cotton was tightly compressed before Shabbath or Yom Tov. (See also paragraph 29 below.)

    c. One may, however, put the oil on the desired part of the baby's body and then gently wipe over it with an absorbent cloth or cotton.

rubbing oil on a baby

29. a. Cotton swabs (absorbent cotton wound tightly around the tip of a stick) required for cleaning a baby's nose or ears must be prepared before the commencement of Shabbath or Yom Tov (where none of the ready-made variety is available).

    b. It is proper to prepare before Shabbath or Yom Tov as many cotton tufts as one is likely to need, since it is best to refrain from tearing them off the wad on Shabbath or Yom Tov.

preparing absorbent cotton

30. a. One is allowed to sprinkle powder on a baby, even on a spot where the skin is particularly sensitive or sore, notwithstanding the general prohibition against applying medicaments on Shabbath and Yom Tov. (See Chapter 37.)

baby powder

b. Concerning the perforation of the lid of a baby-powder container, see Chapter 9, paragraph 6.

insect repellent

31. *a.* One is permitted to rub one's body with a liquid insect repellent (but not a cream or ointment).

b. For the spraying of liquid insecticides see Chapter 25, paragraph 5.

use of perfume

32. *a.* While perfume may be applied to the hands or any other part of the body,

b. it must not be applied to a handkerchief, a cloth or any article of clothing. (See Chapter 15, paragraph 76.)

freshening up with perfumed pads

33. One may freshen up by wiping one's face or hands with an eau-de-cologne-saturated paper towel or pad, since none of the perfume is visibly squeezed out.

cleaning one's teeth

34. *a.* It is the practice not to brush one's teeth on Shabbath or Yom Tov, even without paste.

b. One is permitted to pick one's teeth with a toothpick or with any suitably shaped chip or splinter of wood or stalk that one is not prevented from using by the rules of *muktzeh* set out in Chapter 20.

c. 1) A matchstick may be used as a toothpick, if one has nothing else suitable (as is apparent from Chapter 20, paragraphs 7 and 16), but

2) one must not sharpen it, either with an instrument or by hand, to adapt it for use as a toothpick.

d. See also Chapter 11, paragraph 15 for the use of straw as a toothpick.

false teeth

35. One may not sprinkle false teeth with the special powder which makes them adhere firmly to the palate.

mouthwash

36. *a.* Mouthwash may be used to rinse one's mouth on Shabbath or Yom Tov.

b. The mouthwash should be poured into the water before Shabbath or Yom Tov, but, if one has not done so, one may prepare it on Shabbath or Yom Tov.

37. *a.* One must not weigh or measure oneself or any other *weighing and* person. *measuring*
   b. For the weighing of a baby, when one needs to know how much, if anything, it has gained after a feed, see Chapter 37, paragraph 5.

38. *a.* One should not, as a rule, perform physical exercises on *physical* Shabbath or Yom Tov, whether with or without the use of *exercise* an instrument designed for strengthening muscles, such as a chest-expander.
   b. Likewise, one should not engage in occupational therapy.
   c. It is, however, permitted to do simple, light exercises with one's hands, even if one's object is to ease a pain.
   d. A person who, as a result of his state of health, is advised to engage in physical exercises or occupational therapy ought to consult a qualified rabbinical authority, since the circumstances may be such as to justify performing them even on Shabbath or Yom Tov.

39. *a.* Pliable ear plugs, of the kind used by light sleepers to *ear plugs* prevent their sleep from being disturbed, may not be used on Shabbath or Yom Tov, as it is forbidden to spread the wax-like material of which they are made, so that it should fill the cavity of the ear, and if one does not do so they are not effective.
   b. Tufts of absorbent cotton (cotton wool) may be used as ear plugs, if they are prepared before Shabbath or Yom Tov. (See paragraph 29 above.)

40. *a.* Water which one has used for washing one's hands first *disposal of* thing in the morning may be poured into the sink, and *water used* there is no prohibition against moving it, despite the fact *for washing* that it is not fit to be used for any purpose. *hands in*
   morning
   b. The water must not be poured
      1) onto seeds, due to the prohibition against sowing, which also includes watering seeds, or
      2) onto earth, since this would violate the prohibition against kneading.

[159]

CARE OF THE HAIR ON SHABBATH AND YOM TOV

cutting or removing hair

41. *a.* One may not cut hair on Shabbath or Yom Tov,

    1) whether it be on the head, in a beard or on any other part of the body, and

    2) whether one uses an instrument, such as scissors or a shaver, a powder, an ointment or any other kind of preparation.

b. One may, likewise, not tear out hair, whether by hand, with an instrument or with the aid of one's teeth.

scratching one's head

42. *a.* It is permissible to scratch one's head or beard lightly, and one need not be afraid that one might thereby pull out some of the hairs.

b. It is also permissible to extract the remains of food stuck in one's beard, so long as one takes care not to pull out any of the hair.

dandruff

43. *a.* One is allowed to remove loose dandruff from one's hair with one's hand, but

b. one must be careful not to remove dandruff which is still attached to the skin.

combing and brushing the hair

44. *a.* One may neither

    1) comb one's hair, **nor**

    2) brush one's hair with a hard brush.

b. Combs and hard brushes may not be moved, as they are *muktzeh*. (See Chapter 20, paragraph 16.)

c. 1) While one is permitted to tidy one's hair a little with a soft brush which is not likely to pull out any of the hair,

    2) it is advisable to keep this brush especially for Shabbath and Yom Tov, so that there is a recognizable distinction between the way in which one brushes one's hair on a normal weekday and the way in which one does so on Shabbath and Yom Tov.

combing prior to mikveh

45. A married woman who has forgotten to comb her hair before Shabbath or Yom Tov, as is required before going to the *mikveh* (ritual bath) on Shabbath or Yom Tov, should consult a qualified rabbinical authority who will tell her how to proceed in the circumstances.

46. *a.* It is proper to refrain from combing a wig on Shabbath or Yom Tov.   *combing and brushing a wig*

    b. However, it is perfectly in order to smooth the hair of a wig with a soft-haired brush.

47. *a.* A woman may put hairpins or clips in her hair to hold it in place.   *hairpins and decorative combs*

    b. She may even use decorative combs for the purpose, despite the fact that the mere act of inserting them may, to some extent, arrange her hair.

    c. Regarding the question of whether a woman may go out with hairpins, clips or combs in her hair into a place where there is no *eiruv*, see Chapter 18, paragraphs 8 and 12.

48. *a.* Brilliantine or any other hair oil may be applied to the hair, but only in small quantities so that one should not come to squeeze it out of the hair.   *hair oil and hair cream*

    b. The use of hair cream, in any quantity, is forbidden.

49. The hair may be parted with the fingers, but not with a brush or comb.   *hair parting*

50. *a.* It is forbidden to spray the hair or a wig in order to stiffen and preserve the coiffure.   *hair spray*

    b. It is also forbidden to style one's hair (or a wig).

51. *a.* There are authorities who permit the hair to be sprayed with (non-stiffening) perfume.   *perfuming hair*

    b. Perfume must not be sprayed on a wig.

52. *a.* One may not plait or unplait hair.   *plaits and ribbons*

    b. One may gather up dishevelled hair, arrange it by hand and tie it with a ribbon or hairband.

curling   53. One is not permitted to curl the hair with curlers or in any
               other way.

MANICURE AND COSMETICS

cutting the   54. *a.* On Shabbath and Yom Tov one is not allowed to cut, trim
nails   or file nails, whether with scissors, a nail file or any other
     instrument or by biting them.

     b. Similarly, small pieces of skin which are peeling off
     around the fingernail or on any other part of the body, but
     which are still connected, may not be pulled or cut off
     with an instrument, by hand or even with the teeth.

     c. Nonetheless, if
       1) the end of a nail has become detached for most of its
         width and is, therefore, close to coming off **and**
       2) it is causing, or one is afraid that it will cause, pain,
       it may be removed, either by hand or with the teeth, but
       not with an instrument.

cutting nails 55. A married woman who has forgotten to cut her fingernails or
prior to   toenails before Shabbath or Yom Tov, as is required before
mikveh   going to the *mikveh* (ritual bath) on Shabbath or Yom Tov,
    should consult a qualified rabbinical authority who will tell
    her how to proceed, according to the circumstances of the
    case.

cleaning   56. *a.* Dirt may be cleaned from underneath the tip of a nail,
nails   but

     b. one must not, in doing so, scrape away any part of the nail
     itself.

polishing   57. *a.* It is prohibited to polish (lacquer) one's nails on Shab-
nails   bath or Yom Tov.

     b. The prohibition applies whether the nail polish is colored
     or colorless.

lipstick   58. *a.* It is not permitted to color one's lips (or any other part of
     the body) on Shabbath or Yom Tov, even if one is only

adding color to color which was already there when Shabbath or Yom Tov began.

b. Even the use of colorless lipstick is forbidden.

c. See also Chapter 34, paragraph 13.

59. a. Make-up in the form of cream or a cake, such as rouge or face powder mixed with cream, may not be used on Shabbath or Yom Tov. *face powder*

b. It is also proper not to apply make-up powder to the face, even when it does not adhere well to the skin.

60. The use of face cream or hand cream to soften the skin is not allowed. *face cream and hand cream*

61. A married woman may remove polish (lacquer) from her nails with acetone before going to the *mikveh* on Shabbath or Yom Tov, if she forgot to do so beforehand, but she should not use absorbent cotton (cotton wool) for this purpose. *removing nail polish prior to mikveh*

Chapter 15

Care of Clothes on Shabbath and Yom Tov

*general
prohibition*

1. It is forbidden to clean clothes on Shabbath or on Yom Tov in any of the ways mentioned below.

*forbidden
activities*

2. *a.* Four types of activity are forbidden under the heading of "cleaning":
1) soaking a garment in water or in any other substance which cleans;
2) washing a garment with water or with any other substance which cleans;
3) squeezing or shaking water out of a garment;
4) removing dirt from a garment by rubbing or shaking it.

b. It will be seen below that there is also a rabbinical prohibition against hanging up a wash or any wet clothes to dry.

*distinctions
to be made*

3. As will be explained below, the following distinctions must be made in order to determine the extent to which the prohibition against cleaning applies:

a. between soaking a dirty garment and soaking a clean garment;

b. between the type of soaking which cleans the garment and the type of soaking which soils it;

c. between a black garment and a white garment;

d. between a garment which one is particular to keep clean and a garment which one is not particular to keep clean.

*scope of
prohibition*

4. *a.* With certain exceptions, one may not soak laundry in water, or pour even a small amount of water onto laundry,
1) whether on Shabbath or on Yom Tov,
2) whether the wash is dirty or clean and

3) whether it is white or colored.

b. 1) Consequently, one should take care not to soak in water diapers (nappies) which have become wet or dirty, nor even to spray them with water, but *diapers*

2) it is permitted to remove excrement from them, provided that one does not do so with water.

3) The proper course of action is to put the dirty diapers into a pail, as they are, and cover them, although

4) one is allowed to sprinkle them with insect repellent.

5) If there is any fear of the transmission of a contagious or infectious disease,

   a) one may soak the diapers in disinfectant, in which it is not usual to wash them, but

   b) one may not soak them in bleach or some other substance in which it is usual to wash them, since the prohibition against soaking applies not only in the case of water, but also in the case of any other substance which cleans.

   c) However, it is better to use disposable diapers in such circumstances.

5. a. Plastic or rubber pants or sheets may be soaked in water or cleaned by spraying with water, if *babies' waterproof pants and sheets*

   1) there is no cloth sewn to them,

   2) they are not sewn with thread made from a natural fiber **and**

   3) one actually intends to use them that day.

b. While wet, they must not be cleaned by rubbing one side against the other, or by rubbing them with one's hand or a cloth.

c. A wet cloth must in no event be used, since it is inevitable that, in the process of rubbing, one will squeeze some of the water out of it.

d. See paragraph 11 below regarding the drying of plastic or rubber pants or sheets.

6. a. Socks, shirts and other clothes made from purely synthetic fibers may be soaked in water, if *purely synthetic clothes*

1) there is no intermixture of natural fibers,
2) they are not sewn with thread made from a natural fiber **and**
3) one actually intends to use them that day.

b. While wet, they must not be cleaned by rubbing one side against the other, or by rubbing them with one's hand or a cloth.

c. A wet cloth must not be used under any circumstance, for the reason mentioned in 5c above.

d. It is forbidden to squeeze, or energetically shake, the water out of such clothes.

e. See paragraph 11 below regarding the drying of purely synthetic clothes.

mixture of natural and synthetic fibers

7. Garments
   a. which are made of a mixture of natural and synthetic threads **or**
   b. whose threads are themselves composed of a mixture of natural and artificial fibers
   should be treated as described in paragraph 4 above.

synthetics or rubber sewn with natural thread

8. Where one wishes to soak rubber, plastic or purely synthetic items in water, in accordance with paragraph 5 or paragraph 6 above, but they are sewn with thread made from natural fibers, one may do so only if one takes care not to spray or soak the sewn parts in water.

HANGING UP AND TAKING DOWN LAUNDRY

general prohibition on drying laundry

9. Wet laundry
   a. may not be hung up to dry,
   b. may not be hung up at all in a place where it is usual to hang it to dry and
   c. may not be placed near a heater or radiator.

drying clothes which have become wet

10. Clothes which have become wet, for example in the rain or with sweat, even if only partly, may
    a. neither be hung up to dry
    b. nor be placed near a heater or radiator.

11. Clothes and other items of the kind referred to in paragraphs 5 and 6 above, which one is allowed to soak on Shabbath or Yom Tov, may also be hung up to dry, but not near a heater or radiator. *drying clothes one may soak*

12. Babies' diapers (nappies) which have become partly wet with urine may be hung up to dry, if *wet diapers*
    a. it is obvious from the circumstances or from their appearance that they are not being hung up to dry after being washed,
    b. one indeed intends to use them that same day,
    c. one has no other diapers **and**
    d. one does not hang them near a heater or radiator.

13. Even wet or damp clothes which one is not permitted to hang up to dry may be put or hung away in their usual place, but *putting clothes away in their usual place*
    a. only subject to the limitations set out in paragraph 15 below,
    b. only if that place is not near a heater or radiator **and**
    c. with the reservation that they must not be hung in a place where they are commonly hung up to dry, for example wet towels on a cord over the bath.

14. a. Laundry hanging on the line need not be removed before Shabbath. *laundry hung up before Shabbath*
    b. For its removal on Shabbath see paragraph 17 below.

15. a. 1) With the exceptions mentioned below, wet clothes may not be moved on Shabbath or Yom Tov, for fear that one may come to squeeze them out. *scope of prohibition on moving wet clothes*
    2) The prohibition affects only clothes which are wet to such an extent that a hand touching them would become sufficiently wet to transfer moisture to another object with which it subsequently comes into contact.
    3) It applies
       a) whether the clothes are wet with water or with a different substance which cleans and
       b) even if they are only partly wet.

[167]

   b. The prohibition does not apply to

     1) clothes which are only damp, that is to say not wet to the extent specified in subparagraph *a* above,

     2) wet towels or other wet cloths which are of such a nature that one does not mind them being wet (even if they are wet to the extent specified in subparagraph *a* above), since one does not usually squeeze them out,

     3) diapers (nappies) which have been made wet by a baby (regarding which see also paragraph 12 above) or

     4) clothes which became wet on Shabbath but have dried out again. (See paragraph 9 above.)

wearing wet clothes

16. *a.* A person whose clothes have become wet may continue wearing them and need not be afraid that he will come to squeeze them out.

   b. If one has no other clothes, one may even put on wet clothes.

   c. In neither case may one vigorously shake the water out of the clothes, nor, while wearing them, should one stand or sit near a heater or radiator in a position where the temperature reaches 45 degrees centigrade (113 degrees Fahrenheit), even if one's sole intention in doing so is to warm oneself and not one's clothing.

taking down laundry on Shabbath and Yom Tov

17. *a.* With the exceptions mentioned below, laundry previously hung up to dry may be taken down on Shabbath or Yom Tov only if, when Shabbath or Yom Tov commenced, it was already dry or only damp, that is, not wet to the extent specified in paragraph 15a2 above.

   b. See also Chapter 22, paragraph 3.

   c. Since clothes made of a purely synthetic material, of the kind described in paragraphs 5 and 6 above, may be hung up to dry on Shabbath or Yom Tov (as explained in paragraph 11 above), they may also be taken down, even if, when Shabbath or Yom Tov commenced, they were still wet to the extent stated in paragraph 15a2 above.

18. Diapers (nappies) and other baby clothing may be removed *taking down* from the clothesline on Shabbath or Yom Tov, for use on the *baby clothes* same day, even if, when Shabbath or Yom Tov commenced, *on Shabbath* they were wet to the extent stated in paragraph 15a2 above, *or Yom Tov* so long as one has no other clothing one could use that day.

19. *a.* Clothespins (pegs) are *muktzeh*, since the normal use for *clothespins* which they are intended is prohibited on Shabbath and Yom Tov. (See Chapter 20, paragraph 7.)
   b. They may only be moved
      1) if one wishes to use them for a permitted purpose, such as to hang up items of the kind referred to in paragraphs 5 and 6 above, **or**
      2) if one wishes to use the place which they occupy, or if their presence prevents one from taking some other item, as where they are holding up articles which one desires to remove from the line. (See paragraphs 17 and 18 above.)
   c. For further details, reference should be made to Chapter 20, paragraphs 7 to 12.

20. *a.* Hanging up, or taking down, laundry on Shabbath or *supporting a* Yom Tov, in the circumstances described in paragraphs *clothesline* 11, 12, 17 and 18 above, is allowed only if the clothesline is *on a tree* not supported directly by a tree, because otherwise one is considered to be using the tree, which is forbidden on Shabbath and Yom Tov.
   b. If, however, the clothesline is not supported directly by the tree, but is fixed, for example, to a pulley-wheel which is itself attached to the tree, use of the line is not prohibited, as will be explained in Chapter 26, paragraph 14.

21. Whenever it is permissible to hang up or take down laundry, *clothesline* as detailed above, one may do so even if the line is suspended *overhanging* over a street which is a *reshuth ha-rabbim*. (See Chapter 17, *a street* paragraphs 1, 3 and 6.)

keeping clothes in a washing machine

22. If one is accustomed to keeping one's dirty clothes in the washing machine until they are washed, one may put them in even on Shabbath or Yom Tov, provided that there is no water inside it.

REMOVING DUST, STAINS, OR DIRT FROM CLOTHES ON SHABBATH AND YOM TOV

relevant distinctions

23. *a.* It will be seen below that, in deciding whether or not clothes may be cleaned on Shabbath and Yom Tov, one must distinguish between
   1) the removal of stains,
   2) the removal of dust and
   3) the removal of dirt stuck to clothes.
b. It will also be explained that cleaning may or may not be allowed, depending on
   1) the kind of garment one wishes to clean and
   2) the method of cleaning to be employed.

stain removal

24. *a.* To clean a stain on any garment is forbidden.
b. The prohibition covers
   1) the use of water or any other substance which cleans, including
      a) paraffin (kerosene),
      b) benzine,
      c) special preparations for spraying on stains,
      d) colored liquids which, although they do not make the garment absolutely clean, leave it cleaner than before,
      e) spittle and
      f) talcum powder sprinkled on a garment or cloth, to absorb grease which has spilled on it, and
   2) removing a stain from a garment by rubbing it or by scraping it with an instrument or with one's fingernail.

dust

25. Whether and how one may remove dust from a garment depends on whether or not one is normally particular to keep it clean.

a. If the garment is one which, according to the definition contained in paragraph 26 below, one is normally particular to keep clean, one is not allowed to shake out or remove the dust.

b. If, however, the garment is one which one is not normally particular to keep clean,

1) one may dust it lightly
   a) with one's hand or
   b) with a dry cloth held in one's hand, or
   c) by gently shaking it, but
2) one may not
   a) rub it,
   b) shake it very vigorously or
   c) remove the dust with a brush.

26. *a.* Garments which one is normally particular to keep clean comprise black or dark clothes that are new or look new, unless one in fact does not mind putting them on even without cleaning them first. *classification of garments*

b. 1) Garments which one is not normally particular to keep clean comprise
   a) light-colored clothes and
   b) black or dark-colored clothes which are neither new nor look new.

2) Nevertheless, if one is in fact particular not to wear such clothes when they are not clean, they should be treated like clothes about whose cleanliness one is normally particular.

c. A garment which one would usually wear even if it is dirty, without bothering to clean it, but which one now wishes to dust in honor of Shabbath or a special occasion, is treated as a garment about which one is not normally particular.

27. *a.* Dirt stuck to clothes, even clothes which one is particular to keep clean, may be removed in the ways listed below, provided that *wet, stain-leaving dirt stuck to clothes*

1) the dirt is moist or soft and

2) a stain will remain after the dirt is removed.

b. In these circumstances, it is permissible

1) to rub the reverse side of the cloth until the dirt drops off,

2) to remove the dirt directly, with one's fingernails or the back of a knife, **or**

3) to wipe the dirt off gently with a dry cloth, taking care not to squeeze out the moisture absorbed within the garment.

c. It is forbidden

1) to wipe the garment with a wet cloth, since in the course of doing so one will inevitably squeeze out some of the water absorbed in the cloth, or

2) to wet the garment in order to clean it.

dirt which has dried onto clothes

28. a. Mud or any similar substance which has dried onto a garment may not be taken off at all, as it will crumble while being removed, and this is an infringement of the prohibition against grinding.

b. Nonetheless, if

1) the dry dirt consists of food which either

a) was previously ground, such as dough or farina, or

b) became pulpy in cooking, as beans, for example, sometimes do, **and**

2) the dirt will leave a stain on the garment after it has been taken off,

then it may be removed in one of the permitted ways listed in paragraph 27 above.

non-stain-leaving dirt stuck to clothes

29. a. Dirt which will not leave a stain may be removed from a garment to which it is stuck only if one would not normally be particular to keep the garment free of that kind of dirt.

b. It is irrelevant in this connection whether the dirt is moist or dry (although it must be remembered that dry dirt of the kind mentioned in paragraph 28a above may not be removed at all).

c. The dirt must not be removed in any of the ways set out in paragraph 24 above.

30. *a.* The removal of dirt which is on the surface of—but not absorbed in or stuck to—a garment does not fall under the prohibition against cleaning, and it may accordingly be taken off by hand (but not with a brush) or blown off. *dirt on the surface of a garment*
    b. Consequently, it is in order to pick a feather, wisps of absorbent cotton (cotton wool) or a thread off clothes, even if one is particular about keeping them clean.
    c. A thread which is still sewn into a garment may not be pulled out. (See also paragraphs 65 and 68 below.)

31. *a.* One is allowed to clean the eyeglasses (spectacles) one is using on Shabbath or Yom Tov, but *cleaning eyeglasses*
    b. one must not wet the cloth one employs for that purpose.
    c. On the other hand, one may wet the lenses and wipe them with a dry cloth.

32. *a.* Due to the ease with which one can come to transgress the prohibition against cleaning, it is recommended that one should take care to prevent one's clothes from becoming dirty. *advisability of keeping clothes clean*
    b. Thus,
    1) it is a good idea to put away clothes which one is particular to keep clean, so that they should not fall on the floor and become dirty, and
    2) it is advisable not to take a baby directly onto one's lap, without first putting down a clean diaper (nappy) or cloth to protect one's clothes.

SHAKING RAIN AND SNOW OUT OF CLOTHES
ON SHABBATH AND YOM TOV

33. *a.* 1) It is altogether forbidden to shake out a new garment that has been soaked by rain, regardless of the color of the garment. *shaking out clothes soaked by rain*
    2) This is because one is usually particular that no new

garment should be soaked in water, and shaking it out in effect amounts to cleaning it.

3) The same applies to a garment which, while not new, looks new.

b. 1) If the garment is neither new nor looks new, it may be shaken out gently.

2) Vigorous shaking is not permitted, even if the garment is one which one does not mind being wet, as the result achieved is the same as squeezing the garment out and is equally prohibited.

c. See also paragraphs 9, 15 and 16 above.

d. For the special case of raincoats see paragraph 34 below.

raincoats 34. a. A raincoat, whether old or new, made of or containing cloth may be gently shaken out, since one does not mind its being wet.

b. A raincoat made entirely of non-woven plastic sheeting, and not containing any cloth, may be shaken out even vigorously.

hanging up 35. a. As already mentioned in paragraph 10 above, clothes *rain-soaked* which have become wet in the rain may not be hung up to *clothes* dry (with the exception specified below).

b. This includes raincoats made of or containing cloth.

c. From paragraph 13, it can be seen that rain-soaked clothes may be hung away in their usual place, so long as that is not near a heater or radiator.

d. If one has no other suitable clothes, one may put a rain-soaked garment back on.

e. A raincoat made entirely of a plastic material or of synthetic fibers, without any intermixture of natural threads, may, as explained in paragraph 11 above, be hung up to dry.

snow 36. a. One may gently shake unmelted snow off clothing, but care should be taken not to do so vigorously.

b. Snow may be shaken, even vigorously, off a raincoat made entirely of non-woven, plastic sheeting or off a plastic hat-cover or rain bonnet, so long as they do not contain any cloth.

CLEANING SHOES ON SHABBATH AND YOM TOV

37. *a.* It is forbidden   *polishing and*
   1) to spread polish on shoes,   *shining*
   2) to spray them with any preparation for polishing shoes,
   3) to smear them with oil or
   4) to shine them with a brush or a cloth, even without putting polish on them.
   b. One may, however, remove dust from shoes with one's hand or a cloth, as long as one is careful to do so gently, so as not to shine them.

38. The cleaning of suede or cloth shoes or felt slippers is   *suede shoes* governed by the rules regarding the cleaning of clothes set out in paragraphs 24 to 30 above.

39. *a.* Mud which is still wet may be gently, but not vigorously,   *removing wet* removed from shoes or boots with the aid of a scraper or   *mud* any instrument whose use is permissible on Shabbath or Yom Tov. (See also the rules of *muktzeh* discussed in Chapter 20.)
   b. The composition of the soles and heels, whether they be of leather, plastic, rubber or crepe, is irrelevant.

40. *a.* Dried mud must not be removed from shoes or boots   *removing* either by hand or with an instrument, since causing the   *dried mud* mud to crumble involves a transgression of the prohibition against grinding.
   b. 1) If
      a) the mud hinders one when walking **and**
      b) the shoes or boots are not sewn with any natural thread nor made of suede or cloth,
      then one may wash them by standing them in water or by spraying them with water.

2) Even in this case,
    a) one should refrain from rubbing them with one's hand or a cloth while they are in the water **and**
    b) one should not wipe them clean with a wet cloth, because in the course of doing so one will squeeze out some of the water absorbed in the cloth.

PREPARING AND FOLDING CLOTHES ON SHABBATH AND YOM TOV

tidying jumbled clothes

41. If one has a pile of clothes of different kinds or sizes,
  a. one may not sort them out according to kind or size, but
  b. one may take each article of clothing, as it comes to hand, fold it (in a permitted manner, as set out in paragraphs 44 and 46 below), and then put it in its place, until one has arranged the whole pile. (See also Chapter 3, paragraph 82.)

selecting clothes to be worn

42. *a.* Since selection is only permitted immediately prior to the use of what one picks out (as explained in Chapter 3, paragraph 62), one should not pick out the clothes one requires until just before they are to be put on.
  b. One should, accordingly, take care, on the evening of Shabbath or Yom Tov, not to select clothes for one's children to wear in the morning.
  c. It is permitted
    1) to remove the top clothes from a pile, but only just before they are to be worn, or
    2) to lift the top clothes off a pile, so as to reach clothes underneath which are about to be worn.

ironing

43. Ironing, in any form whatsoever, is forbidden.

folding in an existing crease

44. One must not fold a garment or cloth back into already existing creases, unless all of the following five conditions are met:
  a. The article is being folded for use on the same day.
  b. The article is new, that is to say it has never been washed.

c. The article is white and not colored.

d. One has no similar article, even one less presentable than the first, which is suitable for wear or use on Shabbath.

e. The folding is done by one person, without the assistance of anybody else and without putting the article onto a table or other surface in the process of folding it.

45. Consequently,

a. one should not fold a *tallith* or a tablecloth into its previous creases, unless all of the conditions listed in paragraph 44 above are satisfied, and

b. one should not fold a pair of trousers, although one is permitted to hang them on a hook even if they fall into their existing creases by themselves.

tallitoth, tablecloths and trousers

46. *a.* Any article may be folded if one takes care not to fold it into its original creases, but one should re-fold it into its normal creases after Shabbath or Yom Tov.

b. It is permissible to fold articles in which no recognizable crease is left, as in the case of rubber sheets, certain types of plastic tablecloths and woollen articles.

c. Dry laundry may be folded, provided that one's sole object is to make it easier to put away in its place and that one is not particular about the manner of folding.

d. In all of the instances referred to in this paragraph, folding is allowed even when one has no intention of using the articles folded on the same day, so long as the folding serves some purpose on the Shabbath or Yom Tov, such as keeping the house tidy.

permitted methods of folding

47. The prohibition against folding clothes on Shabbath or Yom Tov is not infringed

a. by restoring the dents in a hat which has been crushed,

b. by turning down a collar which has become turned up or

c. by adjusting to its proper position a trouser cuff (turn-up) which has become turned down.

hats, collars and cuffs

48. Shoe-trees may be inserted into shoes so that they will retain their shape, but not if the intention is to widen the shoe.

shoe-trees

TYING AND UNTYING KNOTS
ON SHABBATH AND YOM TOV

*forbidden
types of
knots*

49. *a.* There is a general prohibition, subject to certain exceptions which are amplified in the succeeding paragraphs,
against tying knots, whether on Shabbath or on Yom Tov.

b. Included within this prohibition are
   1) the tying together of two ends of string, ribbon or the
   like with a double knot,
   2) the tying of even a single knot at the end, or in the
   middle, of a piece of string, as is often done at the ends
   of the threads of *tzitzith,* and
   3) the tying of a single knot in two adjacent ends of
   string.

c. One should be particularly careful to avoid infringing
these rules when tying knots or bows in head scarves, hair
ribbons, dress sashes, children's bibs and the like. (See
paragraph 53 below for the tying of bows.)

*tightening
knots*

50. *a.* Knots which one is not allowed to tie on Shabbath or Yom
Tov must not be tightened if they become loose.

b. An example is a double knot, the top knot of which is
coming undone.

c. As a result, one should beware of tightening knots of
tzitzith which have loosened.

*when single
knots
permitted*

51. *a.* It is permissible to make a single knot in articles one is
accustomed to secure with a double knot, such as *tzitzith,*
since in this case, they cannot be said to be properly tied.

b. It is forbidden to add a single knot
   1) to an already existing single knot—tied on or before
   Shabbath or Yom Tov, whether by oneself or by
   another person—thereby converting it into a double
   knot, or
   2) to an already existing double knot, in order to make it
   more secure.

52. *a.* 1) One may, on Shabbath or Yom Tov, tie a knot (even a *tying*
double knot) *temporary*
   a) which is, both usually and on this particular occa- *knots*
sion, due to be untied again within a period of
twenty-four hours, **but only**
   b) so long as it is not firmly tied.
2) Where there is no practicable alternative and the knot
is being tied to last for a period of less than a week,
even a firm double knot may be tied, provided that
   a) there is a pressing need to tie the knot **or**
   b) it is being tied in order to prevent or alleviate pain
or discomfort **or**
   c) it is being tied in the performance of a mitzva.
  b. Consequently,
1) a dressing may be tied onto a wound
   a) with a loose double knot, if the intention is to
remove it within twenty-four hours, or
   b) even with a firm double knot—that will not necessarily be untied within the day—as long as the
intention is to remove it within seven days and
there is no other practicable way of securing it (for
example, by means of a bow, clips or a loose double
knot).
2) a) A woman may tie her head scarf with a loose
double knot, provided she is in the habit of untying
it every day; however,
   b) if she is used to slipping it off without untying it,
she may not tie it with a double knot, even if, this
time, she does intend to untie it the same day.

53. *a.* 1) It is permissible to tie a bow, that is to say a loop or a *tying bows*
pair of loops, over a single knot, as is customary in
tying shoelaces, but only if one is likely to untie it
within twenty-four hours.
2) Consequently, one should not tie such a bow when
wrapping a *sefer Torah* which one does not intend to
read again on that or the following day, but one should

simply secure the end of the girdle or ribbon by tucking it in.*

b. 1) Even if one intends to untie a bow within twenty-four hours, one must not make it more secure by tying a knot over it.

2) One should beware of this when tying shoelaces.

c. Making a bow without a knot underneath, or one bow over another without a knot underneath, is allowed, even if one's intention is that it should remain tied for an indefinite period of time, provided that one does not tie a knot over it.

d. Tying a knot over a bow is to be treated in the same way as tying a double knot, even if there is no knot underneath.

undoing knots and bows in general

54. a. 1) Just as it is forbidden to tie many types of knots on Shabbath or Yom Tov, or to tie a bow consisting of a loop over a knot with the intention that they should remain tied for more than twenty-four hours, so is it forbidden to untie such knots or to sever them in some other way.

2) The stringency of this rule may be relaxed if one cuts or breaks the securing cord, lace or ribbon in the middle (thereby spoiling it), and not where it is knotted.

b. 1) Knots and bows which, as specified in paragraphs 51 to 53 above, one may tie on Shabbath and Yom Tov may also be untied.

2) Should one be unable to untie them, one may cut or otherwise sever even the knot itself (but, if one severs the knot itself, it should not be done in the presence of a person who is not versed in the laws of Shabbath observance, since, in his ignorance, he may be misled into treating lightly the whole prohibition against tying and untying knots).

---

*There is some justification for the widespread custom to tie the *sefer Torah* with a bow over a single knot, even after reading it on Shabbath afternoon, as one is performing a mitzva.

55. *a.* It follows, from the contents of the previous paragraph, that one may untie knots which

undoing temporary knots

    1) are intended to remain tied for less than twenty-four hours **and**

    2) are not firmly tied.

   b. Knots which are tied to last for longer periods, but for less than seven days, may be untied, but only

    1) if there is a pressing need to do so **or**

    2) in order to prevent or alleviate pain or discomfort **or**

    3) in the performance of a mitzva.

   c. Knots which one is permitted, but is unable, to untie may be severed. (See paragraph 54*b*2 above.)

56. *a.* A bow which has become tangled and knotted may be untied.

untying tangled laces

   b. If one is unable to untie it, it may be severed.

   c. See paragraph 54*b*2 above.

   d. In practice, this situation often arises in the case of shoelaces.

57. Despite the general prohibition against tying and untying knots, one may, in a case of great need, make use of the services of a non-Jew for this purpose, even if the knot is intended to remain tied for a long period, provided that it is not intended to be permanent.

assistance of non-Jews

58. *a.* One may tie a necktie if either

neckties

    1) one is in the habit of untying it every day when removing it **or**

    2) a) it is tied in such a way that pulling the narrow end out of the knot unties it **and**

       b) it is intended to be untied within twenty-four hours.

   b. Otherwise, one should tie it before Shabbath or Yom Tov and enlarge or tighten the loop, to remove it or put it back on.

MISCELLANEOUS RULES RELATING TO CLOTHING
ON SHABBATH AND YOM TOV

threading or
lacing —
when
permitted

59. The insertion of a ribbon, thread or lace into eyelets or loops
is permitted on Shabbath and on Yom Tov only if all three of
the following conditions are fulfilled.

   a. The ribbon, thread or lace was in that particular article of
clothing before Shabbath or Yom Tov. (See paragraph
60c below for exceptions to this condition.)

   b. The ribbon, thread or lace can be easily inserted, without
any difficulty.

   c. The ribbon, thread or lace is of the kind which is not
normally sewn in place or permanently knotted after
insertion (since, otherwise, there is a danger that one may
forget oneself and indeed sew or tie it).

inserting
shoelaces

60. *a.* As a result, a lace which has come out of a shoe may be
rethreaded through the eyelets, so long as either
   1) the eyelets are large enough to enable the lace to be
inserted without undue difficulty **or**
   2) the tip of the lace is encased in a metal or plastic
sheath which facilitates threading.

  b. If the lace has snapped, part of it may be rethreaded,
subject to the same conditions, in order to enable the
continued use of the shoe.

  c. 1) However, a fresh lace may not be inserted, even into
an old shoe, unless
    a) the lace can be easily threaded **and**
    b) the circumstances or the manner in which it is done
make it certain that the lace will not be left in the
shoe, but will be removed.

   2) Examples are
    a) the insertion of a lace so different in color from the
shoe that one would use it only in an emergency
and
    b) threading the lace through only the upper eyelets of
the shoe.

61. Elastic which has come out of underwear may not be *inserting* threaded back, because *elastic*
    a. this is none too easy a task and
    b. it is usual to sew or tie together the ends of the elastic after insertion.

62. a. The rules set out in paragraph 59 above, with regard to *belts* laces, apply also to a belt which is designed to be worn with a particular dress, as the intention is to leave it in its loops, once inserted, so that it becomes part of the dress.
    b. On the other hand, an ordinary belt may be inserted in the loops of a dress or a pair of trousers, even if they are new, since it is not usual to leave it permanently in that particular dress or pair of trousers, and its insertion cannot, therefore, be said to effect an improvement in the actual garment itself.
    c. The same principles apply in the case of suspenders (braces).

63. a. New pairs of socks or gloves, or other new articles of *separating* clothing, which are sewn or tied together should be *new socks or* separated before the commencement of Shabbath or Yom *gloves* Tov.
    b. If one has forgotten to do so, one should not untie any knots, but one may sever the connecting thread in such a way that it is spoiled, as described in paragraph 54a2 above (but not in the presence of a person unversed in the laws of Shabbath observance, who is likely to become confused as to what is and is not permitted).
    c. Articles which have been temporarily stapled together may be taken apart. (See Chapter 28, paragraph 5.)

64. The pins with which new shirts are secured before they leave *removing* the factory, to ensure that they remain properly packed and *pins from* do not become creased, may be removed. *new shirts*

[183]

final touches to new clothes **65.** It is forbidden

     a. to remove temporary tacking, whether stitches or pins, which the tailor has left in new clothes,

     b. to rub off chalk marks made by the tailor to assist him in cutting or sewing new clothes, or

     c. to remove ends of wool left in new knitted garments.

pulling out threads of a weave **66.** *a.* One may not pull out threads forming part of a weave.

     b. Thus, loose ends of thread should not be pulled out of the edge of a bandage to make it look tidier.

tightening loose threads **67.** *a.* One is not allowed to secure a loose stitch by pulling its thread tight.

     b. Similarly, it is prohibited to pull tight the thread securing a loose button.

buttons coming off **68.** *a.* One must not

     1) pull a button off an article of clothing, even if the thread by which it is attached has become very loose, nor

     2) extract the threads remaining in the cloth after a button has dropped off.

     b. While a button which has come off is not *muktzeh*, that is to say it may be moved, it is better not to move it, due to the fact that it is unfit for any other use.

wearing garments with loose buttons **69.** *a.* From Chapter 17 it will be seen that, in general terms, one is not permitted on Shabbath to move articles about in *rᵉshuth ha-rabbim* or *carmᵉlith* (usually, but not invariably, a public thoroughfare or an open area), unless an *eiruv chatzeiroth* has been made.

     b. Accordingly, there is a view that, if one is wearing a garment with a button so loose that one will not fasten it for fear that it will come off, one should not go out on Shabbath into *rᵉshuth ha-rabbim* or *carmᵉlith*.

pinning clothes **70.** *a.* One may

     1) stick a pin or needle through cloth, in order to make a

garment narrower or in order to join together two parts
of a torn garment, or

    2) use a safety-pin in place of a button which has come
off.

b. Nevertheless, if possible, one should stick the pin through
the cloth only once and not through and back again.

71. a. It is generally forbidden to insert feathers or other stuffing *stuffing*
into a pillow or cushion.   *pillows*

   b. However, it is permissible to replace stuffing in the same
pillow or cushion out of which it has fallen.

72. Clothes made of synthetic materials may be worn, even *sparks given*
though they give off sparks when being put on or taken off. *off by synthetic*
                                                                   materials

73. a. One may not apply soap to runs (ladders) in nylon *preventing*
stockings to prevent them from spreading further.   *longer runs*

   b. It is also preferable to refrain from using nail polish *in stockings*
(varnish) for this purpose.

74. a. A broken zipper which is no longer usable may not be *zippers*
repaired.

   b. A zipper may be used on Shabbath or Yom Tov, even if it
is made in such a way that one side can be completely
disconnected from the other and reconnected, as in the
case of a detachable raincoat lining.

   c. It is perfectly in order to go out wearing a coat with such a
lining attached, even where there is no *eiruv chatzeiroth*
(as defined in Chapter 17).

75. Garments or other articles which have been starched to- *opening*
gether may be opened and one side separated from the other *starched*
on Shabbath or Yom Tov.   *articles*

76. a. There is a rabbinical prohibition against transferring *scenting*
scent onto clothes or similar articles.   *clothes*

   b. Consequently, one is not permitted

    1) to spray or sprinkle perfume onto a handkerchief or
any article of clothing or

2) to put lavender among linen or underwear.

c. This is so even if the clothing or linen was previously scented and one's intention is to add to the scent.

d. Nonetheless, lavender may be put back into items of linen or underwear from which it has been removed, if it was inside them before Shabbath or Yom Tov commenced, and the items have already absorbed its scent.

e. An object which gives off scent, such as an *ethrog*, may be wrapped in a cloth which did not previously contain it, only if

1) one's sole intention in so doing is to preserve it, and not to scent the cloth, **and**

2) there is no practical alternative.

repairing eyeglasses

77. a. Whereas

1) it is forbidden to repair eyeglasses (spectacles) by replacing a lens which has fallen out,

2) the lens itself is not *muktzeh* and may be moved. (See Chapter 20, paragraphs 41 and 42.)

b. Straightening the frame of a pair of glasses which has become bent is also prohibited.

use of strips which cling to each other

78. a. Two parts of a garment or two pieces of cloth may be fastened together by means of "velcro" strips (special strips of material which have tiny "teeth" that cling tightly to each other when brought into contact).

b. It is likewise allowed to pull such strips apart.

removing labels from clothes

79. a. One may not remove

1) cleaners' or laundry labels sewn or stuck onto washing or

2) price, quality, grade or similar labels sewn or stuck onto new clothes.

b. See Chapter 18, paragraph 44 regarding the wearing of clothes with such tags or labels in *r^eshuth ha-rabbim* or *carm^elith* (as defined in Chapter 17, paragraphs 3 and 4).

opening plastic bags

80. If one has forgotten to open sealed plastic, or other, bags containing new clothes before Shabbath or Yom Tov, one may tear them open on Shabbath or Yom Tov, provided that one does so in such a way that the bags are spoiled and that one does not tear through lettering or pictures, as explained in Chapter 9, paragraphs 3 and 12.

81. *a.* If one wishes to use disposable diapers (nappies) or other baby clothes which are fastened with an adhesive strip to make sure they stay on, one must peel the protective covering off the tape before the beginning of Shabbath or Yom Tov. *diapers sealed with adhesive tape*

    b. One may then stick the tape down on Shabbath or Yom Tov when putting the diaper on the baby, and, after use, unfasten the tape and dispose of the diaper.

82. Soft contact lenses may on Shabbath and Yom Tov be put into the solution in which it is usual to keep them. *soft contact lenses*

83. A rubber mattress may be inflated, with or without the aid of a pump, but one should do this only if one has already used the mattress before Shabbath or Yom Tov. *inflatable mattresses*

Chapter 16

Games and Toys on Shabbath and Yom Tov

<table>
<tr><td>adults and
older
children</td><td>

1. *a.* Most of the rules set out in this chapter relate to the playing of games by boys under the age of thirteen or girls under the age of twelve.

b. 1) It is highly desirable that older children and adults should refrain from playing games, or with toys, on Shabbath and Yom Tov.

2) While Shabbath, the most precious of days in the Jewish calendar, was given to be enjoyed, that enjoyment should be largely spiritual, a taste of the pleasures of the world to come.

3) We are told that the reward of one who celebrates Shabbath with this approach has no bounds.

</td></tr>
<tr><td>bells, rattles,
whistles, etc.</td><td>

2. *a.* Making a noise with any device designed for that purpose is forbidden. (See further Chapter 28, paragraphs 32 to 41.)

b. The prohibition covers such items as bells, rattles, flutes and whistles.

c. All devices of this nature are *muktzeh,* and may not be moved except in certain circumstances as elaborated in Chapter 20.

d. Whistling with one's mouth, without the use of an instrument, is permitted.

e. See paragraphs 14 and 17 below for additional points regarding this topic.

</td></tr>
<tr><td>giving
rattles, etc.
to babies</td><td>

3. *a.* One may give a baby toys which make a noise when shaken or squeezed, even though such toys are *muktzeh.*

b. It is of course forbidden for an adult to make such toys emit a sound, even if he wishes to do so in order to amuse the baby.

</td></tr>
</table>

4. *a.* One need not prevent children from playing with sand, *sand*
provided the sand
1) is of a fine consistency,
2) is dry **and**
3) was prepared for this use before Shabbath or Yom Tov
(as in a sandbox).

b. It is not permitted to mix the sand with water or to pour
water over it, as this contravenes the prohibition against
kneading.

c. Sand which was not prepared before Shabbath or Yom
Tov for children to play with, such as sand on the beach
or building sand, may not be moved on Shabbath or Yom
Tov.

5. *a.* Children are permitted to play with marbles inside the *marbles*
house (even on the floor, unless it consists of bare,
uncovered earth).

b. They must not play with marbles on the ground outside,
even if the ground is paved or surfaced in some other way.

6. *a.* Subject to the restrictions referred to in paragraphs 7, 8 *ball games*
and 9 below, there is no reason to forbid ball games
played on a hard surface, such as an asphalt or concrete
court or a ping-pong (table-tennis) table, whether indoors or out, provided that, where necessary, an *eiruv
chatzeiroth* has been made properly, as described in
Chapter 17.

b. Ball games should not be played on earth or grass.

7. *a.* A ball which lodges in a tree may not be taken down on *retrieving a*
Shabbath or Yom Tov, either with one's hand or with the *ball from a*
aid of a stick, nor may the tree be shaken to make the ball *tree*
drop out.

b. These acts would fall within the prohibition against
making use of something which is growing from the
ground. (See Chapter 26, paragraphs 14 and 15.)

inflatable
8. *a.* Footballs, water-polo balls and other balls which it is *balls*

[189]

usual to tie after inflating are *muktzeh* and must not be moved on Shabbath and Yom Tov. (See Chapter 20.)

b. Inflatable balls which one does not tie and toys such as plastic animals, the air of which is kept in by the insertion of a rubber or plastic plug, or by means of an elastic band, may be blown up on Shabbath or Yom Tov (but not for the first time).

visiting sports grounds

9. There are at least three reasons for not visiting sports grounds, football stadiums and the like on Shabbath and Yom Tov, even where one gains admission without paying an entrance fee.

a. It is not in keeping with the sanctity of the day and the spirit of tranquility which should prevail.

b. In the event that those participating are Jews, visiting such places amounts to encouraging them in their transgressions and in the public violation of Shabbath.

c. In Israel or in a Jewish neighborhood, public sporting events are usually bound up with the mass desecration of Shabbath, for instance by traveling in motor vehicles or by the sale of tickets.

sticks and stones

10. a. Sticks, stones on the ground, and fruit pits (stones) which are not fit even for animal consumption (for example apricot pits) may not be moved, unless

1) they are actually used for playing with (or for some other purpose) during the week, **or**

2) before the commencement of Shabbath or Yom Tov they were designated for playing with (or for some other use).

b. There are no grounds for permitting pits to be played with on Shabbath and Yom Tov if they have been removed from fruit on the same day.

c. See also Chapter 20, paragraph 26.

"five-stones"

11. a. Playing "five-stones" (a kind of jacks) is allowed on Shabbath and Yom Tov, but,

b. if one of the "stones" is lost, it must not be replaced by a stone which did not serve any use before Shabbath or Yom Tov began.

12. Photographs may be inserted into an album, so long as
    a. the photographs are not sorted before being arranged in the album,
    b. they are not stuck into the album (nor inserted by means of corner-pieces which themselves have to be stuck into the album) **and**
    c. the album is not of the type to which photographs adhere of their own accord when inserted.

    photograph albums

13. It is forbidden
    a. to shape models out of plasticine, clay, wax or the like **and**
    b. to pour plaster into any kind of mold.

    molding

14. a. One need not prevent children from playing with wind-up toys, such as model cars or robots.
    b. However, if they are made in such a way that they always produce sparks or emit a distinctive noise, there are no grounds for permitting children to play with them.

    wind-up toys

15. a. One may not
       1) climb a tree or
       2) ascend a ladder leaning against a tree, even if the ladder has been there since before the start of Shabbath or Yom Tov.
    b. It is permitted to play on a metal, plastic or wooden climbing-frame.
    c. See also Chapter 26, paragraph 14 regarding the use of a tree.

    climbing

16. a. One is allowed to rock on a swing or in a hammock, as long as it is not fixed to a tree, even on one side.
    b. 1) One is also allowed to use a swing or hammock hung from a pole or bar between two trees, provided that
          a) the swing or hammock was in place before Shabbath or Yom Tov **and**

    swings and hammocks

[191]

b) the trees are firm enough not to sway with the
rocking motion.

2) The reason is that in this case no direct use is being
made of the trees, since the swing or hammock is not
attached to them, but rather to the pole or bar, which,
in turn, is attached to the trees.

3) It is forbidden to attach the swing or hammock to the
pole or bar on Shabbath or Yom Tov.

tricycles,
scooters,
skates and
bicycles

17. *a.* One may allow a child to ride a tricycle or scooter with
solid tires or to roller-skate in the house or, where there is
an *eiruv chatzeiroth* (conforming with the rules set out in
Chapter 17), outside, but the following points should be
noted.

1) It is best to remove the bell of the tricycle before
Shabbath or Yom Tov, so that the child should not
come to use it on Shabbath or Yom Tov (in contravention of the prohibition mentioned in paragraph 2
above).

2) A tire which comes off a wheel must not be replaced on
Shabbath or Yom Tov, and the tricycle or scooter itself
becomes *muktzeh* and must not be moved, as explained in Chapter 20, paragraph 42.

3) In a place where the custom is to prohibit the use of a
tricycle, scooter or roller-skates on Shabbath or Yom
Tov one should not permit it.

b. It is forbidden to ride a bicycle, even if it is designed for
use by children.

building
blocks

18. *a.* One need not stop children from playing with ordinary
toy building blocks or interconnecting blocks* of any
kind, unless they have to be screwed together or very

___

*It is prohibited, on Shabbath and Yom Tov, to open sealed bags, boxes
or cartons of toys, if they are made to keep the toys in afterwards, except
in the permitted manner or circumstances specified in Chapter 9,
paragraphs 2, 3, 9, 10, 11, 13, 14 and 16.

tightly fixed together, in which case they may not be used.

b. See also paragraph 34b and c below.

19. One should not make boats, hats or other objects by folding paper. *paper folding*

20. It is not permitted to assemble or dismantle a toy from a *model* model-making kit, such as a model airplane or ship made *building* from plastic, metal or wooden parts, as the parts join together with a great deal of precision and they are normally built with the intention of leaving them assembled for a considerable time. (See also paragraph 18 above.)

21. a. Children's beads may be threaded onto a cord, since the *beads* resulting necklace is not made to last, but care should be taken
    1) not to tie the ends of the cord together **and**
    2) not to tie a knot at either end of the cord.
    b. Pearls and the like may not be threaded onto a cord to make a necklace.

22. One may not impress writing or a pattern onto a special pad *erasable-* on which one can write without a pen and from which the *writing pads* writing can be erased by separating the sheets of which it is composed.

23. One is allowed to play games in which letters, or parts of *word-* letters or of a picture, are placed side-by-side so as to make *building and* up a whole word or picture, provided that *picture-*
    a. this does not involve setting the word or picture in a frame *building* that holds it together **and** *games*
    b. the various sections are not interlocked and fixed to- gether, as they are in most jigsaw puzzles.

24. Playing with a game consisting of (usually) fifteen movable, *arranging* lettered or numbered squares set in a framed board the size *numbered* of sixteen such squares, and rearranging the squares by *squares set in* *a frame*

[193]

moving them about within the board, is permissible on Shabbath and Yom Tov.

rubber stamps 25. It is prohibited

    a. to make an impression with a rubber stamp,

    b. to arrange letters with the object of forming them into a rubber stamp or

    c. to separate letters making up a rubber stamp.

photography 26. One must not

    a. take a photograph with a camera,

    b. develop film or

    c. make prints from film.

non-permanent lettering or patterns 27. *a.* It is forbidden

    1) to write letters or make patterns on a misted or frosted windowpane, or to wipe them off,

    2) to cut letters or designs into the peel of an orange or other fruit or

    3) to write with, or in, sand or dust, or crumbs lying on the table.

    b. One may outline the shape of letters in the air with one's finger.*

cutting and sticking 28. All games involving cutting or sticking, whether with glue or with adhesive tape, are prohibited.

transfers 29. The use of decals or transfers for making pictures is not allowed on Shabbath or Yom Tov.

blowing bubbles 30. Although adults should not blow soap bubbles, one need not stop children from doing so.

---

*The general prohibition against writing during the intermediate days of Yom Tov does not apply to nonpermanent writing, such as writing with chalk on a blackboard or with, or in, sand or dust.

31. Games in which points are awarded to the participants, such as quizzes and "pick-up-sticks," and in which it is usual to note down the score, should not be played on Shabbath or Yom Tov, so that one should not come to write. (Games played for money are prohibited even on a weekday.)

games in which points are noted down

32. a. It is best to refrain from playing games in which imitation money is used, such as "Monopoly."
    b. The same applies to all games in which one stands to make either a gain or a loss (even if not expressed in money), such as *dreidel* (Chanuka spinning-top) and "odds or evens."

imitation money

33. Dice games, for example "chutes and ladders," are permitted, so long, of course, as they do not involve any forbidden activity.

dice games

34. a. Games like chess, dominoes and "fish" (a card game in which four cards are dealt to each player and have to be made into sets) are allowed.
    b. However, care should be taken, when play has ended, not to separate the pieces or cards by color or type, as this contravenes the prohibition against selection.
    c. Pieces or cards may be separated and sorted with a view to playing with them right away.

chess, dominoes and "fish"

35. a. Sorting postage stamps or sticking them onto an envelope or into an album is forbidden.
    b. 1) Mint stamps which are intended to be used and
       2) stamps, whether used or unused, which are intended for dealing
       are *muktzeh* and should not be moved. (See Chapter 20, paragraphs 20, 21 and 23 and compare paragraph 38 there.)

postage stamps

36. Plaiting or weaving together threads, strands or strips of plastic or other material is prohibited on Shabbath and Yom Tov.

plaiting

betting   **37.** Betting is forbidden, whether it be Shabbath or Yom Tov or
              an ordinary weekday.

swimming   **38.** One is not allowed
and boating   *a.* to swim, whether in the sea or in a pool,
              b. to play with the sand on the seashore (as stated above in
                   paragraph 4) or
              c. to board a floating boat or ship, unless it is secured and
                   remains secured to the bank or the quay.

games   **39.** *a.* Running and jumping games, such as tag, hide-and-seek
involving   and skipping with a rope are permitted, but
running or   *b.* the performance of physical exercises is prohibited (as
jumping   detailed in Chapter 14, paragraph 38).
              c. If a jump rope (skipping rope) is used, there must, where
                   necessary, be a properly made *eiruv*. (See Chapter 17.)

hopscotch   **40.** *a.* Hopscotch and similar games may be played, but any
                   stone used must be one which was kept for regular use
                   since before the commencement of Shabbath or Yom Tov.
              b. It is forbidden to draw or scratch marks on the ground.
              c. If a stone (or any other item) is used, there must, where
                   necessary, be a properly made *eiruv*. (See Chapter 17.)

strolling   **41.** *a.* When strolling on Shabbath, one should beware not to
                   carry anything outside in a place where there is no *eiruv
                   chatzeiroth* or beyond the limits within which the *eiruv* is
                   effective. (See Chapter 17.)
              b. It is proper, before going out on Shabbath in a place
                   where there is no *eiruv*, or beyond the bounds of the *eiruv*,
                   to check one's pockets, to make sure that one is not
                   carrying anything.
              c. One should take care, on Shabbath and Yom Tov, not to
                   go more than two thousand *amoth* beyond the boundary
                   of the *eiruv* or, if there is no *eiruv*, more than two
                   thousand *amoth* beyond the last house of the town.

42. Dancing may be permitted only when it is a mitzva, as on *dancing*
    Simchath Torah.

43. One should not clap one's hands except* *clapping*
    a. in celebration of a mitzva **or** *hands*
    b. in a manner which one does not usually adopt on a
    weekday, for instance by clapping one hand on the back
    of the other.

44. a. It is not permitted to make snowballs or a snowman, but *snow*
    b. the snow itself is not *muktzeh*, even if it fell on Shabbath
    or Yom Tov.

45. a. One may look through binoculars on Shabbath or Yom *binoculars*
    Tov.
    b. One may also adjust the focus, as this is done in the
    normal course of use.

46. Concerning the tending of plants, see Chapter 26, para- *plants*
    graphs 1 to 9.

47. It is prohibited to hold raffles or lotteries on Shabbath or *raffles*
    Yom Tov, as is sometimes done at parties, even if one merely
    wishes to do so in order to avoid an argument about who is
    entitled to what.

---

*For a further exception, see Chapter 28, paragraph 36.

Chapter 17

Principles of the Laws Relating to the Transfer of Objects from One Place to Another

THE FOUR CATEGORIES OF PLACE

the four categories

1. *a.* There are various restrictions on Shabbath and, to a limited extent, on Yom Tov on
   1) transferring objects from one place to another and
   2) moving objects about within certain areas.

   b. For the purposes of these restrictions, four categories of "place" have been defined:
   1) r*e*shuth ha-yachid (more often than not, an enclosed property),
   2) r*e*shuth ha-rabbim (in general terms, a public thoroughfare),
   3) carm*e*lith (usually an open area), and
   4) m*e*kom p*e*tur (a space which does not fall within the definitions of any of the other three categories; see paragraph 5 below).

*r*e*shuth ha-yachid*

2. *a.* A r*e*shuth ha-yachid must meet the following requirements:
   1) it must
      a) be surrounded by a fence, wall or other partition, **or**
      b) be on top of something having sides (as in *b*5 below)*;

---

*It is not practicable here to set out all the rules governing the sufficiency or otherwise of the partitions or sides of a r*e*shuth ha-yachid, and it is important to consult with a qualified rabbinical authority whenever there is any doubt, for instance regarding the durability or completeness of a partition or regarding gaps in it.

    2) the partition or sides must be at least ten *t^efachim**
    high;

    3) its dimensions must be such that it can contain a
    square that is four *t^efachim* by four *t^efachim*.

  b. Examples of *r^eshuth ha-yachid* are

    1) a house or an apartment,

    2) a yard having a wall around it,

    3) a town or settlement encompassed by a wall or fence
    (but, in this case, its gates must be closed at night),

    4) even a movable object, having the requisite size, such
    as a large cupboard, a wagon or a car, standing in
    r^eshuth ha-rabbim or *carm^elith*,

    5) the top of a mound or pillar at least ten *t^efachim* high
    and having an upper surface large enough to hold a
    square that is four *t^efachim* by four *t^efachim*,

    6) a pit at least ten *t^efachim* deep and capable of contain-
    ing a four *t^efachim* by four *t^efachim* square,

    7) the roof of a house and

    8) a balcony surrounded by a parapet or railing at least
    ten *t^efachim* high.

  c. The airspace of a *r^eshuth ha-yachid*, to an unlimited
  height, is also *r^eshuth ha-yachid*.

  d. It is normally permissible to move objects about within a
  r^eshuth ha-yachid; however, there are certain places
  covered by the definition of a *r^eshuth ha-yachid* which are
  nevertheless subject to Rabbinical prohibitions in this
  regard. (See paragraph 11 below.)

3. *a.* A place is considered a *r^eshuth ha-rabbim* if it meets the   *r^eshuth*
  following criteria: *ha-rabbim*

    1) it is not covered by a roof;

    2) it is not surrounded by fences, walls or other partitions
    on three or more sides;

---

*A *tefach* is equivalent to 9.6 centimeters (3.8 inches) or 8 centimeters
(3.15 inches), depending upon which of two opinions one adopts. In
practice, one usually follows the view which, in the circumstances of the
case under consideration, is the more restrictive.

3) if it is in a town or city, it passes through from one side to the other;
4) it is at least sixteen *amoth** wide;
5) a) according to some authorities, a place is not classed as *r^eshuth ha-rabbim* unless at least six hundred thousand people walk through it every day;
   b) according to others, large numbers of people (even less than six hundred thousand) walking through a place can make it a *r^eshuth ha-rabbim*;
   c) yet others apply the criterion of six hundred thousand passers-by for a thoroughfare in a town or city, but not in the case of a busy intercity highway.

b. Apart from busy intercity highways, the commonest examples of *r^eshuth ha-rabbim* are the bustling thoroughfares of large cities.

c. The rules which apply to *r^eshuth ha-rabbim* apply also
   1) to anything in *r^eshuth ha-rabbim* that is less than three *t^efachim* in height and
   2) to any depression in *r^eshuth ha-rabbim* that is less than three *t^efachim* in depth.

d. *R^eshuth ha-rabbim* reaches only to a height of ten *t^efachim*, and the space above that is usually treated by Halacha as *m^ekom p^etur*.

carm^elith

4. a. *Carm^elith* is a place which
   1) is neither *r^eshuth ha-yachid* nor *r^eshuth ha-rabbim* **and**
   2) has an area large enough to hold a four *t^efachim* by four *t^efachim* square.

b. Examples of *carm^elith* are
   1) a field,
   2) the sea,

---

*An *amah* is equivalent to 57.6 centimeters (22.7 inches) or 48 centimeters (18.9 inches), depending upon which of two opinions one adopts. In practice, one usually follows the view which, in the circumstances of the case under consideration, is the more restrictive.

3) a desert,

4) a thoroughfare which fails to meet the requirements for r^eshuth ha-rabbim because, for instance,

   a) it is covered,

   b) it is less than sixteen amoth wide **or**

   c) an insufficient number of people pass through it, and

5) an area in r^eshuth ha-rabbim which has the dimensions specified above for carm^elith **and**

   a) is at least three, but not as many as ten, t^efachim high, or

   b) is surrounded by a fence, wall or other partition that is at least three, but not as many as ten, t^efachim high.

c. Carm^elith reaches only to a height of ten t^efachim; the vacant space above that is usually treated by Halacha as m^ekom p^etur.

5. a. M^ekom p^etur is a space   *m^ekom p^etur*

1) in r^eshuth ha-rabbim,

2) having an area into which there cannot be fitted a four t^efachim by four t^efachim square **and**

3) raised at least three t^efachim above the ground level of r^eshuth ha-rabbim.

b. As already mentioned, the vacant space above the ten t^efachim occupied by r^eshuth ha-rabbim and carm^elith is also usually treated by Halacha as m^ekom p^etur.

PROHIBITIONS UPON THE TRANSFER OF OBJECTS
FROM ONE PLACE TO ANOTHER ON SHABBATH

6. a. The Torah prohibits the transfer of objects, on Shabbath, from r^eshuth ha-rabbim to r^eshuth ha-yachid or vice versa.   *transfer between r^eshuth ha-rabbim and r^eshuth ha-yachid*

b. The transfer is prohibited, regardless of whether the object

1) is carried in the hand or in one's pocket,

2) is dragged along the ground,

[201]

3) is passed over into the hand of another person or

4) is thrown or rolled from one *r^eshuth* to the other.

c. The transfer is prohibited even if the person performing it remains in the same spot.

transfer
within
r^eshuth
ha-rabbim

7. The Torah also forbids one to transfer objects a distance of four *amoth* or more within *r^eshuth ha-rabbim*, by any method whatsoever.

forbidden
transfers
involving
carm^elith

8. In addition, Rabbinical prohibitions were imposed upon the transfer of an object

a. from *r^eshuth ha-rabbim* to *carm^elith* or vice versa,

b. from *r^eshuth ha-yachid* to *carm^elith* or vice versa, or

c. a distance of four *amoth* or more within *carm^elith*.

transfers
involving
m^ekom p^etur

9. a. 1) One may transfer an object

    a) from *m^ekom p^etur* to *r^eshuth ha-rabbim*, *r^eshuth ha-yachid* or *carm^elith* or

    b) from *r^eshuth ha-rabbim*, *r^eshuth ha-yachid* or *carm^elith* to *m^ekom p^etur*.

2) However, one is not permitted to transfer an object from *r^eshuth ha-yachid* to *r^eshuth ha-rabbim*, or vice versa, through *m^ekom p^etur*, even if

    a) one is standing in the *m^ekom p^etur* or

    b) one puts the object down in the *m^ekom p^etur* before transferring it onward into the second *r^eshuth*.

transfers
from one
carm^elith to
another

b. 1) One may transfer an object, within a distance of four *amoth*, from one *carm^elith* to another.

2) An example would be the transfer of an object from the side of a narrow country road into an adjacent, open field.

elements
within scope
of
prohibition

10. a. To be forbidden by the Torah (as opposed to being the subject of a Rabbinical prohibition), a transfer must contain three elements:

1) the **displacement** of the object from its former position, with the intention of transferring it,

2) the actual **transfer** of the object, either from one

r^eshuth to the other or for a distance of four amoth within r^eshuth ha-rabbim, as the case may be, **and**

3) the subsequent **depositing** of the object.

b. If a person has an object in his hand or in his pocket,

1) commencing to walk is regarded as the displacement of the object, while

2) stopping is regarded as depositing it.

c. The Rabbis have forbidden transfers even in circumstances where one does not perform all three of the above activities, so that it is not permitted

1) a) for one person to pick up an article and transfer it into the other r^eshuth, even without depositing it there, and

b) for a second person then to take it from his hand in the other r^eshuth and put it down or stand with it there, or

2) a) for one person to pick up an article (intending it to be transferred into the other r^eshuth) and, rather than transfer it himself, put it into a second person's hand and

b) for that second person then to transfer the article into the other r^eshuth and put it down or stand with it there.

LAWS OF EIRUV CHATZEIROTH AND SHITUFEI MEVO'OTH
(TRANSFERS INVOLVING PROPERTY OWNED IN COMMON)

11. a. It is permissible to transfer an object between two adjacent r^eshuyoth ha-yachid, if both have the same owners or, where the premises are rented, the same tenants.*

b. 1) Subject to the contents of paragraph 12 below, it is forbidden to transfer an object from one r^eshuth ha-yachid to another which is not in the identical owner-

prohibitions against transfers from one r^eshuth ha-yachid to another

---

*In the case of rented houses or apartments, the determining factor, for the purpose of the rules contained in this and the following paragraphs, is the identity of the tenant-occupiers, and not of the owners, unless the owners retain some right of use.

ship or tenancy, unless an *eiruv chatzeiroth* is made in accordance with the procedure outlined in paragraphs 13 to 17 below.

2) The prohibition includes

a) taking an object out of an apartment and putting it on the landing of the staircase which is owned in common, or which belongs to the landlord of the whole building,

b) bringing an object into an apartment from such a staircase, or from a similarly owned entrance hall, or

c) a transfer from one room to another in the same apartment, where they are separately and exclusively rented by different individuals, even if the rooms are adjacent to each other and are owned by the same landlord.

c. 1) It is likewise forbidden, where there is no *eiruv chatzeiroth*, to transfer an object from one apartment to another through a staircase or courtyard owned or used in common by the occupiers of all the apartments.

2) This is so even if

a) the courtyard is surrounded by walls on all four sides and

b) both apartments are in the same ownership or tenancy.

transfers within commonly owned property

12. a. The general rule is that one may transfer an article without restriction of distance within a *r^eshuth ha-yachid*.

b. Nonetheless, where the *r^eshuth ha-yachid* is owned and used in common by the different occupants of a number of houses or apartments, this is permitted only if the article was in that commonly-owned *r^eshuth ha-yachid* at the commencement of Shabbath.

c. Examples of such a *r^eshuth ha-yachid* are

1) the common staircase of an apartment building and

2) a commonly owned courtyard which is walled in on all sides.

d. 1) Two adjacent *reshuyoth ha-yachid* of this kind are, for the purpose of the rule stated in this paragraph, regarded as one, even if there is a wall between them.

2) An example of this situation occurs in the case of two adjacent, walled courtyards, each serving a separate apartment building.

13. a. In order to avoid the restrictions on transfer mentioned in paragraphs 11 and 12 above, one should make an *eiruv chatzeiroth*.

making an eiruv chatzeiroth

b. An *eiruv chatzeiroth* may be made in either of two ways.

1) a) Before Shabbath, one collects from each of the owners or tenants a whole loaf of bread, roll or matza.

b) All of the food is put inside one receptacle and kept in one of the houses, apartments or rooms, as the case may be (but not in any commonly owned property in which no one lives, such as an entrance hall).

c) The blessing to be said on making the *eiruv*,

בָּרוּךְ אַתָּה ה', אֱלֹקֵינוּ מֶלֶךְ הָעוֹלָם, אֲשֶׁר קִדְּשָׁנוּ בְּמִצְוֹתָיו וְצִוָּנוּ עַל מִצְוַת עֵרוּב

is recited at the stage where one collects the food.

d) When making the *eiruv*, one says, "By virtue of this *eiruv*, it shall be permitted to transfer articles between the houses, apartments or rooms [as the case may be] of the participants."

2) a) Alternatively, one of the owners or tenants provides the bread, rolls or matzoth for all the others.

b) Before Shabbath, he takes the quantity mentioned in paragraph 15 below and says the blessing set out above.

c) He then requests a second person (other than his wife or his children who regularly eat at his table) to take possession of the food, on behalf of all of the owners or tenants, by raising it at least one *tefach*.

d) Next, he says, "This food shall belong to all of the present and future owners or tenants of the houses, apartments or rooms [as the case may be], for the purpose of the *eiruv* I am now making, permitting the transfer of articles between them."

e) The *eiruv chatzeiroth* is effective and the other owners and tenants may take advantage of it, even if they did not know it was being made, in conformity with the principle that a benefit may be conferred upon a person without his knowledge.

c. The theory upon which the Rabbinical institution of *eiruv chatzeiroth* is based is that all of the owners and tenants are considered to have a right of access to the house, apartment or room in which the food belonging to them all is kept, and all of the *r^eshuyoth ha-yachid*, whether owned or tenanted by individuals or in common, are therefore treated as being within the same common ownership, forming one, large *r^eshuth ha-yachid*.

when eiruv chatzeiroth may be used

14. *a.* 1) An *eiruv chatzeiroth* can be effective to permit the transfer of objects, for example, from a house to a common courtyard in front of it.

2) This is because the right to use the courtyard belongs in common to the owners and occupiers of all the properties within the *eiruv*, to the exclusion of other persons.

b. 1) An *eiruv chatzeiroth* cannot be effective to permit the transfer of objects from a house or from a common courtyard to the street outside.

2) This is because the right to use the street is shared with other persons, who do not own or occupy properties included within the *eiruv*.

3) It makes no difference that the street in question fits, or has been converted to fit, the definition of a *r^eshuth ha-yachid*.

c. The transfer of objects to the street can only be rendered permissible by means of *shitufei m^evo'oth*, as explained in paragraph 19 below.

[206]

15. The amount of food to be provided for the *eiruv chatzeiroth* depends on the number of separately owned or tenanted properties which it covers.

amount of food required for eiruv chatzeiroth

 a. If there are less than eighteen, the amount required is the equivalent in volume of about four-ninths of an egg for each property.

 b. If there are eighteen or more, irrespective of how many more there may be, the total amount of food required is the equivalent in volume of about eight eggs.

16. a. The required quantity of bread, rolls or matzoth must continue to exist until after the commencement of Shabbath.

how long food for eiruv chatzeiroth must last

 b. 1) The same *eiruv* can be made to cover more than one Shabbath, even all the Shabbathoth in the year.

 2) In this case, one must use food which lasts, such as matzoth, since it must continue to exist in an edible state for the whole of the period.

17. Since the *eiruv chatzeiroth* operates on the basis that all of the owners and tenants have rights of ownership in the food provided, none of them ought to raise any objection if one of the others wishes to exercise his rights by eating the food before Shabbath, or at its commencement, which is when the *eiruv* comes into effect.

extent of partnership in food of eiruv chatzeiroth

18. a. One should make an *eiruv chatzeiroth* wherever appropriate, so as to limit the possibility of transgressing the prohibition against the transfer of objects.

importance of eiruv chatzeiroth

 b. It is important to consult a qualified rabbinical authority on the detailed application of the rules relating to *eiruv chatzeiroth*.

19. a. Wherever possible, one should make similar arrangements, by way of *shitufei mevo'oth*, for all of the occupants of a street, a district, or even a whole town.

how and where to make shitufei mevo'oth

 b. This can only be done if the area included does not, for one reason or another, fall within the definition of a r^eshuth ha-rabbim, but is only a carm^elith. (See paragraphs 3 and 4 above.)

c. The rules relating to the making of *shitufei m^evo'oth* are detailed and complicated, and a qualified rabbinical authority must be consulted before the task is undertaken.

d. It involves

   1) surrounding the whole of the area in question by a fence, either real or nominal,* fulfilling specified requirements, and

   2) providing food for the owners and tenants in a manner similar to that set out in paragraphs 13 to 17 above.

duplication of shitufei m^evo'oth and eiruv chatzeiroth

20. *a.* There is no need for those participating in *shitufei m^evo'oth* to make an *eiruv chatzeiroth* as well.

b. Nevertheless, it is recommended that the person making the *shitufei m^evo'oth* should have in mind, when putting the bread, rolls or matzoth in place, that they should serve, not only for *shitufei m^evo'oth*, but also for *eiruv chatzeiroth*.

importance of shitufei m^evo'oth

21. *a.* It is important for every community to make *shitufei m^evo'oth*, wherever the possibility exists, in order to save the public from transgressing the prohibitions against the transfer of objects on Shabbath, but,

b. as previously mentioned, it is essential that a properly qualified rabbinical authority be consulted, both with regard to the way in which a real or nominal* partition should be erected around the area and concerning all the other details indispensable for the validity of *shitufei m^evo'oth*.

large cities

22. *a.* A mere nominal* partition cannot be used to make *shitufei m^evo'oth*

---

*See paragraph 25 below.

1) in an area which is *reshuth ha-rabbim*, as defined in paragraph 3 above, or even

2) in the case of a road which is thirteen and one-third *amoth* or more wide and leads into *reshuth ha-rabbim* in both directions.

b. Consequently, there is no practicable way of making *shitufei mevo'oth* to permit the transfer of objects in the main streets of very large cities.

c. 1) However, even in large cities, one can make *shitufei mevo'oth* or an *eiruv chatzeiroth* in order to permit the transfer of objects between a number of apartments or houses or in a particular vicinity, as mentioned in paragraph 19 above, but

2) this is possible only if the area covered is not traversed either

a) by *reshuth ha-rabbim* or

b) by a road thirteen and one-third *amoth* or more in width, leading into *reshuth ha-rabbim* at both ends.

23. a. All of the rules regarding *shitufei mevo'oth* and *eiruv chatzeiroth* are equally applicable on Shabbath and Yom Kippur. *Yom Kippur and Yom Tov*

b. Regarding the transfer of objects from one place to another on Yom Tov see Chapter 19.

24. Neither an *eiruv chatzeiroth* nor *shitufei mevo'oth* may be made on Shabbath or Yom Tov. *not to be made on Shabbath*

25. a. The nominal partition delineating the area covered by *shitufei mevo'oth* may (subject to scrupulous compliance with detailed regulations too numerous to set out here) consist of a wire running right around this area along the tops of a series of poles. *breaks in a nominal partition*

b. Should the wire break, the partition becomes ineffective and the transfer of objects is once more forbidden.

c. 1) In such an event, one is allowed to ask a non-Jew to repair the wire, in order to prevent the widespread breach, by the general public, of the prohibition against the transfer of objects.

2) Where the non-Jew can repair the wire in such a way that only Rabbinical prohibitions are transgressed, for example if he is able to tie the ends of the wire together solely by means of a bow over a single knot, that is the preferred course.

3) If this is not possible, then he may tie the ends together with a double knot or twine them together and, where the need arises, the non-Jew may even dig holes in the ground in which to stand the posts supporting the wire.

4) This aspect of the matter is also dealt with in Chapter 30, paragraph 22.

5) It is irrelevant whether the wire was torn on Shabbath itself or whether it was torn before Shabbath but not repaired prior to its commencement.

d. 1) In the absence of a non-Jew, a Jew may repair the wire, but only by tying the ends in a bow (over a single knot).

2) He is not permitted to tie a double knot, nor to twine the ends of the wire together, nor, for the purpose of repairing the wire, to perform any act prohibited by the Torah (as opposed to an act which is the subject of a Rabbinical prohibition).

e. Whenever it proves impossible to repair the wire on Shabbath,

1) it is better not to make any public announcement to the effect that the transfer of objects is forbidden, but

2) one should inform individuals who one is sure will pay attention and will refrain from a breach of the prohibition.

Chapter 18

Specific Laws Relating to the Transfer of Objects from One Place to Another on Shabbath, Where There Is No Eiruv*

Specific laws relating to the transfer of objects from one place to another on Yom Tov are dealt with in Chapter 19.

ARTICLES WHICH ARE WORN

1. *a.* 1) As mentioned in Chapter 17, paragraphs 6 and 7, the *significance* Torah prohibits the transfer of objects on Shabbath *of manner of*
      a) from r*e*shuth ha-rabbim to r*e*shuth ha-yachid, *transfer*
      b) from r*e*shuth ha-yachid to r*e*shuth ha-rabbim or
      c) within r*e*shuth ha-rabbim over a distance of four *amoth* or more.
   2) This Torah prohibition (as distinct from the wider Rabbinical prohibition) is contravened only if one transfers an object in the same way as one would during the rest of the week.
   b. It will be seen in the succeeding paragraphs that there is no prohibition against the transfer of an article of clothing or an ornament (or, to be more precise, a *tachshit*, as defined in paragraph 11 below) in the manner in which it is usually worn.
   c. There is a Rabbinical prohibition against the transfer of articles in a manner not commonly employed during the rest of the week.

2. *a.* The Torah prohibition includes *common*
   1) going out into r*e*shuth ha-rabbim with something in *methods of* one's pocket, *transfer*

---

*See Chapter 17, paragraphs 11 to 25 for a discussion of the subject of *eiruv*.

2) going out with a candy (sweet), chewing gum or any other food in one's mouth,

3) a tailor's going out with a needle stuck in his lapel,

4) going out with a bundle balanced on one's head, in countries where this is the custom, or on one's shoulder,

5) going out with a thread or rubber band around one's wrist, since many people habitually slip them around the wrist for convenience and then walk about with them still on, and

6) a woman's going into *r^eshuth ha-rabbim* with a handkerchief stuck under her gold wristwatch or bracelet, where this is the practice.

b. A person who goes into *r^eshuth ha-rabbim*

   1) with something other than food in his mouth or

   2) carrying on his head something which it is not usual to carry in this way

   transgresses a Rabbinical, but not a Torah, prohibition.

c. Whether or not one may wear false teeth in *r^eshuth ha-rabbim* is dealt with in paragraph 15 below.

d. One may go out into *r^eshuth ha-rabbim* wearing a dental plate or brace. (See Chapter 34, paragraph 29.)

definition of article of clothing

3. a. As already mentioned, it is permitted to transfer an article of clothing from one place to another in the course of wearing it in the usual way.

   b. For this purpose, an article of clothing comprises anything which a person wears

      1) that either

         a) protects his body or

         b) serves the needs of his body in some other way

         and

      2) that it is the custom of the time to wear in that way, in that particular place.

coats, gloves, and muffs

4. It is, consequently, permitted to go out into *r^eshuth ha-rabbim*

a. with a coat worn over one's shoulders like a cape (that is to say without one's arms in the sleeves),

b. wearing gloves or a muff on one's hands (although it is best to attach them to one's coat by means of a cord, so that one will not be carrying them in the usual way if one unthinkingly removes them in r*e*shuth ha-rabbim), or

c. wearing earmuffs in very cold weather.

5. a. One may wear two similar articles of clothing, one over the other, in a place where one does indeed sometimes go out dressed in such a manner. *wearing one garment over another*

 b. This is so, even though

 1) one's sole purpose is, in this way, to take one of the garments through r*e*shuth ha-rabbim to another person or

 2) it is the underneath article which is serving the function of a garment, whereas the upper is being worn over it only because it looks more dignified.

 c. Accordingly,

 1) a doctor may go out wearing a white coat over his clothes and

 2) a person may go out wearing a *gartel* (special belt worn by some during prayer), even if his trousers are already supported by an ordinary belt or suspenders (braces).

 d. See also paragraph 9 below.

6. a. One is allowed to bring a *tallith* to the synagogue by wearing it, even under one's coat. *tallith*

 b. One may fold the sides of one's *tallith* up onto one's shoulders so that it should not hang down too far.

 c. One should not go out with one's *tallith* folded and wound around one's neck.

7. a. A woman may go out into r*e*shuth ha-rabbim wearing a scarf or wig over her hair. *head scarves and wigs*

 b. She is also allowed to keep it on by means of a pin.

 hairpins and ribbons

8. a. Furthermore a woman is allowed to go out into r*e*shuth

ha-rabbim with her hair kept in place by hairpins or a ribbon.

b. She should not, however, use more hairpins than are necessary to hold her hair.

rule
regarding
protection of
clothes

9. a. One may go out into *r^eshuth ha-rabbim* wearing an article of clothing in the normal manner, even if it only serves the purpose of protecting the rest of one's clothes from dust or rain.

b. 1) Something which is not worn as an article of clothing in the normal manner (for examples, see paragraph 10*b* below) should not be put on, unless it will serve the purpose of keeping one's body clean or dry.

2) In that event, it does not matter that it will also incidentally protect one's clothing.

examples of
protection of
clothes

10. a. With the important reservation mentioned at the end of this paragraph, it is therefore permissible

1) to wear a raincoat over a winter coat, even if one does so only in order that the winter coat should not become wet,

2) to wear galoshes,

3) to wear a specially made, fitted, plastic rain-cover over one's hat and

4) for a woman to protect her head from the rain by covering it with a rain-hood or head scarf.

(See paragraph 31 below regarding hoods attached to coats.)

b. On the other hand, it is forbidden to go out

1) with a handkerchief laid over one's collar to prevent it from being soiled by perspiration or

2) with a handkerchief (or a plastic bag) on one's hat to protect it from the rain,

since in neither case is the handkerchief (or the plastic bag) being worn as an article of clothing in the normal manner.

c. An article should not be worn in *r^eshuth ha-rabbim* (as distinct from *carm^elith*) for protection against the rain, if there is a reasonable possibility that one may come to take it off when the rain stops.

11. *a.* The following paragraphs deal with the conditions under which one may go out into *reshuth ha-rabbim* with a *tachshit*. *scope of definition of tachshit*

    b. The term *tachshit* (literally "an ornament") is applied to anything worn
      1) which is not an article of clothing, but
      2) which is required for the purposes of the human body,
      3) whether or not it is worn in a position in which it is visible.

12. *a.* There are two types of *tachshitim,*
      1) items of a purely ornamental or decorative nature, such as jewelry, and *two types of tachshit*
      2) other items (not being articles of clothing) which are required for the purposes of the human body.

    b. 1) It is the common practice to go out into *reshuth ha-rabbim* wearing *tachshitim* of the first kind (decorative).
      2) They must not, however, be carried in the hand.
      3) While the practice of wearing *tachshitim* of this kind is widespread and justifiable on a few grounds, the halachic authorities nonetheless indicate that, where possible, it is preferable not to follow it.

    c. 1) In most cases, it is perfectly in order to go out into *reshuth ha-rabbim* with *tachshitim* of the second kind, so long as one is wearing them in the way they are usually worn on an ordinary day of the week.
      2) A few exceptions to this rule will be apparent from the succeeding paragraphs.

13. *a.* A person who is unable to walk at all without the aid of a cane may go out into *reshuth ha-rabbim* carrying his cane in his hand. *walking-sticks*

    b. The following are not permitted to go out into *reshuth ha-rabbim,* cane in hand, where there is no *eiruv:*

1) a person who can walk without a cane, but whose step is firmer when he carries a cane in his hand;

2) a blind person (although, if he cannot walk about at all without a cane, he should consult a qualified rabbinical authority);

3) a person who is afraid to walk unaided on a wet or frozen surface, lest he slip and fall.

c. 1) All of these persons may go out carrying a cane where there is an *eiruv*.

2) The same applies to a person who carries a cane or a baton for ornamental purposes or as a mark of authority.

3) One may not carry a cane on Shabbath, even where there is an *eiruv*, if one has no use for it whatsoever.

d. See also paragraph 23 below concerning ornamental walking-sticks and batons.

therapeutic and hearing aids

14. The wearing of therapeutic necklaces and bracelets (against rheumatic pains) and of hearing aids is discussed in Chapter 34, paragraphs 15 and 28.

artificial limbs and false teeth

15. It is permitted for a person who has an artificial limb or false teeth to go out wearing them on Shabbath.

eyeglasses

16. a. A person who wears glasses (spectacles) all the time because he cannot see as clearly without them may go out into *r^eshuth ha-rabbim* wearing them.

b. There are also valid grounds for permitting a person who wears glasses purely for ornamental purposes, and not because he has any difficulty in seeing, to go out into *r^eshuth ha-rabbim* wearing them, but see paragraph 12*b* above.

c. It is forbidden to go out wearing reading glasses, since one will certainly come to remove them in the street and carry them for a distance of four *amoth* or more in *r^eshuth ha-rabbim*.

d. This does not apply in the case of glasses containing

bifocal lenses and one may, accordingly, go out into _reshuth ha-rabbim_ wearing them.

17. _a._ 1) A person who has not yet grown used to wearing his contact lenses may not go out into _reshuth ha-rabbim_ wearing them.

   2) This is because it is reasonable to suppose that, after a while, he may feel so uncomfortable that he will come to remove them and carry them for a distance of four _amoth_ or more.

   _b._ The wearing of contact lenses by a person who is used to wearing them is permitted.

18. Whether or not one may wear sunglasses in _reshuth ha-rabbim_ depends on their type.

   _a._ 1) One should not go out into _reshuth ha-rabbim_ with ordinary sunglasses which are worn to protect one's eyes from the sun, since one may come to remove them in the shade and carry them for a distance of four _amoth_ or more.

   2) The prohibition extends also to sunglasses which one clips on to one's everyday spectacles.

   _b._ One may go out into _reshuth ha-rabbim_ wearing sunglasses which are attached to ordinary spectacles by means of a hinge, because if one walks into the shade one simply swings them upwards without removing them.

   _c._ The rules set out in paragraph 16 above apply to ordinary optical spectacles, worn in order to improve defective vision, even if they have tinted lenses and thus serve also as sunglasses.*

   _d._ Dark glasses which are worn for medical reasons and are not removed even indoors are treated as ordinary spectacles, and one may go out into _reshuth ha-rabbim_ wearing them.

---

*Spectacles with photogrey lenses that change color with the strength of the light may be worn on Shabbath and Yom Tov.

dressings on wounds

19. *a.* It is permitted to go out wearing a dressing over a wound, as the dressing is required for the purposes of the body and is thus considered to be a *tachshit*.

b. One may even wrap a handkerchief around a wound as a protection and go out with it in this way.

c. The dressing may be secured with an item which has no intrinsic value and is normally thrown away after use, such as a piece of thread.

d. One should not go out with a dressing secured by something which does have some value in itself and is not thrown away afterwards, such as a handkerchief.

e. 1) If one winds an item around a dressing, not with the purpose of securing the dressing, but rather of transferring that item from one *r^eshuth* to another, it is forbidden to go out with it into *r^eshuth ha-rabbim*.

   2) This is so even if the item is merely a piece of thread, or some other item which has no intrinsic value.

   3) The reason for this is that

      a) on the one hand, one is in fact attributing a separate value to the thread, so that its identity is not merged within that of the dressing, and

      b) on the other hand, it does not by itself fall within the definition of a *tachshit*.

f. One may not go out into *r^eshuth ha-rabbim* wearing a dressing whose only purpose is to keep one's clothing from being soiled with blood, rather than to protect or heal the wound.

g. It is also forbidden to go out into *r^eshuth ha-rabbim* wearing a dressing which is not firmly attached, if it is worn not to protect or heal a wound but merely to cover a blemish so as to prevent its being seen.

arm slings, cotton in ears, sanitary napkins, and trusses

20. One is allowed to go out into *r^eshuth ha-rabbim* wearing

a. a sling to support a painful arm,

b. absorbent cotton (cotton-wool)* in an aching ear,

---

*One may not roll up absorbent cotton into a ball on Shabbath or Yom Tov and insert it into the ear, but there is nothing wrong with thrusting a piece of absorbent cotton, in its existing form, into the ear.

    c. a sanitary napkin (towel) or tampon, to prevent discomfort through the body's being soiled at the time of menstruation, or

    d. a rupture belt or other surgical belt.

21. One may also go out into *reshuth ha-rabbim* wearing *orthopedic supports and insoles*

    a. orthopedic supports inside one's shoes (but not in open sandals, unless the support is built-in or firmly attached),

    b. insoles inside one's shoes (but not in open sandals), whether they are intended

        1) to keep the feet warm,

        2) to absorb perspiration or

        3) to provide a better fit,

    or

    c. a hat with paper tucked into its lining to reduce its size.

22. *a.* A soldier may, if the need arises in the performance of his security duties, go out into *reshuth ha-rabbim* wearing a chain with an identification disc (bearing his name, number, blood group and so forth) around his neck. *identification discs and identity cards*

    b. Subject to the following two conditions, a person is allowed to go out into *reshuth ha-rabbim* with an identity card or certificate, during time of war or emergency.

        1) It must be carried in an unusual way, for example stuck into one's hat.

        2) One must be on one's way to perform a mitzva, for example to prayers or to study Torah.

23. *a.* We have already seen, in paragraph 12 above, that it is the common practice to go out into *reshuth ha-rabbim* wearing jewelry or other items of an ornamental or decorative nature in the normal way. *decorative items carried in the hand*

    b. It is, however, forbidden to carry these items in the hand, even if that is the normal way in which they are used.

    c. It is, consequently, not permitted

        1) for a man to go out into *reshuth ha-rabbim* carrying a stick or cane in his hand (except as mentioned in paragraph 13 above), even if it is decorated with a silver

knob or some similar ornament and serves as a mark of authority or dignity, or

2) for a woman to go out into *r^eshuth ha-rabbim* with a handbag or purse in her hand or over her arm, even if its only use is ornamental or decorative, as in the case of an evening bag.

three categories of personal ornament

24. One must distinguish between three different types of personal ornament.

    a. 1) The first type consists of ornaments proper, such as rings, bracelets, necklaces and brooches, which are worn for decorative purposes.

        2) The practice is to take a lenient attitude with regard to ornaments of this nature and to go out into *r^eshuth ha-rabbim* wearing them, as stated in paragraph 12 above.

        3) One may rely on the practice even if the ornament is not visible, as where gloves are worn over rings.

    b. 1) The second type consists of ornaments serving a dual purpose, only one of which is decorative.

        2) An example is a gold brooch or clip in the shape of a key. (See paragraph 48 below.)

        3) No objection need be raised if a person goes out into *r^eshuth ha-rabbim* wearing an ornament of this kind, provided his principal intention is to wear it for decorative purposes.

    c. 1) The third type consists of ornaments which

        a) in fact serve a decorative purpose but

        b) are attached to articles that are used for other purposes and which themselves may not be transferred from one *r^eshuth* to another.

        2) There are no grounds for permitting a person to go out into *r^eshuth ha-rabbim* wearing such an ornament.

decorative handker-chiefs, feathers, badges and medals

        3) For illustration, see paragraph 26 below.

25. *a.* In accordance with the contents of paragraph 24*a* and *b* above, a lenient attitude is taken to a man's going out into *r^eshuth ha-rabbim* wearing

1) a handkerchief solely for decorative purposes in the top pocket of his jacket,
2) a feather stuck in his hatband or
3) the badge of a movement or organization or a medal or other sign of distinction on his lapel.

(But see paragraph 12 above.)

b. However,
1) a doctor should not go out into *reshuth ha-rabbim* with a name-tag pinned to his clothing and
2) a person should not go out wearing a ribbon or tag to identify his position or function, as in the case of a steward or usher,

since these are not, strictly speaking, decorative or ornamental in nature.

26. A woman is forbidden to go out wearing
a. a key attached to a bracelet, even if the bracelet is made of gold, or
b. a watch hanging from a chain around her neck, even if both the watch and the chain are made of gold.

keys on bracelets and watches on chains

27. a. 1) It is a common practice to go out into *reshuth ha-rabbim* wearing a gold wristwatch, as long as one would not take it off if it stopped. (See, however, paragraph 12 above.)
2) In this case, the watch is considered to be an ornament proper.
3) It is irrelevant whether or not the bracelet of the watch is also made of gold.

wristwatches and pocket-watches

b. 1) One should not go out into *reshuth ha-rabbim* wearing an ordinary wristwatch, even if it has a gold bracelet, because one would normally take it off if it stopped.
2) Nonetheless, one should not object to a person's adopting a more lenient approach and going out into *reshuth ha-rabbim* wearing an ordinary watch, with an ordinary strap or bracelet, since there are some authorities who permit this.

c. 1) By way of contrast, there are no valid grounds for

allowing a person to go out into *reshuth ha-rabbim* wearing a pocket-watch on a chain.

2) Since the watch is carried inside the pocket, one cannot be said to be wearing an ornament.

3) This is so even where both the watch and the chain are made of gold.

decorative ribbons, buttons and fringes

28. *a.* One is allowed to go out into *reshuth ha-rabbim* with ribbons, buttons or fringes attached to one's clothes, even if the only purpose served by them is decorative.

b. From paragraph 30 below it will be seen that the case of spare buttons is different.

c. See paragraph 38 below with regard to *tzitzith*.

belts, suspenders, cuff-links, safety pins, neckties, etc.

29. *a.* 1) One may go out into *reshuth ha-rabbim* wearing any item which

a) is worn to serve the requirements of an article of clothing **or**

b) is normally attached to a particular article of clothing.

2) This is because, even if the item is of value in itself, it is considered to be ancillary to the garment.

b. Accordingly, one may go out into *reshuth ha-rabbim* wearing

1) a belt or suspenders (braces) to hold up one's trousers,

2) garters or a garter belt (suspender-belt) to support one's socks or stockings,

3) cuff links,

4) shirt-collar stiffeners,

5) a safety pin joining together two parts of a garment,

6) a pin or hair-grip to secure a head-scarf or *yarmulke* or

7) a necktie.

c. One is allowed to go out wearing a belt sewn onto a garment or threaded through its loops, even while it is unbuckled or untied and is hanging loose.

d. Similarly, one may go out wearing a support-girdle with the suspender straps dangling from it, even though they are not holding up one's stockings.

    e. It is, however, prohibited to go out wearing garters or a suspender-belt without socks or stockings.

    f. See also paragraph 32 below.

30. *a.* One is not permitted to go out wearing a garment which has spare buttons sewn onto it.

     spare buttons

    b. Contrast the case in paragraph 28 above, where the buttons, while not made to be fastened at all, do serve a function, namely a decorative one.

    c. See also paragraph 33 below.

31. *a.* One may go out wearing

     coats with hoods or detachable linings

      1) a coat to which a hood is attached, even if the hood is not covering one's head, but is hanging down from the back of the coat, or

      2) a raincoat with a zipper or buttons intended for attaching a lining in cold weather.

    b. See Chapter 15, paragraph 74 with regard to attaching a lining to a coat on Shabbath or Yom Tov.

32. *a.* Some authorities hold that it is permissible to go out with a handkerchief wound around one's shirt sleeve to hold the cuffs together in place of a cuff link or a button.

     handker- chiefs used to secure cuffs or socks

    b. One may wind a handkerchief around one's leg to hold up a sock or stocking, in place of a garter or suspenders.

    c. In both of these cases, the handkerchief must be performing the relevant function alone, and these devices cannot be adopted if the cuffs are connected by means of a cuff link or are buttoned together, or if the sock or stocking is supported by a garter or suspenders.

    d. Care should be taken, in winding the handkerchief around one's arm or leg, not to violate the prohibition against tying knots on Shabbath and Yom Tov. (See Chapter 15, paragraphs 52 and 53.)

    e. See further paragraph 47 below.

33. *a.* 1) It is forbidden to go out into *reshuth ha-rabbim* (or *carmelith*) with any item which is attached to one's clothing, if that item

     useless or un- usual attach- ments on garments

        a) does not serve the requirements of the garment to which it is attached,

        b) would not be attached to it in the usual course of events **and**

        c) is of value in one's eyes and retains an identity distinct from that of the garment.

2) If, however, an item attached to one's clothing is of no value in one's eyes and its identity can be said to merge within that of the garment, one may go out into *r*e*shuth ha-rabbim* wearing it.

garments with defective attachments

b. 1) a) It is also forbidden to go out into *r*e*shuth ha-rabbim* wearing, attached to one's clothing, an item that is unusable due to some defect or deficiency which one intends to remedy after Shabbath in order to render it fit for use again.

        b) In such circumstances, the item retains an identity separate from that of the garment, even if it is sewn on.

        c) This is so whether or not the item itself has any intrinsic worth, since the intention to repair it lends it importance.

2) a) One may likewise not go out into *r*e*shuth ha-rabbim* if the defective or deficient item is unusable in its existing state, but does have some intrinsic value.

        b) In this case, its identity does not merge within that of one's clothing.

        c) This is so even if one has no intention of repairing the item after Shabbath.

tallith with one of its tzitzith spoiled is not to be worn

34. a. From what has been said above, it follows that one must not go out into *r*e*shuth ha-rabbim* wearing a *tallith* or *arba kanfoth* one of whose *tzitzith* has been damaged to the extent where it is no longer fit for use.

b. This is because one values the remaining three *tzitzith* and intends to use them when a fourth is attached.

c. The result is that, although at present serving no purpose, the *tzitzith* retain their separate identity and are not regarded as merely part of the *tallith* or *arba kanfoth*.

d. Apart from being a desecration of Shabbath, the wearing of the *tallith* or *arba kanfoth* would be a transgression of the general prohibition against wearing such a garment without proper *tzitzith*.

35. a. 1) If all of the *tzitzith* of a *tallith* or *arba kanfoth* have been damaged and not a single thread remains fit for use, what is left has lost its separate identity and is regarded as part of the *tallith* or *arba kanfoth*. *tallith with all tzitzith spoiled*

   2) Thus, wearing it would not give rise to any breach of the prohibitions against transferring items from one *reshuth* to another or within *reshuth ha-rabbim*. (But see paragraph 34d above.)

   b. The same applies when some threads are left which are fit for use but one has no intention of using them again because they are ragged.

36. a. 1) It is forbidden to go out on Shabbath, in a place where there is no *eiruv,* wearing *garment to which*

      a) a garment to which one has been obliged to attach *tzitzith* solely in order to satisfy a doubt as to whether Jewish religious law requires one to have *tzitzith* on that particular type of garment or *tzitzith are unnecessarily or improperly attached*

      b) a garment to which the *tzitzith* have not been attached in the proper position or fully in accordance with the demands of Jewish religious law.

   2) In the latter case, one would, in addition, be transgressing the prohibition against wearing the garment without proper *tzitzith*.

   b. It is also better not to go out on Shabbath, in a place where there is no *eiruv,* wearing *arba kanfoth* that are below the required size or any other garment which, according to Jewish religious law, does not need *tzitzith*, but nevertheless has them.

[225]

tzitzith on **37.** *a.* Some authorities hold that the Torah required one to
garments not   have *tzitzith* only on garments made of wool or linen and
made of wool   that the requirement for *tzitzith* on garments made of
or linen   other materials is only a Rabbinical one.

          b. 1) Even according to this view, however, one may go out
into *r^eshuth ha-rabbim* wearing a garment made of
other materials, to which *tzitzith* have been attached.

             2) This is because, whether the source of the requirement
is the Torah or Rabbinical, the wearing of the *tzitzith*
on the garment is obligatory.

wearing **38.** *a.* Although the obligation to wear *tzitzith* does not apply at
tzitzith at   night, there is nothing wrong with going out on Friday
night   night wearing one's *arba kanfoth*, its *tzitzith* being
regarded as a decorative accessory.

          b. The same applies to going out wearing a *tallith,* for
instance in the evening at the commencement of Yom
Kippur.

checking **39.** *a.* It is proper to examine one's *tzitzith* for defects before
tzitzith on   putting on one's *tallith* or *arba kanfoth* on Shabbath, if
Shabbath   one has in mind to go out wearing it in a place where there
is no *eiruv.*

          b. One should take care

             1) not to untie any threads which have become tangled
together in a double knot, and

             2) not to tighten any loosened knots in the *tzitzith.* (See
Chapter 15, paragraph 50.)

loose buttons **40.** *a.* 1) A button which has become so loose that one does not
fasten it, for fear that it will come off, is not considered
to be part of the garment.

             2) As a result, it is better not to wear the garment on
Shabbath when one intends to go out into *r^eshuth ha-
rabbim* in a place where there is no *eiruv.*

          b. From Chapter 15, paragraph 68a it is seen that on
Shabbath and Yom Tov it is forbidden to detach a loose

button, or to extract threads left after a button has fallen off.

41. *a.* It is prohibited to go into *reshuth ha-rabbim* wearing an article of clothing if

   1) a cord with which it is secured has torn and is unusable in its existing state, **and**

   2) one intends to repair, after Shabbath, the remains of the cord still attached to the garment.

  b. The rule is identical when the loop by which one hangs up a garment has snapped.

  c. The principle is the same where

   1) one of two ribbons which are tied together to secure an article of clothing is torn or pulled off,

   2) the ribbon which is still attached to the garment is useless by itself **and**

   3) one intends to replace the torn or missing ribbon.

  d. 1) In the above cases, the intention to repair lends importance to the remains of the cord or the loop or to the surviving ribbon.

   2) Consequently, one is considered to be carrying them about as separate items, and not wearing them as part of the garment.

  e. 1) If one does not intend to repair the remains of the cord, sew together the remains of the loop or replace the missing ribbon, then one may go into *reshuth ha-rabbim* wearing the garment.

   2) This is because the remains of the cord or of the loop or the surviving ribbon no longer retain any importance, and their identity merges within that of the garment.

  f. 1) On the other hand, if a silver chain which is used to hold together the two sides of a *tallith* has snapped or is defective to the point where it cannot be used, one may not go out into *reshuth ha-rabbim* wearing the *tallith*.

   2) This is so even if one does not intend to repair the chain.

   3) The reason is that the chain has an intrinsic value,

clothes with torn hangers, cords, etc.

despite the fact that it is broken, and cannot be said to be merely ancillary to the *tallith*.

pins in clothes

42. *a.* One may go out into *r^eshuth ha-rabbim* with a pin holding together two parts of a garment one is wearing. (See also paragraph 29 above.)

b. It is a common practice to go out into *r^eshuth ha-rabbim* with an ornamental brooch pinned to one's clothing. (See paragraphs 12 and 24 above and paragraph 48 below.)

c. However, there is no justification for going out into *r^eshuth ha-rabbim* with pins which are neither securing an article of clothing nor decorative.

torn buttonholes and loops and missing buttons

43. *a.* It is forbidden to go out into *r^eshuth ha-rabbim* on Shabbath wearing a garment with a button whose corresponding loop or buttonhole is torn, if one has the intention of repairing it after Shabbath.

b. The same is the case if a button corresponding to a loop sewn to the garment is missing.

c. See paragraph 30 above concerning garments with spare buttons.

labels

44. One is allowed to go out into *r^eshuth ha-rabbim* wearing clothes onto which there are sewn or stuck such items as

a. laundry labels,

b. price tags,

c. quality labels,

d. labels showing that the garment has been checked for *shaatnez* or

e. identification labels or tags.

MISCELLANEOUS RULES CONCERNING
THE TRANSFER OF OBJECTS

precautions against forgetting items in pockets

45. *a.* A person should not go out into *r^eshuth ha-rabbim* on Friday afternoon, close to the commencement of Shabbath, with something in his pocket or held in his hand, lest he forget and continue to carry it about with him on Shabbath.

b. Similarly, one should refrain from putting a watch, a handkerchief or any other article into one's pocket on Shabbath, even in the house, lest one forget to remove it before going out into *reshuth ha-rabbim*.

46. a. At the commencement of Shabbath, clothes should be checked to see that one is not carrying anything which one might come to take out into *reshuth ha-rabbim* (or which is *muktzeh* and must not be moved on Shabbath). *checking pockets*

b. On Shabbath too, one should look through one's clothes before going out into a place where carrying things about is forbidden.

47. a. 1) Unfortunately, there are many people who, through ignorance, carry handkerchiefs about with them in a forbidden manner on Shabbath; it is therefore worth emphasizing that, as a rule, it is no less prohibited to carry a handkerchief into *reshuth ha-rabbim* than it is any other item. *methods of carrying a handkerchief*

2) It makes no difference whether the handkerchief is carried in the hand or in a pocket, and we have already seen (in paragraph 2 above) that it is equally forbidden for a woman to carry her handkerchief tucked under her watch-strap or bracelet, and (in paragraph 10 above) that one must not go into *reshuth ha-rabbim* with a handkerchief on one's collar to protect it from perspiration.

b. A handkerchief may be carried in one of the following ways.

1) It may be wrapped around the neck, like a scarf.

a) If it is too small to wind like a scarf, one should at least tie the ends at the neck and not leave them hanging free.

b) As explained in Chapter 15, paragraph 52, the ends may even be tied with an ordinary knot.

2) It may be used as a belt for a garment which is not already secured or supported by a belt or by some other means.

3) According to some authorities, it can be wound around one's sleeve to hold one's shirt cuffs together, as in paragraph 32 above.

4) It can serve as a garter, as in paragraph 32 above.

5) It may be firmly sewn into a pocket before Shabbath, so that it becomes part of the garment.

   a) The use of a safety pin to attach the handkerchief to the pocket is insufficient.

   b) Should the handkerchief be of linen, one must be careful not to sew it into a woolen garment, because of the prohibition against wearing a mixture of wool and linen (*shaatnez*).

6) Where

   a) it is not possible to adopt any of the above methods **and**

   b) one badly needs a handkerchief, as when one has a severe cold,

one may go out into r^eshuth ha-rabbim with it inside one's hat or wound around one's wrist.

methods of carrying a key

48. *a.* In the case of keys (as in the case of handkerchiefs), lack of knowledge has led to widespread inadvertent transgressions in the methods of transfer from one r^eshuth to another, for example by the forbidden practice of simply hanging a key on a belt without its serving any purpose in helping to secure the garment.

b. A key may be carried, as part of a belt, in one of the following ways.

1) a) A length of cord or elastic should be passed through the hole of the key and the ends tied (in a bow, but not with an ordinary knot, if it is already Shabbath).

   b) The result will be a piece of cord or elastic in the shape of a loop with a key hanging on it.

   c) Holding the key in one hand, one should then take the double cord or elastic forming the loop around one's waist with the other hand, and fasten the "belt" by inserting the teeth of the key in the end of the loop coming around one's waist from the opposite direction, so that the key serves as a buckle.

2) a) A different method is to tie one end of a cord or elastic to the key (with a bow, if it is Shabbath).

b) The result is a single length of cord or elastic with a key attached to one end.

c) The single cord or elastic is put around one's body and the free end is either tied to the teeth of the key with a bow, or wound around them, in such a way that the key serves as an integral part of the "belt," namely its buckle.

3) a) If one requires two keys, one should tie one at each end of the cord or elastic (by means of a bow, if it is Shabbath) and fasten the "belt" by hooking the teeth of the two keys into one another, so that they serve as a buckle.

b) Alternatively, one key can be used as a connection between two separate pieces of cord or elastic, while the second serves the function of a buckle, in the same manner as if it were the only key.

4) Where a key has no teeth which can be used in the above ways, the free end or ends of the cord or elastic can be attached to another part of the key, so long as it is the key which is holding the "belt" together.

c. One must, of course, not fasten a "key-belt" over one's usual belt. (Compare paragraph 47*b*2 above.)

d. One need not raise any objection if a person goes into *reshuth ha-rabbim* wearing a silver or gold key made in the form of a brooch or tie-clip, as this is permitted by some authorities.

49. a. One must always take care, when using a key carried as *use of key* part of a belt (as described in paragraph 48 above),

1) not to leave the key in the lock when opening a door away from oneself into a different *reshuth* **and**

2) that the "belt" is properly fastened or re-fastened

before going in or out, or before moving away in *r^eshuth ha-rabbim* or *carm^elith*.

b. 1) Where the distance between the outside edge of the lintel and the closed door is four *t^efachim* or more and one wishes to remove the key one is wearing before using it, then one must not do so until one is standing under the lintel.

2) Even though the area beneath the lintel is *r^eshuth ha-yachid*, one must remember
   a) not to leave the key in the lock when opening the door into the house **and**
   b) to re-fasten the "belt" before going in.

c. Where the keyhole penetrates the door into the house from one side to the other,* the key may be inserted into it from the outside only while it is attached to the (even unfastened) "belt" still around one's body.

carrying a healthy child

50. Subject to the contents of paragraph 51 below, the prohibitions against transferring objects from one *r^eshuth* to another, or within *r^eshuth ha-rabbim* or *carm^elith*, apply also to carrying a child in one's arms or pushing a child in a baby carriage (perambulator), whether by oneself or with the assistance of another person.

carrying a sick child

51. a. A sick child who knows how to walk by himself, but who finds it difficult under the circumstances, may be carried to the doctor even through a place which meets all the criteria of *r^eshuth ha-rabbim*. (See Chapter 17, paragraph 3.)

b. A sick child who does not yet know how to walk by himself may, if necessary, be carried through *carm^elith*, but not through *r^eshuth ha-rabbim*.

c. Whenever it is permitted to carry a child through a place where the transfer of objects is otherwise not allowed,
   1) one should make sure that the child does not have

---

*This is the case with most locks, other than padlocks and Yale locks of the type which, on the inside, have only a knob or a lever but no keyhole.

anything in his hands or pockets, except items which might be necessary to avoid his being endangered, and

   2) one may take him in a baby carriage.

d. When a baby carriage is used,

   1) one should be careful to remove everything from it except items

     a) which might be necessary to avoid the child's being endangered or

     b) whose use is ancillary to that of the baby carriage, such as a sheet or a small mattress, and

   2) one should, if possible, make a point of not carrying the child and the baby carriage separately (as one might do when going down steps), but should leave the child inside all the time.

e. It cannot be over-emphasized that, if there is any chance of danger to the child's life, he may be taken to the doctor by any means whatsoever, whether or not he knows how to walk and regardless of the *r^eshuyoth* through which one must pass on the way.

52. *a.* If one finds oneself walking in *r^eshuth ha-rabbim* on Shabbath with something in one's hand or pocket, one should act as follows:

   1) One should not cease walking, even for an instant.

   2) One should rid oneself of the object in a manner which one would not normally adopt; for example,

     a) if the object is in one's hand, one should not put it down, but should let it slip out, and

     b) if it is in one's pocket, one should turn the pocket inside out until the object drops out.

   3) One should preferably leave the object where it falls, until after Shabbath.

b. The same rules apply

   1) whether one was out on Friday afternoon and was unable to reach home before Shabbath commenced or

   2) whether one realizes, while walking in *r^eshuth ha-rabbim* on Shabbath, that one has something in one's hand or pocket.

discovering articles in one's hand or pocket

c. If
1) the object is valuable,
2) one is afraid it will be lost if left where it is,
3) one is unable to remain with the object to look after it until Shabbath is over **and**
4) there is no non-Jew available who could look after it,* the object need not be left where it falls, but one may pick it up and bring it to a secure place, in one of the ways described below.

d. When one is permitted to bring the object to a place of safety, one should transfer it through *r^eshuth ha-rabbim* in the following manner.
1) Where possible, one should carry the object for a distance of less than four *amoth* and then hand it to a friend, who will do likewise before handing it back, and so on, until one approaches the house.
2) Otherwise, one may carry the object oneself for a distance of less than four *amoth*, put it down, pick it up again, walk with it for less than another four *amoth* and so on.
3) a) If, for some reason, it is not practicable to put the object down each time, one should at least stand still for a few moments after every space of just under four *amoth*.
   b) In this way, one avoids making a continuous transfer of four *amoth* in *r^eshuth ha-rabbim*.

e. 1) If one can, one should not bring the object into a *r^eshuth ha-yachid*, but should leave it outside, in a safe place, until after Shabbath.
2) If one is afraid that the object will not be safe outside, and that one will sustain a loss, one may bring it in, so long as one does so in an unusual manner, for instance

---

*a. One may ask a non-Jew to look after the object even if one knows that he will afterwards bring it to one's house.
b. Moreover, if the non-Jew is not willing, or cannot be trusted, to remain with the object until after Shabbath, one may even ask him to bring it to one's house.

a) by letting it slip into r^eshuth ha-yachid from one's hand or pocket,

b) by putting it in one's shoe,

c) by tying it to one's leg or

d) by placing it between one's clothing and one's body.

f. 1) Sometimes, the circumstances can be such that one has no time to transfer the object for a distance of less than four *amoth* at a time.

2) This may occur, for instance, where it is dangerous to be outside or when one is being pursued.

3) In such a situation, if one stands still in r^eshuth ha-rabbim after realizing that one is carrying the object, there is no alternative but to leave it where it is.

4) On the other hand, if one is still walking when one realizes one is carrying the object, then one should,

a) without stopping, quickly run home, or to any house on the way, and,

b) again without stopping, throw the object into r^eshuth ha-yachid in a manner one would not normally employ.

53. a. A person who goes from r^eshuth ha-yachid into r^eshuth ha-rabbim and then remembers that he has a handkerchief or a *yarmulke* in his pocket

what to do with a handkerchief or yarmulke found in a pocket

1) should, without stopping, let it drop to the ground in the fashion described in paragraph 52 above and he

2) may subsequently pick it up and, while standing still,

a) if it is a handkerchief, wrap it around his neck or otherwise put it on in one of the permitted ways set out in paragraph 47 above, or,

b) if it is a *yarmulke*, place it on his head.

b. He should not put it on while continuing to walk, since this very act is regarded as depositing the object in r^eshuth ha-rabbim.

54. a. 1) It is permitted to give a prayer book to a child (under thirteen if a boy and under twelve if a girl) to take to

children carrying

[235]

the synagogue for his or her own use, provided the child will not have to take it through an area which fits the definition of *r^e^shuth ha-rabbim* contained in Chapter 17, paragraph 3.

2) Once the prayer book is in the synagogue, an adult may share its use with the child.

b. With this exception, there is no justification for giving an article to a child so that he should carry it in a place where the transfer of objects is forbidden.

urinating   **55.** *a.* One should not urinate against a wall in *r^e^shuth ha-rabbim*, if there is a possibility that the urine might traverse a distance of four *amoth* or more.

b. Similarly, one must not urinate in *r^e^shuth ha-yachid*, in a place where the urine might run out into *r^e^shuth ha-rabbim*, and vice versa.

c. One may, however, urinate in *carm^e^lith* regardless of the possibility that the urine may run into *r^e^shuth ha-rabbim* or *r^e^shuth ha-yachid* or traverse a distance of four *amoth* or more.

consequences   **56.** *a.* If one has transferred an article between *r^e^shuth ha-*
of forbidden   *rabbim* and *r^e^shuth ha-yachid*, in either direction, one
transfer   ought to take a strict view and refrain from using the article on that Shabbath in the place to which it has been brought.

b. Nevertheless, if the subject of the transfer was a key with which one proceeded to unlock a door, one is not prohibited from entering the house.

Chapter 19

Specific Laws Relating to the Transfer of Objects from One Place to Another on Yom Tov, Where There Is No Eiruv*

1. a. It is not customary to make an *eiruv chatzeiroth* for Yom Tov alone.

   b. Nevertheless, it is advisable to include Yom Tov in an *eiruv chatzeiroth* made before Shabbath to cover an extended period. (See Chapter 17, paragraph 16.)

   c. Having done so, one will be permitted to transfer an object from the house to the common courtyard or to another place covered by the *eiruv*, even if one does not need it for any purpose.

   advisability of eiruv chatzeiroth on Yom Tov

2. a. In a place where there is no *eiruv*, one may, on Yom Tov, transfer an article from one *reshuth* to another, or for a distance of four *amoth* or more in *reshuth ha-rabbim*, only if

   1) one has, or thinks that one may perhaps have, some use, however small, for the article on that day **and**

   2) that use is one commonly adopted by most people.

   b. An article for which one has no need at all should not be taken outside on Yom Tov where there is no *eiruv*.

   extent to which transfers permitted without eiruv

3. It is therefore allowed on Yom Tov, even where there is no *eiruv*, to

   a. wear jewelry or ornaments of all kinds,

   b. go out with a handkerchief or the keys of the house in one's pocket and

   c. take a baby out in a baby carriage (perambulator).

   jewelry, handkerchiefs, keys and baby carriages

---

*See Chapter 17, paragraphs 11 to 25 for a discussion of the subject of *eiruv*.

prayer books   **4.** *a.* One may take a prayer book back home, even where there is no *eiruv*, if
1) it was brought to the synagogue on the Festival and
2) one is afraid to leave it in case it will be lost.
b. If it was left in the synagogue before the Festival, one should not take it home on Yom Tov, unless one intends to use it there on the same day (before evening).

walking-sticks   **5.** A person who generally goes out with a walking-stick, but for whom a stick is not absolutely essential to enable him to walk, should not go out into *r^eshuth ha-rabbim* or *carm^elith* with it on Yom Tov. (Compare Chapter 18, paragraph 13.)

boxes of matches and packets of cigarettes   **6.** *a.* One may carry a box of matches or a packet of cigarettes from one *r^eshuth* to another, whether or not there is an *eiruv*, even though one only needs part of the contents for Yom Tov.
b. Regarding smoking on Yom Tov see Chapter 13, paragraph 7.

for whom transfer may be made   **7.** Where there is no *eiruv* and transfers from one place to another are prohibited on Shabbath, one should transfer nothing on Yom Tov, not even food, unless it is for the use or benefit of a human being (not just for an animal), and then only if it is for a Jew who does not violate Shabbath in public. (See Chapter 2, paragraphs 5 and 6.)

Chapter 20

Categories of Muktzeh

Laws specifically relating to *muktzeh* on Yom Tov are explained in Chapter 21.

NATURE OF MUKTZEH

1. *a.* Maimonides (*Mishneh Torah, Hilchoth Shabbath* 24:12) explains what the laws of *muktzeh* are in the following manner: "The Sages forbade one to handle some objects on Shabbath as one does during the week."

a reason for muktzeh

 b. He says that one of the reasons for the laws of *muktzeh* is that they follow logically from the prohibitions derived from the Prophet Isaiah: Chapter 58, verses 13 and 14.

 c. Pursuant to these prohibitions, one's manner of walking and one's conversation should not be the same on Shabbath as on other days of the week, but should be subject to restriction. (See Chapter 29.)

 d. All the more so, concluded the Sages, should one be restricted in handling objects on Shabbath.

 e. Otherwise, one would find something to do with every object one picked up, having little else to occupy one on Shabbath, and the purpose of our being granted a Shabbath day of rest would be defeated.

2. There are two distinct types of prohibitions involved in the laws of *muktzeh*:

muktzeh involves two prohibitions

 a. a prohibition against eating or using an object and

 b. a prohibition against moving it.

3. *a.* Since the rules relating to the laws of *muktzeh* are too numerous to be listed in detail in a work of this nature,

treatment of muktzeh in this book

this book limits itself to setting out the general principles and to specific practical examples.

b. The rules concerning *muktzeh* on Shabbath and Yom Tov are identical, with the exception of certain differences mentioned in Chapter 21.

categories of muktzeh

4. *a.* There are four main categories of *muktzeh*:

1) *k^eli she-m^elachto l^e-issur;*
2) *muktzeh mei-chamath chesron kis;*
3) *muktzeh mei-chamath gufo;*
4) *basis la-davar ha-assur.*

b. These categories are the subject of the following paragraphs.

KELI SHE-MELACHTO LE-ISSUR

definition

5. A *k^eli she-m^elachto l^e-issur* is an object which is used for performing an activity that is forbidden on Shabbath, for example

a. a pen, because it is used for writing,
b. a pair of scissors, because they are used for cutting (but see paragraph 16 below regarding kitchen scissors),
c. notepaper, because one writes on it, or
d. a pot used primarily for cooking.

objects used for both forbidden and permitted activities

6. *a.* An object which is more often than not used for performing a forbidden activity, and is only occasionally used for performing a permitted activity, is treated as a *k^eli she-m^elachto l^e-issur.*

b. An object

1) which is more often than not used for performing a permitted activity, although it is also occasionally used for performing a forbidden activity, or even
2) which is used with equal frequency in the performance of forbidden and permitted activities,

is not treated as a *k^eli she-m^elachto l^e-issur* (but is treated in the manner outlined in paragraph 80 below).

7. *a.* A *keli she-melachto le-issur* may be moved, subject to the limitations contained in the following paragraphs,
   1) if one needs to use it on Shabbath for a permitted purpose **or**
   2) if, on Shabbath, one needs to make use of the place which it occupies.
   b. Otherwise, it may not be moved, even if one fears that in its present position it is liable to be spoiled or lost.

scope of prohibition against moving

8. *a.* Examples of the use of a *keli she-melachto le-issur* for a permitted purpose are
   1) the use of a hammer to crack nuts,
   2) the use of a matchstick to pick one's teeth and
   3) the use of a needle to extract a thorn from one's finger.
   b. One must not do anything to adapt the *keli she-melachto le-issur* to its permitted use, for instance trimming the end of a matchstick with which one wishes to pick one's teeth.
   c. A *keli she-melachto le-issur* ought not to be used if one has available, and could use for the same purpose, an article whose use is not restricted.

use for a permitted purpose

9. One is also allowed to move a *keli she-melachto le-issur*
   a. in order to give it to another person who wishes to use it for a permitted purpose, or
   b. if one needs to use it (in a permitted manner) for an animal.

use by another person or for an animal

10. *a.* A typical example where one is allowed to move a *keli she-melachto le-issur* in order to make use of the place which it occupies occurs when a hammer is lying on a table over which one wishes to spread a cloth.
   b. Similarly, one may move the hammer if one wishes to use or move something else and is physically prevented from doing so by the hammer's presence, as where it is lying on a tablecloth which one needs.
   c. One is not permitted to move the hammer merely because its very presence in a particular place disturbs one's peace

use of place which it occupies

of mind, for instance if the fact that it is lying on the table will cause one embarrassment in front of guests.

putting down after permitted handling

11. A *k^eli she-m^elachto l^e-issur* which has been picked up in circumstances where this is permissible, as described in paragraphs 7 to 10 above, and which is still in one's hand after one has finished using it or moving it out of the way, need not be thrown aside immediately, but may be put down wherever one wishes.

preservation of the k^eli

12. *a.* We have seen, in paragraph 7 above, that it is forbidden to move a *k^eli she-m^elachto l^e-issur* which one does not need to use, if one's intention is merely to save it from being spoiled or lost.

b. Nevertheless, one may move a *k^eli she-m^elachto l^e-issur* if one does so

1) in order to preserve it for a permitted use later on during the same Shabbath, **or**

2) for some permitted purpose, despite the fact that one's primary objective is its preservation, and not the achievement of that purpose.

when object becomes k^eli she-m^elachto l^e-issur

13. *a.* 1) An object whose primary use is obviously for performing an activity that is forbidden on Shabbath is considered to be a *k^eli she-m^elachto l^e-issur*, even if it has never been used for that purpose.

2) Examples of such objects are pens, hammers and matchsticks.

b. 1) An object which is not recognizable as being designated for use in a forbidden activity is not considered to be a *k^eli she-m^elachto l^e-issur*, even if it has been set aside for that purpose, until it has actually been used in the performance of such an activity.

2) Examples of such objects are

a) a liqueur bottle which one has decided to use as the base of a table-lamp and

b) a jar which one has decided to use as a children's piggy bank.

14. *a.* *T^efillin* should be treated, for most purposes, as a *k^eli she- t^efillin* *m^elachto l^e-issur.*

   b. Consequently, one may remove *t^efillin* inadvertently left inside a *tallith* bag,

   1) if one wishes to use the *tallith* and cannot easily take it out while the *t^efillin* are still inside, or

   2) if one needs to put one's *tallith* into the bag for taking to the synagogue (where there is an *eiruv chatzeiroth*).

   c. Although they are *muktzeh, t^efillin* may be picked up and moved if

   1) they have fallen down or are lying in a degrading position or

   2) there is a danger that they will fall down or come to be in a degrading position or that they will be stolen.

15. *a.* A utensil which is used for cooking, and not usually for *cooking* keeping food in, is a *k^eli she-m^elachto l^e-issur.* *utensils*

   b. One may move it

   1) in the circumstances set out in paragraphs 7 to 10 above **or**

   2) if it contains food.

   c. Examples of such utensils are

   1) a frying pan and

   2) a spit on which liver is roasted.

   d. The lid of a pan is treated in the same manner as the pan.

16. *a.* The category of *k^eli she-m^elachto l^e-issur* includes such *purses,* items as matchsticks, purses used for carrying money *scissors,* (while there is no money inside), oil lamps (provided they *combs, etc.* were not burning when Shabbath commenced), rulers, combs, nails, cigarettes, soap and washing-powder.*

   b. A purse made for holding money may be opened when there is no money inside, in order to take out a key.

   c. 1) Kitchen scissors are regarded in the same way as an ordinary knife and are not a *k^eli she-m^elachto l^e-issur.*

---

*For the use of washing powder see Chapter 12, paragraph 5 and Chapter 14, paragraph 16.

2) This is because they are intended to be used mainly for purposes which are permitted on Shabbath, such as cutting up food or opening bags containing food.

telephone directories

17. a. A telephone directory is a k^eli she-m^elachto l^e-issur. (See also Chapter 28, paragraph 14.)

b. However, one may use it to look for an address one needs on Shabbath.

printer's proofs

18. a. Printer's proofs are a k^eli she-m^elachto l^e-issur.

b. Since they are printed with the specific object of being corrected (if necessary), and one could come to insert amendments in the process of reading, one must not read them, unless one's attention is directed solely to understanding their contents as when reading an ordinary book.

MUKTZEH MEI-CHAMATH CHESRON KIS

basic rule

19. a. Anything
1) which has an appreciable value,
2) which is meant to be used in a manner that is forbidden on Shabbath **and**
3) whose owner is particular not to use it for any other purpose, lest it be damaged,
is *muktzeh mei-chamath chesron kis.*

b. Examples are
1) a circumcision knife,*
2) a knife used for slaughtering animals or poultry,
3) a special butchers' knife,
4) valuable candlesticks (even if no candles have been lit in them on the Shabbath in question),
5) a length of cloth intended to be made into a garment,
6) a typewriter,
7) a radio,
8) a camera,

---

*From Chapter 37, paragraph 13, it will be seen that circumcision is forbidden on Shabbath except under the conditions set out there.

9) delicate instruments designed for a use which is prohibited on Shabbath,

10) mint stamps which one wishes to use for postage,

11) good quality writing paper and

12) parchment awaiting use by a scribe.

c. An item which is *muktzeh mei-chamath chesron kis* may not be moved, even if one desires to use it for a permitted purpose and wishes to make use of the place which it occupies.

20. The category of *muktzeh mei-chamath chesron kis* includes

    commercial papers

a. business letters and invoices,

b. checks,

c. bank-notes,

d. stock certificates,

e. valid bus tickets and

f. any other document whose use on Shabbath is prohibited and which a person looks after carefully.

21. a. Items

    goods intended for sale

1) which are intended for sale **and**

2) which their owner is particular not to use, even for his own purposes,

are treated as *muktzeh mei-chamath chesron kis.*

b. They may not be moved, even though, on this occasion, the owner wishes to make use of them for his own requirements.

c. This is so even if the items

1) are designed for use in an activity which is permitted on Shabbath **and**

2) have no great value.

d. Food as such (see *g* below regarding *ethrogim*), even if it forms part of one's stock-in-trade, is not *muktzeh mei-chamath chesron kis,* since one always has in mind the possibility of eating it should the occasion arise.

e. It follows from the above that

1) the owner of a hardware store may not use a dinner set that forms part of his stock for sale, **but**

2) if part of his business also consists of renting out cutlery and crockery, he (or anyone else) may use a set belonging to that part of his stock which is for hire.

f. Postage stamps, whether used or unused, which are intended for dealing are regarded as *muktzeh mei-chamath chesron kis.*

g. *Ethrogim* which are intended to be sold for ritual use on Sukkoth are treated as *muktzeh mei-chamath chesron kis* and may not be moved.

objects having a fixed position

22. *a.* Anything

1) to which a person allots a fixed place on account of its special value **and**

2) which one is particular not to move about, lest it be damaged,

is also *muktzeh mei-chamath chesron kis.*

b. Examples are

1) a wall clock and

2) a valuable painting.

c. Similarly, a heavy cupboard which one is careful not to move from the position in which it stands, for fear that this may result in its being damaged, is *muktzeh* and may not be moved, although one may open and close its doors.

d. 1) Threads of *tzitzith* which have not yet been attached to a garment are *muktzeh mei-chamath chesron kis;*

2) however, *tzitzith* which have become torn and unfit to be used as such are not *muktzeh*, provided that

a) they were not, before Shabbath commenced, put away in a special place used for disposing of disused items of a sacred nature (*g^eniza*) **and**

b) one is accustomed to making some permitted use of them, for instance as a bookmark.

e. 1) Eating utensils which one uses on Passover are *muktzeh mei-chamath chesron kis* (except on Passover of course), as one is normally particular not to use them during the rest of the year.

2) Matzoth which one wishes to use on the first night of Passover, in order to fulfill the mitzva of eating matza,

are *muktzeh mei-chamath chesron kis* on Shabbath which falls on the day before Passover.

23. *a.* An object which would otherwise be *muktzeh mei-chamath chesron kis* is not so if, before the commencement of Shabbath, one designates it for some permanent use that is permitted on Shabbath.

designation for a permitted use

b. It is sufficient if this designation is in thought.

c. Accordingly, one is allowed to move mint stamps which, before Shabbath, one had in mind not to use for postage, but to add to one's collection.

24. If an article which is *muktzeh mei-chamath chesron kis* breaks on Shabbath, it may not be moved on that day, even though its owner no longer minds if it is used for a purpose other than that originally intended.

broken articles

MUKTZEH MEI-CHAMATH GUFO

25. *a.* Subject to the qualifications contained in the succeeding paragraphs, items

definition

    1) neither designed nor designated for any use

    2) nor consisting of food or fodder which is fit for human or animal consumption

are *muktzeh mei-chamath gufo.*

b. Examples are stones in the street and sand on the seashore.

26. *a.* 1) Peels, shells, fruit pits (stones), and bones are *muktzeh* and, except in certain circumstances, may not be moved, if

inedible peels, shells, pits and bones

    a) they are fit for neither human nor animal consumption **or**

    b) they are fit for animal consumption, but there is no animal in the vicinity to whom they could be given.

    2) Nevertheless, one may remove such peels, shells, pits, or bones from one's mouth with one's fingers and put them on the plate.

3) When cracking nuts, one should not retain the shells in one's hand for throwing away afterwards, but should throw them away or put them on the plate immediately upon cracking.

4) See Chapter 22, paragraphs 36 and 42, for the circumstances and manner in which inedible peels, shells, pits, and bones may be cleared away.

5) For playing games with apricot pits see Chapter 16, paragraph 10.

b. 1) The following are not *muktzeh* and may be moved, unless one threw them away before Shabbath:
   a) peels, shells, pits, or bones to which some of the fruit or meat is still attached;
   b) pits which contain some edible material inside them (as is the case with certain kinds of apricot);
   c) bones which contain marrow.

2) It is irrelevant that one has no intention of eating the remaining fruit or meat, the contents of the pit or the marrow.

edible peels, seeds and bones

27. a. Peels, seeds (pips) and bones are not *muktzeh* and may be moved, if
   1) they are fit for human consumption **or**
   2) they are fit for animal consumption and there is an animal in the vicinity to whom they could be given.

b. Examples are orange peels, watermelon seeds and soft bones.

c. Peels, seeds and bones of this kind do become *muktzeh* if they are thrown away (for instance into a refuse bin or the street) before Shabbath commences, but not if they are thrown away on Shabbath.

d. By contrast, normal foodstuffs do not become *muktzeh* when one throws them into the refuse bin, even if one does so before Shabbath.

foodstuffs not yet made fit for eating

28. a. Foodstuffs which are not fit to be eaten because they have yet to be cooked or baked are *muktzeh*.

b. Examples are flour, uncooked beans or potatoes, and raw meat.

29. a. Food which one is forbidden to eat and from which one is not permitted to derive any benefit is *muktzeh*.

food from which all benefit is forbidden

b. Examples are
  1) *chametz* on the first and last days of Passover and on Shabbath occurring on one of the intermediate days of Passover,
  2) *chametz* which on Passover remainèd in the possession of a Jew,
  3) fruit which grows on a tree in the first three years after planting (*orla*) and
  4) the produce which grows from seeds sown within a given distance of vines, and the grapes which grow on those vines (*kil'ei kerem*).

c. One is not allowed to pick up *chametz* which one finds in the street on Passover, but it is still regarded as food to the extent that one may not, by treading on it, treat it in a manner not befitting food given to us by the Almighty for our sustenance.

30. T*e*ruma, t*e*rumath ma'aser and *challa* are *muktzeh*, since

*t*e*rumoth and challa*

  a. one is not nowadays permitted to eat them **and**
  b. due to the sanctity attaching to them, one does not give them to a non-Jew to eat nor feed them to an animal.

31. a. Food which, before it may be eaten, has to be dealt with in a manner not permitted on Shabbath is *muktzeh*.

*food from which t*e*rumoth, ma'asroth or challa not yet separated*

  b. Examples are fruits and vegetables from which one has not yet separated t*e*rumoth and ma'asroth (where this is required).
  c. 1) Bread from which *challa* has not been separated, and which is made from dough kneaded within the boundaries of what Halacha regards as the Land of Israel, also falls within this category.
     2) This is not so if the dough was kneaded outside the Land of Israel, since, in that case, one is allowed to eat

the bread, as long as one leaves over enough for *challa* to be separated after Shabbath.

food which may not be eaten till after Shabbath

32. *a.* Food which it is forbidden to eat on Shabbath is *muktzeh* even if, when Shabbath terminates, it will be permissible to eat it without dealing with it in any special way.

b. The following are examples of such food:
1) an egg which was laid on Shabbath;
2) milk which was milked on Shabbath, albeit in a permitted manner (for instance by a non-Jew or by means of a milking machine, as explained in Chapter 27, paragraphs 46 and 48);
3) fruit which has fallen, or which one suspects may have fallen, from a tree on that Shabbath;
4) fruit which has been picked, or which one suspects may have been picked, by a non-Jew on that Shabbath;
5) juice which has oozed out by itself on Shabbath from
   a) grapes or
   b) other fruit, if not intended specifically for eating (as distinct from pressing).
(See Chapter 5, paragraph 11.)

c. For similar reasons, the following are *muktzeh*:
1) oil remaining in a lamp which was burning at the commencement of Shabbath and subsequently went out;
2) oil which drips from a burning lamp on Shabbath.

forbidden food fit for a non-Jew

33. *a.* 1) Food which one is forbidden to eat both during and after Shabbath, but which is fit for a non-Jew to eat, is not *muktzeh mei-chamath gufo.*
2) Consequently one may move a piece of cooked meat which does not comply with the halachic requirements for consumption by a Jew, since it is fit to be eaten by a non-Jew.

b. 1) The same applies to non-kosher food which is fit to be fed only to an animal (if there is an animal in the vicinity to whom it could be given).

    2) One may, therefore, move a piece of meat which is unfit for human consumption, but which is fit to be given to an animal, even if the meat is uncooked.

   c. For the case of meat which has been cooked with milk, see paragraph 35 below.

34. *a.* Food which may not be eaten by its owner, but which other persons are allowed to eat, is not *muktzeh* and may be moved even by its owner. *food forbidden to particular individuals*

   b. 1) One example of this is food from which its owner has vowed that he personally will derive no benefit.

    2) a) There is a further instance, which will be relevant when the rules of purity and defilement will again be observed to the extent that they were in Temple times.

      b) This is the case of undefiled t^eruma or challa, which may only be eaten by kohanim who themselves are in a state of purity.

35. *a.* One is forbidden to eat, or derive any benefit from, meat cooked with milk, and it is accordingly *muktzeh.* (See paragraph 29 above.) *meat mixed with milk*

   b. 1) On the other hand, meat which has merely had milk spilled on it is not *muktzeh.*

    2) This is because, while there are grounds for forbidding it to be eaten, one is permitted to derive a benefit from it and may give it to a non-Jew to eat or may feed it to an animal.

   c. For the same reason, fowl which has been cooked with milk is not *muktzeh.*

36. *a.* A healthy person is not allowed to take medicines on Shabbath, and they are consequently *muktzeh* for him. *medicines*

   b. The medicines of a person who was ill at the commencement of Shabbath are not *muktzeh.*

   c. See also Chapter 33, paragraph 4, and Chapter 34, paragraph 3, regarding the taking of medicine.

[251]

clothes made
from a
combination
of wool and
linen

37. *a.* Since a Jew may not wear an article of clothing which contains a combination of wool and linen, such a garment is *muktzeh* and may not be moved if it belongs to a Jew.

b. However, if it belongs to a non-Jew, it is not *muktzeh* and may be moved.

c. Accordingly, if a non-Jew visits a Jew on Shabbath, wearing a coat which contains, or may contain, a combination of wool and linen, the Jew may take his coat from him and hang it on a hook.

coins

38. *a.* Coins, and tokens which are used in place of coins, are *muktzeh.*

b. 1) Nevertheless, one may move a coin which is attached for ornamental purposes to a necklace or key ring.

2) Owing to the fact that it is permanently fixed in position, it is no longer regarded as a coin and ceases to be *muktzeh.* (See paragraph 44 below.)

c. 1) The important factor for consideration is whether or not the coin continues to be used as such.

2) Thus, even a coin suspended from a necklace or key ring would remain *muktzeh* if it were employed for the purpose of removing the sanctity from *ma'aser sheini,* for which an actual coin is essential. (With regard to moving the necklace or key ring see paragraphs 81 and 82 below.)

human
corpse

39. *a.* A human corpse is *muktzeh.*

b. The specific laws relating to the treatment of a dead person on Shabbath and Yom Tov are dealt with in a subsequent chapter.

animals

40. *a.* Animals are *muktzeh.*

b. See Chapter 27, paragraphs 21 to 30, for the care of animals on Shabbath and Yom Tov.

broken and
discarded
articles

41. *a.* 1) The pieces of a broken article which, in their existing state, are not fit to be used for any purpose are

muktzeh and may not be moved, whether the article
was broken on Shabbath or during the week.

2) An example is a shoe from which the sole or the heel
has become totally detached, so that it cannot be worn
at all.

3) Nevertheless, if such pieces of a broken article are in a
position where they might cause injury to passers-by,
one may move them to the side.

b. 1) The pieces of a broken article which are fit to be used
(even for a purpose other than that for which the
original article was designed) are not *muktzeh*,
whether or not one has the intention of using them
again, unless

a) fragments of this kind are normally thrown away **or**

b) their owner actually threw them away before Shabbath commenced.

2) The mere act of throwing usable fragments away on
Shabbath itself does not make them *muktzeh*.

c. Unbroken articles are not made *muktzeh* by being thrown
away, even before Shabbath.

42. a. 1) It is forbidden to move a piece of furniture or any other *reparable* object which is broken, or part of which has become *items* detached, if it can easily be repaired.

2) This is so despite the fact that it may still be fit for
use.

3) The reason is that, if one were allowed to use it, one
might come to repair it.

4) However, should it be in a position where it may injure
someone, it may be moved aside.

b. Subject to the reservations mentioned in paragraph 41
above, it is permissible to move or use a piece of furniture
or another object

1) which is broken and not easy to repair **or**

2) part of which has become detached and lost.

doors, door handles and

43. a. 1) The door of a house or of a large cupboard or a window *windows*

which has come off its hinges may not be replaced on Shabbath.

2) Such a door or window is *muktzeh* and may not be moved, unless

a) it came off its hinges before the beginning of Shabbath **and**

b) one had in mind, before Shabbath, to make use of it, on Shabbath, for some permitted purpose.

b. 1) Likewise, an ordinary handle which has come out of a door may not be replaced and is *muktzeh*, but

2) a handle of a type that is made to be inserted in, and withdrawn from, the door when opening and closing it may be moved and used in the same way as a key. (See also Chapter 23, paragraph 32.)

c. 1) While one may, on Shabbath, take the door of a small cabinet or locker, such as a first-aid box, off its hinges,

2) it is forbidden to replace it.

3) Yet the door, even after removal, is not *muktzeh*.

designation for a permitted use

44. a. An object which would otherwise be *muktzeh mei-chamath gufo* is not so if, before the commencement of Shabbath, one designates it for some permanent use that is permitted on Shabbath.

b. It is sufficient if this designation is in thought.

c. 1) If the object is of a kind which, when used, is used in its existing condition, then, in case of need, it is enough that the designation was for use only on one Shabbath.

2) An example is a stone conveniently shaped for cracking nuts.

d. 1) Similarly, designation for use on just one Shabbath is enough in the case of things which are used on a one-time basis.

2) An instance would occur where, before Shabbath, one designated sand for use in temporarily covering up an oily patch on the floor.

sand, watches and buttons

45. a. 1) Sand on the seashore is *muktzeh*.

2) The same applies to sand which is intended to be used for building (even if children are accustomed to playing with it).

3) On the other hand, sand which has been put into a sandbox for children to play with is not *muktzeh* and may be moved, subject to the limitations mentioned in Chapter 16, paragraph 4.

b. Regarding the handling of a watch which has stopped going see Chapter 28, paragraph 25.

c. Regarding the handling of a button which has come off an article of clothing on Shabbath, see Chapter 15, paragraph 68.

BASIS LA-DAVAR HA-ASSUR

46. a. Subject to the qualifications contained in the following paragraphs, a *basis la-davar ha-assur* is an article on which there was placed or hung, before Shabbath, an object which is *muktzeh*. *(general definition)*

b. An article may be a *basis la-davar ha-assur* even if, by itself, it would in no way be *muktzeh*, as for example food.

c. 1) A *basis la-davar ha-assur* acquires the same status as the *muktzeh* object which has been placed or hung on it.

2) It may not be moved during the whole of Shabbath, except in circumstances in which it would be permitted to move that *muktzeh* object.

3) This is so notwithstanding that the *muktzeh* object may have been removed from the *basis la-davar ha-assur* during the course of the Shabbath by a non-Jew or a child, or may have dropped off by itself.

47. a. An article becomes a *basis la-davar ha-assur* only if a number of conditions, explained in paragraphs 50 to 56 below, are fulfilled. *(article which supports a muktzeh object but is not a basis la-davar ha-assur)*

b. If not all of these conditions are met, an article which supports an object that is *muktzeh* does not become a *basis la-davar ha-assur*, but the following rules apply.

1) One may move the article once the object that is *muktzeh* has been removed, for example by a non-Jew.
2) One may oneself tilt the article so that the *muktzeh* object falls off, provided that one needs to use the article or the place which it occupies.
3) One may even move the article while the *muktzeh* object is still on it, if
   a) one needs to use the article or the place which it occupies and
   b) one is afraid to make the *muktzeh* object fall off, lest it become spoiled or spoil something else.
4) Likewise, one may move the article with the *muktzeh* object still on it, if
   a) one requires the *muktzeh* object in the place to which the article is being taken, so long as
   b) one's principal aim is to use the article itself or the place which it occupies.
5) One may **neither**
   a) move the article with the *muktzeh* object still on it, **nor**
   b) tilt it to make the *muktzeh* object drop off,
   if one does not require the article or the place which it occupies but wants to prevent the *muktzeh* object from being lost, stolen or damaged.

basis supporting k^eli she-m^elachto l^e-issur

48. *a.* Some authorities hold that an article supporting a *k^eli she-m^elachto l^e-issur* does not become *muktzeh* as a *basis la-davar ha-assur* at all.

b. 1) In any case, one certainly cannot apply more stringent restrictions to the *basis* than to the *muktzeh* object which it supports.
2) One may therefore move the *basis* in the same way as if it were a *k^eli she-m^elachto l^e-issur*, that is to say
   a) if one needs to use if for a permitted purpose or
   b) if one needs to make use of the place which it occupies.

existence of pre-requisites

49. The succeeding paragraphs contain the conditions laid down

by the Rabbis as prerequisites before any article becomes a
basis la-davar ha-assur subject to the same restrictions as
the *muktzeh* object that it supports.

50. *a.* An article does not become a *basis la-davar ha-assur* *(1) muktzeh*
unless an object which is *muktzeh* is placed or hung *placed on*
on it *basis by or*
1) by the article's owner, *for owner*
2) by somebody who received his permission to put the
muktzeh object there or
3) by somebody who puts it there for the owner's benefit,
albeit without his knowledge and consent, so long as it
is plain that he would be pleased with what has been
done if he knew of it.
b. If one has placed or hung a *muktzeh* object on an article
belonging to another person without his knowledge and
consent and without its being for his benefit,
1) that article does not become a *basis la-davar ha-assur*
and
2) it may be moved, subject to the rules set out in paragraph 47*b* above.

51. *a.* An article does not become a *basis la-davar ha-assur* *(2) muktzeh*
unless *inten-*
1) one's specific intention in placing or hanging the *tionally*
muktzeh object on the article is that the *muktzeh* *placed on*
object should be in that position **or** *basis*
2) the *muktzeh* object is normally kept in or on the
article, as in the case of money kept in a purse.
b. If
1) one has unintentionally placed or hung a *muktzeh*
object on an article, without any specific desire that
the *muktzeh* object should be there, or if
2) the *muktzeh* object has fallen onto it,
the article does not become a *basis la-davar ha-assur*,
but is subject to the rules set out in paragraph 47*b*
above.

(3) basis serving purposes of muktzeh

52. *a.* 1) An article does not become a *basis la-davar ha-assur* unless an object which is *muktzeh* is placed or hung on it with the intention that it should serve the purposes of the *muktzeh* object.

2) Thus, a table can become a *basis la-davar ha-assur* if candlesticks are placed on it.

b. 1) If, on the contrary, the *muktzeh* object serves the purposes of the article on which it is placed or hung, the article may be moved, subject to the rules set out in paragraph 47*b* above.

2) This would be so in the case of a stone which is placed

   a) on the lid of a receptacle to prevent cats from opening it or

   b) on sheets of paper to stop them from being scattered in the wind.

c. 1) Where neither the object which is *muktzeh* nor the article on which it is placed or hung serves the purposes of the other,

   a) one should treat the article as a *basis la-davar ha-assur*, but,

   b) in case of need, one may rely on the opinion that the article does not become a *basis la-davar ha-assur* in such circumstances, and may move it, subject to the rules set out in paragraph 47*b* above.

2) An example occurs where the *muktzeh* object is placed on the article merely because there is no other practical possibility available, as where

   a) the *muktzeh* object is put on top of another article in a drawer, for lack of space in the bottom of the drawer (as in paragraph 68 below), or

   b) candlesticks are placed on a tablecloth (as in paragraph 60 below).

3) In the above illustrations, it is intended that the *muktzeh* object and the candlesticks should be supported by the drawer and the table respectively, and the fact that they are supported by an article which is already in the drawer, or by the tablecloth, is merely incidental.

53. *a.* An article does not become a *basis la-davar ha-assur* unless an object which is *muktzeh*

    1) is placed or hung on it before sunset, with the intention that it remain there continuously until the stars come out on Friday night, **and**

    2) in fact remains there throughout that period.

  b. An article does not become a *basis la-davar ha-assur*, and may be moved, subject to the rules set out in paragraph 47*b* above,

    1) if the *muktzeh* object was put into position with the intention of removing it before the commencement of Shabbath, but one subsequently forgot about it, **or**

    2) even if the *muktzeh* object was simply put into position without any intention of leaving it there for the period from sunset until the stars come out, and one subsequently forgot about it, **or**

    3) if the *muktzeh* object was put into position with the intention that it should be removed during the period from sunset until the stars come out on Friday night (for instance by a non-Jew or by being shaken off), **or**

    4) if a non-Jew or a child removed the *muktzeh* object during the period between sunset and the time when the stars come out on Friday night, **or**

    5) if a non-Jew or a child put the *muktzeh* object into position on Shabbath itself (whether with or without the knowledge and consent of the article's owner), **or**

    6) even if the owner of the article himself mistakenly placed or hung a *muktzeh* object on it on Shabbath.

  c. 1) In certain circumstances where a loss would otherwise be suffered, one may be permitted to rely on authorities who hold the view that an article does not become a *basis la-davar ha-assur* if one's intention is that the *muktzeh* object

      a) should remain on it for the whole of the period between sunset and the time when the stars come out on Friday night, **but**

      b) should be removed by a non-Jew or shaken off during the course of the Shabbath.

(4) muktzeh placed on basis before Shabbath and intended to remain there

2) A duly qualified rabbi who is competent to give a decision in such matters should be consulted to ascertain whether such circumstances exist.

(5) muktzeh object of some importance in relation to basis

54. *a.* An article does not become a *basis la-davar ha-assur* unless the *muktzeh* object which is on it is of some consequence when viewed in relation to that article.

b. If the *muktzeh* object is of no consequence when viewed in relation to the article which supports it, the article is not a *basis la-davar ha-assur*, and may be moved, subject to the rules set out in paragraph 47*b* above.

c. Instances of the latter situation occur when
1) a low-denomination coin is put on a table or
2) an object which is *muktzeh* is hung on the door of a room. (See paragraph 74 below.)

(6) basis not also supporting more important non-muktzeh object

55. *a.* An article does not become a *basis la-davar ha-assur* unless, at the commencement of Shabbath,
1) there is nothing on it apart from the *muktzeh* object
   or
2) the *muktzeh* object is not less important to the owner of the article than any other object (which is not *muktzeh*) that is also on the article at the time.

b. 1) In other words, an article is not a *basis la-davar ha-assur* (and may be moved subject to the rules set out in paragraph 47*b* above) if, in addition to the *muktzeh* object, there is also on it, at the commencement of Shabbath, an object which
   a) is not *muktzeh* and
   b) is more important to one than the *muktzeh* object.

2) It is sufficient if the importance of the object which is not *muktzeh* lies in the fact that one needs it for Shabbath, as in paragraph 59 below.

3) The article will not subsequently become a *basis la-davar ha-assur*, even if, during the course of the Shabbath, the object which is not *muktzeh* is removed, leaving the *muktzeh* object by itself in place.

4) It makes no difference
   a) whether the *muktzeh* object and the object which is not *muktzeh* are both lying on the article or
   b) whether one of them is lying on it and the other is suspended at the side of it or underneath it.

56. *a.* An article does not become a *basis la-davar ha-assur* unless the *muktzeh* object is directly placed on, or suspended from, the article itself. *(7) muktzeh object directly supported by basis*

   b. 1) If the *muktzeh* object is placed on a subsidiary part of the article which serves a separate function, only the subsidiary part would become a *basis la-davar ha-assur*.

   2) One would thus be permitted to move the article as a whole, subject to the rules set out in paragraph 47*b* above.

   3) An example is the putting of a *muktzeh* object into an ordinary pocket of the type which is sewn into a garment and hangs inside it. (See paragraph 71 below, from which it will be seen that a great deal of importance attaches to the way in which the pocket is made.)

57. The application of the rules relating to *basis la-davar ha-assur* can only be understood by reference to practical examples, a variety of which is contained in the following paragraphs. *application of rules in practice*

58. *a.* 1) If one has placed an object which is *muktzeh* on the lid of a container *muktzeh on lid of container*
   a) with the intention that it should remain there for the whole of the period from sunset until the stars come out on Friday night **and**
   b) in such a way that the container serves the purposes of the *muktzeh* object and not the reverse, the container becomes a *basis la-davar ha-assur* and remains so, even after the *muktzeh* object has been removed from it (for example by a non-Jew).

2) It is also forbidden to lift the lid in order to take food or any other item out of the container.

b. 1) The actual contents of the container are not, however, considered to be a *basis la-davar ha-assur*.

2) Consequently, they may be taken out and moved if there is a possibility of doing this without removing the lid.

3) This would be the case if, for instance,

   a) the container was a barrel of wine fitted with a tap

   or

   b) the lid, together with the *muktzeh* object, fell off by itself or was removed by a non-Jew.

table serving as basis for candlesticks **59.** *a.* If, at the commencement of Shabbath, a table has on it candlesticks containing burning candles, the table becomes a *basis la-davar ha-assur*.

b. The table may not be moved, even after the candles have gone out and the candlesticks have been removed (for example by a non-Jew), unless, at the commencement of Shabbath, there is also on the table a non-*muktzeh* item of importance which one requires for Shabbath, such as the Shabbath loaves.*

c. At all events, one may eat at the table and use it without moving it from its present position. (See Chapter 22, paragraph 32.)

d. Drawers contained in the table may be opened, closed and used.

e. One may also lengthen or shorten the table, if it is of the expanding kind, by inserting or extracting leaves, or by raising or lowering extension flaps, so long as, in so doing, one does not move that section on which the candlesticks are (or were) standing.

tablecloth serving as basis for candlesticks **60.** *a.* That part of the tablecloth on which the candles stand is also treated as a *basis la-davar ha-assur*.

b. The same applies to the special cloth which some people

---

*The rule for Yom Kippur is dealt with in a subsequent chapter.

are accustomed to place underneath the candlesticks in honor of the Shabbath candles.

c. On the other hand, that part of the tablecloth which is not underneath the candlesticks does not become a *basis la-davar ha-assur* and may be moved.

d. 1) In case of need, one may rely on the opinion that even that part of the tablecloth which is underneath the candlesticks does not become a *basis la-davar ha-assur*.*

2) The result is that the rules set out in paragraph 47*b* above apply, and one may, for example, move the whole tablecloth once the candlesticks have been removed by a non-Jew.

61. a. 1) It is customary to place on the table, before the commencement of Shabbath, the Shabbath loaves or some other item of importance which one needs for Shabbath.

2) In this way, one prevents the candlesticks standing on the table from turning it into a *basis la-davar ha-assur*.

table serving as basis for candlesticks and Shabbath loaves

b. If one does this, the table may be moved, but one should first have the candlesticks removed by a non-Jew or should tilt the table until they fall off.

c. 1) Sometimes it is not practicable to remove the candlesticks, for example where there is no non-Jew available and

a) one is afraid the candlesticks will be damaged if one tilts the table to make them fall off, or

b) the candles are burning and may be extinguished if made to fall off.

2) In those circumstances, the table may be moved with

---

*The grounds for this opinion are either

a. that the cloth serves the purpose not of the candlesticks but of the table, or

b. that one's intention in putting the candlesticks in position is not that they should specifically stand on the cloth, but that the candles should cast their light over the table.

the candlesticks still on it (subject to what is stated below and in paragraph 47 above),

a) even while the candles are still burning and

b) even if the Shabbath loaves have been taken off and the candlesticks are left on the table by themselves.

d. Nevertheless, the table may not be moved while the candlesticks are still on it if one requires neither the table nor the space which it occupies, but wishes to move it only for purposes connected with the candlesticks, for example

1) because one is afraid that in their present position they may be damaged or stolen or

2) because one wishes to make use of the light elsewhere.

candle falling on table

62. For the rules applicable to a burning candle which falls onto the table see Chapter 41, paragraph 17.

candlesticks on tray

63. If, before Shabbath, one has placed on the table a tray containing not only the candlesticks, but also a non-*muktzeh* item of importance that one requires for Shabbath (as in paragraph 59 above), then

a. the tray, with the candlesticks still standing on it,* may be moved when

1) one needs the place occupied by the tray **or**

2) one wants to change or remove the tablecloth, but

b. it is forbidden to move the tray for the purpose of the candlesticks, for instance to prevent them from being damaged or lost.

a drawer as a basis la-davar ha-assur

64. a. A drawer containing a *muktzeh* object is a *basis la-davar ha-assur*, and may not be opened, if all of the prerequisites listed in paragraphs 50 to 56 above are present.

---

*The tray may of course be moved with the candlesticks still on it if it is not practicable for them to be removed. (See paragraphs 47 and 61 above.)

b. The drawer may become a *basis la-davar ha-assur* even if the *muktzeh* object has not been put inside intentionally, as long as that is the place in which it is normally kept.

c. Paragraph 67 below deals with the case of a drawer also containing items which are not *muktzeh* and which are more important to one than the *muktzeh* object.

65. With regard to moving a table whose drawer has become a *basis la-davar ha-assur*, the position is as follows:

a. If the drawer cannot be pulled completely out of the table, it is in effect a subsidiary part of the table, with the result that

   1) the presence of the drawer does not also turn the table into a *basis la-davar ha-assur*,

   2) the table may be moved, should one need it or the place which it occupies (as in paragraph 56 above), and

   3) the drawer alone may not be moved.

b. If the drawer can be pulled completely out of the table, it is considered to have an identity distinct from that of the table, with the result that

   1) the presence of the *muktzeh* drawer makes the table a *basis la-davar ha-assur* and

   2) the table may consequently not be moved, unless, at the beginning of Shabbath, it also had on it an item which is not *muktzeh* and which is more important to one than the *muktzeh* object inside the drawer.

66. *a.* 1) Neither the drawer nor the table becomes a *basis la-davar ha-assur* if the *muktzeh* contents of the drawer are of little consequence, as where they consist of a few low-denomination coins. (See paragraph 54 above.)

   2) In such a case, should one require to do so, one may open and close the drawer and move the table (subject to the conditions set out in paragraph 47*b* above).

b. If the *muktzeh* contents of the drawer are *keilim she-melachtam le-issur*, such as a hammer, a screwdriver or matches,

moving table whose drawer is a basis la-davar ha-assur

muktzeh which makes neither drawer nor table a basis la-davar ha-assur

drawer with keli she-melachto le-issur

1) the drawer may be opened and closed in order to put things in and take them out and
2) the table may be moved if one needs to use it or the place which it occupies.

(See paragraphs 7 and 48 above.)

drawer containing muktzeh and non-muktzeh objects

67. When a drawer containing *muktzeh* objects also has in it non-*muktzeh* objects which are of more importance to one, it is not a *basis la-davar ha-assur* and may be opened and closed. (See paragraphs 47 and 55 above.)

muktzeh lying on non-muktzeh object in drawer

68. *a.* Where a *muktzeh* object is lying in a drawer on top of an object which is not *muktzeh*—not because one particularly wants it to be on the non-*muktzeh* object but because there is not enough room elsewhere in the drawer— one may, in case of need, shake off the *muktzeh* object, in order to take out the non-*muktzeh* object underneath. (See paragraph 52 above.)

b. 1) This is so even when the *muktzeh* object is more important to one than the non-*muktzeh* objects in the drawer.

2) However, in that event the drawer must already be open, since it is a *basis la-davar ha-assur* and one would not be permitted to open it. (See paragraph 64 above.)

use of drawer in table which is basis la-davar ha-assur

69. *a.* Even when a *muktzeh* object is lying on a table in such circumstances that the table is a *basis la-davar ha-assur*, one may use a drawer in it.

b. That is to say, one may take things out and put them in, so long as one does not move the table from its present position. (See paragraph 59 above.)

when pocket is basis la-davar ha-assur

70. *a.* 1) If,

a) before the commencement of Shabbath, one put into one's pocket a *muktzeh* and a non-*muktzeh* object, and

b) the latter has more importance for one than the former,

neither the pocket nor the garment in which it is contained becomes a *basis la-davar ha-assur.*

  2) a) Nonetheless, where possible, one should shake the *muktzeh* object out of the garment before putting it on.

   b) This should be done as described in paragraph 72*b* below.

 b. 1) If the pocket has in it

   a) only a *muktzeh* object or

   b) a *muktzeh* and a non-*muktzeh* object, but the latter does not have more importance for one than the former,

   the pocket becomes a *basis la-davar ha-assur,* provided the various conditions set out in paragraphs 50 to 56 above are fulfilled.

  2) In that event, one may not

   a) move the pocket, **nor**

   b) put anything into it, **nor even**

   c) insert one's hand into it.

  3) It should be noted that this situation is unlikely to arise, due to the circumstances mentioned in paragraph 72*a* below.

71. The following rules apply to the garment itself:

 a. 1) Where the pocket is a patch-pocket,* the whole garment becomes a *basis la-davar ha-assur* (subject to fulfillment of the conditions set out in paragraphs 50 to 56 above) and may not be moved even after the *muktzeh* object has been taken out.

  2) It is worth noting that this situation will not usually arise, as explained in paragraph 72*a* below.

 b. 1) If (as in the case of ordinary trouser pockets and most

when garment with muktzeh in pocket is basis la-davar ha-assur

---

*a. A patch-pocket consists of a piece of cloth sewn onto the garment in such a way that the garment itself constitutes one wall of the pocket.

 b. Shirt and cardigan pockets are usually patch-pockets, and sometimes the top pockets of jackets are as well.

jacket pockets) the pocket is of the type which is sewn around its opening to attach it to the garment and is self-contained in that the garment itself does not constitute one of its walls, the whole garment does not become a *basis la-davar ha-assur* even where, as explained in paragraph 70*b*, the pocket does.

2) Should one wish to wear the garment or move it about, one should first shake it to make the *muktzeh* object drop out by itself—as described in paragraph 72*b* below—but one should not try to achieve this by turning the pocket inside out (if the pocket itself is *muktzeh*).

c. 1) If the pocket containing the *muktzeh* object is the small pocket for loose change one often finds sewn inside a larger pocket, whether or not the larger pocket or the whole garment becomes a *basis la-davar ha-assur* depends on considerations parallel to those set out in *a* and *b* above.

2) Thus, if the small pocket containing the *muktzeh* object shares a wall with the large pocket (as in *a* above) and the large pocket is of the type which hangs inside the garment (as in *b* above), then

a) both pockets may become a *basis la-davar ha-assur*, but

b) the garment as a whole is not *muktzeh*.

finding
muktzeh
object in
one's pocket

72. *a.* 1) Notwithstanding the contents of the last two paragraphs, a person who finds a *muktzeh* object in his pocket on Shabbath need not usually fear that either the pocket or the particular article of clothing has become a *basis la-davar ha-assur*.

2) a) This is because he almost certainly had no intention that the *muktzeh* object should remain in the pocket on Shabbath, but merely forgot to take it out before.

b) In those circumstances, as explained in paragraph 53 above, an article does not become a *basis la-davar ha-assur*.

3) Nevertheless, he should shake the *muktzeh* object out of the garment before wearing it.

b. 1) Whenever possible, he should shake the *muktzeh* object out of his pocket in the place where he happens to be when he discovers it.

2) If he is unable to shake the object out there, for example because

    a) he is afraid that the *muktzeh* object will be lost or damaged **or**

    b) he is wearing the garment and it is unbecoming to take it off and shake it out in front of other people **or**

    c) he is in a place where it is embarrassing to shake out the *muktzeh* object,

he may — if there is an *eiruv* or it is otherwise permissible to transfer objects from one place to another — take the garment, with the *muktzeh* object still in its pocket, and shake it out elsewhere.

73. *a.* A garment bag or portable wardrobe in which a *muktzeh* object, such as a garment made of a combination of wool and linen (as to which see paragraph 37 above) or a camera, is hanging is a *basis la-davar ha-assur* (if the other conditions set out in paragraphs 50 to 56 above are fulfilled). *(garment bags)*

b. It may not be moved unless other, more important items which are not *muktzeh* are also hanging in it.

74. *a.* A *muktzeh* object hanging on the door of a closet (cupboard) or of a house does not make the door a *basis la-davar ha-assur* and it may be opened and closed. *(muktzeh objects hanging on doors)*

b. The reason is that the door is important as an integral part of the closet or the house, so that, in relation to the door, the *muktzeh* object is not regarded as an item of any consequence. (See paragraph 54 above.)

75. *a.* A kitchen cupboard with a range of gas or electric burners on it is *muktzeh* and may not be moved. *(cupboard supporting burners)*

b. Its doors and drawers may, however, be opened and it is
perfectly in order to move its contents.

refrigerator
and oven
doors

76. One may open the door of

a. an electric refrigerator (subject to the restrictions detailed
in Chapter 10, paragraphs 12 and 14) or

b. an oven which is not turned on, and will not be turned on
by the act of opening,

in order to remove or insert food, even if there is a *muktzeh*
object in or on the refrigerator or oven.

car doors and
keys

77. a. 1) It is permissible to open the door of a car in order to
take something out, so long as

a) opening the door does not turn on a light **and**

b) there is an *eiruv* or it is otherwise permissible to
transfer objects out of the car.

2) a) It is even permitted to sit in the car, but

b) it is proper to refrain from doing so, since people
generally regard this as being forbidden and it is
advisable to avoid situations in which one can be
suspected of doing something wrong.

b. 1) An ignition key which is not designed to serve any
other purpose is considered to be a *k^eli she-m^elachto l^e-
issur* and may not be moved, unless one wishes to use
it for a permitted purpose or one needs the space which
it occupies.

2) If, however, it also opens the car door or the baggage
compartment, it is not a *k^eli she-m^elachto l^e-issur* and
may be moved.

3) See also paragraph 83 below.

fruit and
other food

78. a. As mentioned in paragraph 46 above, even food which is
fit to be eaten in its existing state can become a *basis la-
davar ha-assur*.

b. Whether or not it becomes a *basis* is governed by the rules
outlined in paragraphs 50 to 56 above.

c. By way of example, where raw potatoes (which, as
explained in paragraph 28 above, are *muktzeh*) happen to

be on top of fruit in a crate or basket, in the circumstances described in paragraph 52c above, one may, in
case of need, rely on the opinion that the fruit has not
become a *basis la-davar ha-assur.*

79. *a.* 1) Except in the case mentioned immediately below, a *articles*
muktzeh object that a non-Jew places on an article of *belonging to*
his own which is not *muktzeh* does not make the *non-Jews*
article a *basis la-davar ha-assur,* even if it remains
there for the whole of the period between sunset and
the time when the stars come out on Friday night.
2) The article should be treated as described in paragraph 47b above.
b. The exception occurs where the non-Jew puts the
muktzeh object in position for the purposes of a Jew, in
which case the article on which it is placed can indeed
become a *basis la-davar ha-assur.*
c. See also Chapter 22, paragraph 52.

MISCELLANEOUS CASES CONNECTED WITH MUKTZEH

80. *a.* 1) a) An object which is normally, or more often than *moving non-*
not, used for performing activities which are *muktzeh*
permitted on Shabbath, or even *objects*
b) an object which is used with equal frequency
for performing both permitted and prohibited
activities,
may be moved for any purpose whatsoever.
2) This means that it may be moved
a) in order to use it right away,
b) in order to have it ready for use later that same
Shabbath,
c) because one wishes to use the space which it
occupies,
d) because one is afraid it may be spoiled or lost if left
where it is or
e) if one derives pleasure or some benefit from the
very act of moving or handling the object, even

though one cannot be said to be actually using it.

   3) On the other hand, with the exceptions mentioned immediately below, moving such an object for no purpose at all is forbidden.

  b. The following objects are exceptions to this rule and may be moved even without any purpose:

   1) books that one is allowed to read on Shabbath;

   2) food that is ready to be eaten;

   3) clothing and decorative accessories;

   4) according to some authorities, objects which are in common use, such as knives, cups and dishes.

penknives with muktzeh attachments

81. *a.* A penknife sometimes has fixed attachments which may not be used on Shabbath, such as scissors or a nail-file.

  b. Even if one is particular not to use these attachments for any other than their intended purpose, one may move the penknife in order to use its blade.

  c. One must not, however, open those attachments that it is forbidden to use.

key rings with muktzeh attachments

82. *a.* A key ring on which there also hangs a *muktzeh* object, such as a nail clipper, may be used on Shabbath, since additional objects on a key ring are merely of secondary importance.

  b. Nonetheless, one would do well to separate the keys from the *muktzeh* object before Shabbath.

muktzeh keys on a bunch

83. If one has a bunch of keys including a key which is *muktzeh*, such as a key used exclusively for a car's ignition or for operating an elevator (lift), one should extract the *muktzeh* key before Shabbath. (See paragraph 77*b* above.)

notebooks

84. *a.* An empty notebook (exercise book) is *muktzeh*. (See paragraph 5 above.)

  b. Where an exercise book is partly empty, then,

   1) if the written pages are of some importance to one and one sometimes reads them,

    a) it is not prohibited to move the exercise book on

account of the blank pages that it contains, although

b) it is best to refrain from leafing through the unused sheets, whereas,

2) if one attaches no importance whatever to what is written and never reads it, one should not move the exercise book at all.

Chapter 21

Laws of Muktzeh on Yom Tov

general

1. *a.* As mentioned in Chapter 20, paragraph 3, rules concerning *muktzeh* apply both on Shabbath and on Yom Tov.

b. However, in certain respects, the rules imposed by the Rabbis with regard to Yom Tov are stricter than the rules imposed with regard to Shabbath, as will be explained below.

peels and bones fit only for animal consumption, and spoiled items

2. *a.* Although, as we have seen in Chapter 20, paragraph 27, peels and bones which could be fed to an animal are not *muktzeh* on Shabbath, on Yom Tov one should adopt a stricter approach and treat as *muktzeh*

1) peels of this kind which have been separated from fruits or vegetables on Yom Tov and

2) bones of this kind from which the meat has been removed on Yom Tov.

b. Such peels and bones should not be moved on Yom Tov, except

1) in the circumstances where this is permitted in accordance with the rule set out in paragraph 3 below, for example if one needs the space which they occupy on the dining table, **or**

2) in the circumstances described in Chapter 22, paragraph 42, that is to say, where one finds the presence of the peels or bones offensive.

c. 1) Furthermore, food which is fit for human consumption, but spoils on Yom Tov to the extent that it becomes fit only for animals, is *muktzeh*.

2) Indeed, any article which breaks or spoils on Yom Tov and is no longer fit for its original use is *muktzeh*, even if it can be used for another purpose.

3. *a.* 1) One may move a *muktzeh* object on Yom Tov in order to facilitate the consumption of food.

   2) One may not, however, eat the *muktzeh* object itself, nor may one use it, except within the limits set out in Chapter 20, paragraphs 7 to 12 (when the object is a *keli she-melachto le-issur*).

b. By way of illustration,

   1) one may

   a) remove a stone which is *muktzeh* (as mentioned in Chapter 20, paragraph 25) from on top of a container, in order to reach the food inside, and

   b) move a purse used for holding money, in order to take out the key of a locked cupboard or pantry containing food one requires, but

   2) one may not

   a) eat an egg which was laid on Yom Tov,

   b) use the oil remaining in a lamp which was lit in honor of Yom Tov,

   c) crack nuts with a stone which is *muktzeh mei-chamath gufo* or

   d) move something which is *muktzeh* in order to feed it to an animal.

c. A *muktzeh* object which is lying on food in circumstances which make the food a *basis la-davar ha-assur* (as explained in Chapter 20, paragraph 78) may not be moved, even if one wants to move it in order to eat the food.

moving muktzeh objects to facilitate the consumption of food

4. *a.* An article which is used for performing an activity that is forbidden on Shabbath, but permitted on Yom Tov, such as a candle or a paraffin heater, is not *muktzeh* on Yom Tov.

b. It may be moved for any purpose whatsoever, but not for no purpose at all. (See Chapter 20, paragraph 80.)

articles used for activities forbidden on Shabbath but permitted on Yom Tov

5. *a.* The lighting of a "new" fire, including the striking of a match, is prohibited on Yom Tov, as explained in Chapter 13, paragraph 2.

matches

b. Nevertheless, it is the practice to permit the moving of matches on Yom Tov, so long as they are fit to be used for lighting a fire from a flame which is already burning.

small logs   **6.** *a.* Small logs which were not designed or designated for any
contrasted   use and are fit only for firewood may not be moved, except
with paraffin   in order to burn them.
and candles   *b.* By contrast, paraffin and candles, since they are specially made for burning, are treated like matches (in paragraph 5 above) and may be moved for any purpose.

Yom Tov   **7.** *a.* On a Yom Tov which occurs on Shabbath, it is possible to
occurring on   relax the rules of *muktzeh* and apply the same rules as
Shabbath   on any other Shabbath, so that
               1) whatever is allowed on a normal Shabbath is also allowed when Shabbath coincides with Yom Tov, whereas
               2) whatever is forbidden on a normal Shabbath is also forbidden when Shabbath coincides with Yom Tov.
         b. The laws of *muktzeh* that apply on Yom Kippur are those applicable on Shabbath.

Chapter 22

General Principles Relating to Muktzeh
on Shabbath and Yom Tov

1. *a.* An item which was *muktzeh* at the commencement of *the principle*
   Shabbath or Yom Tov remains so for the whole day, even
   after the reason for its being *muktzeh* has ceased to exist.
   (But see the qualification set out in *c* of this paragraph
   and the exception in paragraph 11 below.)

   b. It is irrelevant whether the item was *muktzeh*
   1) due to the application of a halachic prohibition
      forbidding it to be eaten, used in any way or moved or
   2) because its physical state made it unfit to be eaten,
      used or moved.

   c. 1) The principle only applies if the item was *muktzeh,*
      and could not be used at the commencement of
      Shabbath or Yom Tov, as a result of a deliberate act.
      2) If, however, the fact that the item was *muktzeh* at the
      commencement of Shabbath was not due to the
      deliberate act of any person, it ceases to be *muktzeh*
      once the reason for its being so no longer exists, and it
      may then be moved, or even eaten. (See paragraph 6
      below for an example.)

2. *a.* It follows from the above that oil in a lamp which was lit *oil in a lamp*
   before Shabbath may not be moved, even after the flame
   has gone out.

   b. This is because, by kindling the flame before the beginning of Shabbath, one physically rejected the possibility
   of using the oil and put any thought of such use out of
   one's mind, since it would have involved an infringement
   of the prohibition against extinguishing a flame.

wet laundry

3. Laundry which was wet when Shabbath or Yom Tov commenced and was not then fit to be worn (because of the prohibitions referred to in Chapter 15, paragraphs 15 and 17) may not be moved on Shabbath or Yom Tov, even after it has dried out during the course of the day.

broken article which is muktzeh mei-chamath chesron kis

4. If an article which is *muktzeh mei-chamath chesron kis* breaks on Shabbath, and one is no longer particular about using it for a purpose other than the one for which it was intended, it nevertheless remains *muktzeh* and may not be moved. (See Chapter 20, paragraph 24.)

basis la-davar ha-assur

5. An article which is a *basis la-davar ha-assur* at the commencement of Shabbath or Yom Tov remains so for the whole day, even after the *muktzeh* object which it supports has been removed. (See Chapter 20, paragraphs 46 and 53.)

animals

6. *a.* An animal which is alive at the commencement of Shabbath is *muktzeh* because of its inherent state as a live animal and not because of an act performed by any person.

   b. Consequently, if the animal dies on Shabbath, it ceases to be *muktzeh* and one may cut up its carcass to feed to a dog.

   c. 1) As can be seen from Chapter 21, paragraphs 1 and 2, a stricter attitude is taken on Yom Tov to the rules of *muktzeh* than on Shabbath.

   2) Thus, an animal which has died that day should not be handled on Yom Tov, unless it was fatally ill when Yom Tov began.

*fruit from which t*e*rumoth and ma'asroth separated on Shabbath*

7. Although fruit from which t*e*rumoth and ma'asroth have not been separated is *muktzeh* (as explained in Chapter 20, paragraph 31), if one has made the separation on Shabbath without realizing that what one is doing is wrong, the fruit may be eaten, even on the same day. (See also Chapter 11, paragraph 17.)

OBJECTS BECOMING MUKTZEH
AFTER THE COMMENCEMENT OF SHABBATH

8. *a.* An item which was fit to be used at the commencement of   *the principle*
Shabbath, but during the course of Shabbath became
muktzeh, may be moved once the reason for its being
muktzeh has ceased to exist.

  b. As a result, clothes which were dry at the commencement   *wet clothes*
of Shabbath, but became wet (and *muktzeh*) during the
course of Shabbath, may be moved once they have dried
out again. (See Chapter 15, paragraphs 9 to 13 for restrictions on the drying of clothes.)

9. *a.* A table does not become a *basis la-davar ha-assur* merely   *table*
   1) because a *muktzeh* object has fallen onto it on   *supporting*
     Shabbath or even   *muktzeh*
   2) because one has mistakenly placed a *muktzeh* object   *object*
     on it on Shabbath, or a *muktzeh* object has been put
     there by a child or a non-Jew.

  b. In such a case, should one need to use the place occupied
by the *muktzeh* object, one may tilt the table to make the
object drop off.

  c. See further Chapter 20, paragraphs 47 and 53.

10. *a.* If, on Shabbath,   *items*
   1) one decides to keep a particular item for sale **and**   *intended for*
   2) from then on, one is particular not to use it, even for   *sale*
     one's own purposes,
   it becomes *muktzeh mei-chamath chesron kis*. (See
   Chapter 20, paragraph 21.)

  b. If one reverses one's original decision later on the same
Shabbath, the item in question ceases to be *muktzeh mei-
chamath chesron kis*.

OBJECTS WHICH, ON SHABBATH,
BECOME FIT FOR USE

11. *a.* An item which is not fit for use at the commencement of   *the principle*

Shabbath is, nevertheless, not *muktzeh* and may be moved or even eaten if

1) it is clear that it will, during the course of that Shabbath, become fit for use **and**

2) the existing conditions in which the article is unusable are not to the liking of its owner, who, on the contrary, is looking forward to the moment when the article can be used.

b. Where, however, the existing conditions are to the owner's liking at the beginning of Shabbath, such an item is and remains *muktzeh,*

1) even if it is clear that, during the course of the Shabbath, conditions will change and the item will become fit for use and

2) even if the change which will take place later is also to the owner's liking and

3) even after the change has occurred and the item is fit to be used.

c. Similarly, if it is not clear that the item will become fit for use during the course of the Shabbath, it is *muktzeh,* even if

1) the existing conditions are not to its owner's liking and

2) he would like them to change so that the item will become usable.

(In this light, see paragraph 3 above.)

d. The rules stated in this paragraph are illustrated in paragraphs 12 and 13 below.

food cooking on Shabbath

12. a. 1) In certain circumstances, even uncooked food may be left on the fire when Shabbath commences. (See, however, Chapter 1, paragraph 63a.)

2) Although the food was unfit to eat at the commencement of Shabbath, it follows from what is stated in paragraph 11a that the food may be eaten on Shabbath when it is ready.

separation of t^erumoth and ma'asroth

b. 1) As explained in Chapter 20, paragraph 31, food from which *t^erumoth* and *ma'asroth* have yet to be separated is *muktzeh.*

2) From Chapter 11, paragraphs 18 to 23, it can be seen that, where one has made the appropriate stipulation before the beginning of Shabbath or Yom Tov, *terumoth* and *ma'asroth* may, nonetheless, be separated on Shabbath or Yom Tov.

3) When one has made such a stipulation, one may move the food, if one needs to do so, even before one has separated the *terumoth* and *ma'asroth*.

13. *a.* The rule set out in paragraph 11*b* above applies in the case of the lighting of the Shabbath candles.   *candlesticks*

b. Since one wishes the candles to be burning at the commencement of Shabbath, the candlesticks supporting them become a *basis la-davar ha-assur* and may not be moved,

1) even after the candles have gone out,

2) even though one knew the candles would go out after a while, during the course of Shabbath, and

3) even if one wanted the candles to go out afterwards, so that one should be able to sleep.

OBJECTS WHICH, FOR EXTRANEOUS REASONS, MAY NOT BE MOVED

14. *a.* An item which is not in itself *muktzeh*, but which, for some extraneous reason, one is not permitted to move when Shabbath commences, may not be moved on Shabbath even after that reason has ceased to exist, except   *the principle*

1) in case of pressing need **or**

2) if there was a possibility, however remote, of moving the item in a permissible manner at the commencement of Shabbath.

b. 1) If the extraneous reason is bound up with the infringement of a prohibition which is purely Rabbinical (and not a Rabbinical extension of a Torah prohibition), then the item may be moved once that reason has ceased to exist.

2) Consequently, an item which is not itself *muktzeh*, and supports a *muktzeh* object in circumstances which do not make it a *basis la-davar ha-assur*, may be moved once the *muktzeh* object has been taken away, as stated in Chapter 20, paragraph 47*b*1.

candle burning near door

15. It follows from paragraph 14*a* above that a door which one is not allowed to open because there is a burning candle close to it (in the circumstances detailed in Chapter 13, paragraph 33) may be opened—after the candle has gone out—only
   a. in case of pressing need, for instance if one has to do so in order to enter one's apartment, **or**
   b. in the event that when the candle was still burning there existed a possibility, however remote or inconvenient, of opening the door in such a way that the candle would not be extinguished.

refrigerators with interior lighting

16. a. As explained in Chapter 10, paragraph 14, it is forbidden to open the door of a refrigerator if this will automatically result in the turning on of an internal light.
   b. However, it follows from paragraph 14*a*2 above that if the refrigerator is designed in such a way that
      1) the motor ceases to operate from time to time and there is a possibility, during such a break in operation, of disconnecting the electricity supply in the manner and circumstances detailed in Chapter 10, paragraph 14, **or**
      2) one can prevent the bulb from being turned on, by carefully inserting the blade of a knife through the hinge-side of the closed door and holding the switch in a depressed position,
   then it is not forbidden to eat the food inside—even if one has opened the door of the refrigerator on Shabbath in the usual way, without taking these steps, and discovered that the light has come on. (One should consult a qualified rabbinical authority on what to do with regard to closing the door again.)

OBJECTS MISTAKENLY THOUGHT TO BE MUKTZEH

17. *a.* An object which at the commencement of Shabbath one *the principle* has no intention of using, because one erroneously believes it to be *muktzeh*, may be moved or even eaten on Shabbath when one realizes one's mistake.

   b. By way of contrast, an object which at the commencement of Shabbath one intended to use, erroneously believing it not to be *muktzeh*, may not be moved on Shabbath when one realizes one's mistake, even after the reason for the object's being *muktzeh* has ceased to exist.

18. Consequently, if one erroneously believed that fruit in one's *fruit thought* possession was not allowed to be eaten because it was *orla*, *to be orla* and on Shabbath one discovered that the fruit was not *orla* after all, it is not *muktzeh* and may be eaten.

19. *a.* Where a doubt arises as to whether one may eat food into *effect of* which something forbidden has fallen, one should ask the *halachic* opinion of an appropriately qualified rabbi. *ruling on*

   b. Even if the doubt arose before Shabbath and the rabbi's *Shabbath* ruling, permitting the food, was not obtained until Shabbath, one may both move and eat the food on Shabbath.

20. Wet clothes which became dry before Shabbath commenced *clothes* may be worn or moved, even if, at the beginning of *thought to be* Shabbath, one mistakenly thought they were still wet. *wet*

21. It also follows from paragraph 17 above that one is permitted *misunder-* to move an article which one previously decided not to use or *standing the* move because one thought it was *muktzeh*, if, during the *halacha* course of Shabbath, it becomes apparent that one's decision was based on a mistaken view of the *halacha*.

22. *a.* If one has the intention at the beginning of Shabbath *prior intention* to move a *basis la-davar ha-assur*, on the mistaken *to move a* assumption that it is permissible to do so, this intention *basis la-davar* *ha-assur*

does not affect the article's status as a *basis la-davar ha-assur*.

b. It may, therefore, not be moved, even if the *muktzeh* object is removed from it during the course of the day (for example by a non-Jew).

clothes **23.** One may not move newly washed clothes
thought to be   *a.* which one intended to wear on Shabbath, but
dry   *b.* which one finds out were in fact wet when Shabbath commenced and dried out only subsequently.

MAKING IT PROHIBITED FOR AN ARTICLE TO BE MOVED

the principle **24.** *a.* It is forbidden to put an article into a particular position on Shabbath in order that an object which is *muktzeh* should fall into it, thereby making it prohibited for one to move the article.

b. This applies even if the article is itself a *k^eli she-m^elachto l^e-issur* which one wants to position (after using it for a permitted purpose or after moving it because one wished to make use of the place it occupied) where an object that is *muktzeh* to a more stringent degree (such as *muktzeh mei-chamath chesron kis* or *muktzeh mei-chamath gufo*) will fall into it.

c. Covering a *muktzeh* object with an article is permitted, as long as one does not thereby move the *muktzeh* object.

eggs laid on **25.** For example,
Shabbath   *a.* it is forbidden to put a receptacle under a hen on Shabbath so that it should lay an egg into it, but

b. it is permitted to put a vessel over an egg which has already been laid on Shabbath, so long as this does not move the egg.

dripping **26.** *a.* One must not place a tray, plate or other receptacle next
candles   to or under a candle on Shabbath to catch dripping wax, as the wax is *muktzeh*.

b. On the other hand, one may put a receptacle (not containing water) in such a position in order to catch sparks, since they are not of any consequence, and the receptacle may be moved even after they have fallen into it.

27. *a.* It is prohibited to do an act, in relation to an article that is not *muktzeh*, which will result in its no longer being fit for its normal use on Shabbath. *water on clothing or linens*

    b. For example, even where the prohibition referred to in Chapter 15, paragraph 4*a* is inapplicable, it is forbidden to wet articles of clothing or linens if, as a result, they will be unfit for use as such that day.

MUKTZEH MEI-CHAMATH MITZVA

28. Any object which has been set aside for use in the performance of a mitzva, and from which it is forbidden, as a result, to derive benefit, is *muktzeh mei-chamath mitzva* on Shabbath and Yom Tov. *the principle*

29. *a.* By way of illustration, on the days of Yom Tov and Shabbath occurring during Sukkoth, the s^echach and decorations of the *sukka* may not be moved, even after they have fallen from the *sukka*. *s^echach and sukka decorations*

    b. On the intermediate days of Sukkoth, one may move them, but one must not derive benefit from them by

        1) breaking a splinter of wood off the s^echach to pick one's teeth, or

        2) eating fruits with which one decorated the *sukka*, even after they have fallen down.

30. *a.* On a day of Sukkoth which occurs on Shabbath, *lulav,*

        1) it is forbidden to move the *lulav*, the *aravoth* or the *hadassim*, but *aravoth, hadassim*

        2) one may move the *ethrog*, since it is permitted to inhale its scent on Shabbath. *and ethrog*

    b. On the other days of Sukkoth, including the intermediate days, one may not derive benefit from any of the four species by using it for the purpose for which it is principally intended (other than the performance of the mitzva).

1) a) Consequently, one may not on Sukkoth deliberately inhale the scent of a *hadass* which forms part of the *arba'a minim*, since the only benefit one can normally derive from it is to inhale its scent.

   b) The reasoning behind this prohibition is that, by using the *hadass* in the performance of the mitzva, one put out of one's mind all thought of using it to inhale its scent.

2) a) Similarly, one may not on Sukkoth eat an *ethrog* which one uses as part of the *arba'a minim*, even after one has performed the mitzva with it.

   b) The reason is that, by using the *ethrog* in the performance of the mitzva, one put out of one's mind all thought of eating it.

   c) It is also desirable—except on Shabbath—to refrain from deliberately inhaling its scent on Sukkoth (since there is an unresolved difference of opinion among the authorities as to whether one should recite a blessing when doing so).

shofar   **31.** *a.* One should not use a *shofar* on Rosh Hashana for any purpose other than the fulfillment of the mitzva of blowing it.

   b. On Shabbath (including a Shabbath on which Rosh Hashana happens to fall), a *shofar* is treated as a *k^eli she-m^elachto l^e-issur* and may therefore be moved in the circumstances set out in Chapter 20, paragraph 7.

USING, TOUCHING AND MOVING OBJECTS
WHICH ARE MUKTZEH

using and touching without moving   **32.** *a.* Subject to what is stated below an object which is *muktzeh* may not be moved, but may be used in its present position.

[286]

1) One may, for instance, sit on a *muktzeh* object.*
2) One may likewise place articles on a *muktzeh* object. (See further paragraph 38 below.)

b. 1) One is not allowed to use a *muktzeh* object, even without moving it, if, in the process of such use, one performs an act whose direct result is the destruction of the object.
2) An example of such use is burning, on Yom Tov, an object which broke on Yom Tov and is *muktzeh* because it is no longer fit to be used for its original purpose.

c. 1) In general, one may touch a *muktzeh* object, even with one's hand, but only so long as this will not make it move.
2) One may, therefore, not touch a lamp hanging from the ceiling.

33. a. A keli she-melachto le-issur which one has picked up in permissible circumstances, and which is still in one's hand after one has finished using it or moving it out of the way, may be put down wherever one wishes. (See Chapter 20, paragraph 11.) *objects already in one's hand*

1) Thus, if one has picked it up in order to use it for a permitted purpose, one is not obliged to throw it down then and there as soon as one has finished using it.
2) Likewise, if one has removed it in order to use the place it occupied, one need not drop it the moment it reaches a position in which it will no longer be a hindrance.

b. 1) This is not so in the case of
   a) a keli she-melachto le-issur which has come into one's hand in circumstances where this is not allowed (for instance where one has picked it up by mistake and needs neither to use the object itself

---

*It is, however, as well not to do so where there is no need, if sitting on it will cause it to move.

for a permitted purpose nor the place which it occupies), or of

b) a *muktzeh* object of any other category which has come into one's hand in a forbidden manner.

2) In these cases, the *muktzeh* object must be put down right away, unless this would cause one financial loss, in which event one may take it to a safe place (provided there are no other prohibitions involved in doing so) and leave it there.

c. 1) As explained in Chapter 20, paragraph 26, shells, fruit pits (stones) and bones which are not fit to be eaten even by an animal are *muktzeh mei-chamath gufo*.

2) They may, nonetheless, be taken out of one's mouth with one's hand and put on the plate.

d. 1) Similar considerations apply to *t^eruma*, *t^erumath ma'aser* and *challa* which have been separated on Shabbath or Yom Tov (in the permitted ways described in Chapter 11, paragraphs 16 and 18 to 28).

2) Although they too are *muktzeh*, as explained in Chapter 20, paragraph 30, they may be moved in the course of separating and putting them aside.

3) However, once they have been put down, they may not be moved again.

moving an object with one's body

34. a. A *muktzeh* object may be moved with a part of the body which one does not generally use for that purpose on an ordinary weekday.

b. For example, one may move a *muktzeh* object

1) with one's foot,
2) with one's elbow,
3) with the backs of one's hands,
4) with one's arms or
5) by blowing it,

provided these are not the usual methods of moving an object of the kind in question.

c. A *muktzeh* object may be moved in this way even for the purposes of the *muktzeh* object itself.

d. Thus, if one finds money in the street, one may push it

with one's foot into a hiding place from where one will be able to collect it after Shabbath (but, if there is no *eiruv*, one should push it only for a distance of less than four *amoth* and then let a friend push it for a like distance, after which a third friend can do the same, and so on, each person only moving the object over a distance of less than four *amoth*, until it reaches its destination).

35. a. A *muktzeh* object may also be moved, subject to the limitation stated in *b* below, if one does so by means of another article which one holds in one's hands, so that one's hands do not come into direct contact with the *muktzeh* object.
moving an object with something held in the hand

b. A *muktzeh* object may be moved in this way only for the purposes of another article which is not *muktzeh*.

c. It may not be moved in this way for the purposes of an article which is *muktzeh*, for example in order to prevent the *muktzeh* object itself from being lost or stolen, or because one needs it elsewhere.

36. a. It follows from the above that bones, shells and the like, although they are not fit for consumption even by animals, may be cleared off a table which one requires to be clean
removing inedible bones, shells, etc., from the table

 1) by sweeping them off with a knife or with a dry cloth or brush or

 2) by shaking out the tablecloth on which they are lying.

b. Similarly, one may sweep the floor of a room one is using, even if, in the act of sweeping, one will move an object which is *muktzeh*. (See, however, Chapter 23, paragraphs 1 and 2.)

c. If one finds the litter of bones or shells on a table offensive, one may remove them

 1) even with one's hands and

 2) even if one does not need to use the clean table,

in accordance with the principles set out in paragraph 42 below.

[289]

  d. On Yom Tov, bones and shells may be removed from the
   table,
   1) even if they are inedible to animals as well as to
    human beings,
   2) even if one does not find their presence offensive and
   3) even with one's hands,
   so long as one requires the table to be cleared for the Yom
   Tov meal. (See Chapter 21, paragraph 3.)

candlesticks **37.** *a.* 1) A table with candlesticks standing on it is not a *basis*
on a table   *la-davar ha-assur* if the Shabbath loaves were also on
    the table when Shabbath began, or if any of the
    conditions stated in Chapter 20, paragraphs 50 to 56 is
    unfulfilled.
   2) In that case, following the rules set out in Chapter 20,
    paragraph 47*b*, the table may be moved while the
    candlesticks are still on it, if in fact
    a) one needs the place occupied by the table, or needs
     to use the table itself elsewhere, and
    b) one cannot first tilt the table to make the candle-
     sticks fall off, for fear that they will be damaged.
   3) The reason why this is permitted is that one is moving
    muktzeh objects (the candlesticks) by means of
    another article (the table) which one holds in one's
    hands, for the purposes of something (the floor or the
    table, as the case may be) which is not *muktzeh*.
  b. 1) It is forbidden to pull or push the table with one's
    hands for the purposes of the candlesticks, for example
    in order to avoid the risk of their being stolen or
    damaged.
   2) The reason why this is forbidden is that one would
    thereby be moving the candlesticks with an article
    held in one's hands (the table) for the purposes of
    something which is *muktzeh* (namely the candlesticks
    themselves).
  c. One may move the table with the candlesticks still on it,
   even for the purposes of the candlesticks, if one does so
   with one's foot, one's body, or any other part of the

anatomy one would not normally use, as explained in paragraph 34 above.

38. *a.* 1) One may take an article that is not *muktzeh* off an object which is *muktzeh*, even if this will cause the *muktzeh* object to move.

taking things off a muktzeh object or putting them on

2) One may not, however, touch the *muktzeh* object itself if this will make it move, as explained in paragraph 32 above.

b. 1) One may put an article on a *muktzeh* object, even if this will cause the *muktzeh* object to move, so long as one does so for the purposes of something which is not *muktzeh*.

2) One must not put the article there for the purposes of the *muktzeh* object.

39. A further example of the rule stated in paragraph 35 above is that one is not permitted to push a *muktzeh* object with a broom or a similar article to a place where it will be secure until one can take it after Shabbath.

sweeping a muktzeh object to a place of safety

40. *a.* 1) As a rule, a person should not pick up a child who is holding a stone or some other *muktzeh* object in his hand.

holding a child with a muktzeh object in his hand

2) The child should first put the *muktzeh* object down, without the adult's touching the object.

b. Only if it is obvious that the child is extremely anxious to be picked up, and must be pacified to stop him from screaming, may one pick up the child and carry him while the *muktzeh* object is in his hand and, even then, only

1) when the *muktzeh* object is of no value **and**

2) in a place where there is an *eiruv* or where it is otherwise permissible to carry objects about.

c. While a child is holding a *muktzeh* object, one is allowed to hold his hand (without picking him up), provided the object has no value.

d. 1) If the *muktzeh* object which the child is holding has some value, one may neither lift him up nor hold his hand, even when he is extremely anxious that one should do so.

2) This is because there is a risk that one will pick up the *muktzeh* object should it drop out of the child's hand.

telling a non-Jew to move a muktzeh object

41. *a.* One may ask a non-Jew to move a *k^eli she-m^elachto l^e-issur*, even if one's sole purpose is to prevent it from being spoiled or stolen.

b. One may ask a non-Jew to move other categories of *muktzeh* objects only

1) if one needs to use the *muktzeh* object or requires the place which it occupies **or**

2) in order to avoid a serious loss.

MATTER OF A REPULSIVE NATURE

the principle

42. *a.* Anything which one finds offensive because of its repulsive nature may be removed on Shabbath, even with one's hand—despite the fact that it is *muktzeh*—from a place where it disturbs one and thrown in the garbage or down the toilet.

b. Instances of items which could fall within this category are excrement, refuse, bones (including those which are not fit even for animal consumption), a dead mouse and the carcass of a cat.

c. Items of this kind may be removed not only from the house, but also if they are, for example,

1) in such a position in the street* that they disturb passers-by, or

2) in a place where their smell is a nuisance to people in the vicinity.

dirty pots

43. A dirty pot, even if it is a *k^eli she-m^elachto l^e-issur* (see Chapter 20, paragraph 15), may be taken back from the dining room to the kitchen after it has been emptied.

---

*in a place where there is an *eiruv*.

44. Garbage pails and chamber-pots made of metal or synthetic materials are not *muktzeh* after they have been washed. *clean garbage pails, etc.*

45. *a.* 1) A chamber-pot may be emptied after use.
  2) A domestic garbage pail may be emptied if
    a) it is hard to bear the smell given off by it **or**
    b) it is full to the top and one has no other garbage pail one could use.
emptying garbage pails and chamber-pots

b. 1) If the chamber-pot or garbage pail is made of material other than metal or plastic, one should not bring it back to its place after emptying—even if it is clean—unless
    a) one is still holding it in one's hand **or**
    b) one puts into it water which is fit to be drunk at least by an animal.
  2) Even then, one should not bring it back if
    a) it is safe in the place to which it has been taken **and**
    b) one does not need to use it again.

ARTICLES WHICH NOT EVERYBODY WOULD USE

46. *a.* 1) An article which is fit to be used on Shabbath is nonetheless *muktzeh* if it is not worth very much and is considered valueless by its well-to-do owner, who would not normally use it at all.
  2) This is despite the fact that someone less well-off would make use of it.
articles whose well-to-do owner would not use them

b. An example is a piece of a broken object which, although still usable, was thrown away by its owner before Shabbath.

c. Such an article is *muktzeh* even for persons who are not as well-to-do as its owner and still consider it to have some value.

47. *a.* An article which is not worth very much, but is fit to be used on Shabbath, is not *muktzeh* if it has some value in the eyes of its owner, despite the fact that a richer person would not use it.
articles of one person which another, richer person would not use

   b. The article is, however, treated as *muktzeh* for such a
   richer person, unless he happens to be a member of the
   owner's household.

articles **48.** *a.* 1) Something which its owner considers to be of value,
whose owner   but which he would not use because it is prohibited to
is not   him personally, is not *muktzeh*.
allowed to   2) It may be moved by anyone, since it is fit to be used by
use them   other people.
        b. Examples of things of this kind which are not *muktzeh*
            are
            1) articles from which their owner has vowed not to
               derive any personal benefit and
            2) undefiled *t^eruma* owned by a person who is not a
               kohen, at a period in time when the laws of purity and
               defilement are observed.
            (See Chapter 20, paragraph 34.)

MUKTZEH OBJECTS BELONGING TO A NON-JEW

objects not **49.** An item which is *muktzeh* because it was not prepared for
ready for use   use before Shabbath, and was not fit for use by a Jew when
at com-   Shabbath commenced, is *muktzeh*,
mencement   *a.* even if it belongs to a non-Jew **and**
of Shabbath   *b.* even if it is fit, or has become fit, for use by the non-Jew.

milk, fruit, **50.** Consequently, the following items are all *muktzeh*:
stones and   *a.* milk which has been milked from the cow on Shabbath,
sand   even by a non-Jew for his own use;
               b. fruit which fell off the tree on Shabbath, even if it belongs
                   to a non-Jew;
               c. fruit which was picked from the tree on Shabbath, even
                   by a non-Jew for his own use;
               d. stones and sand, even in the possession of a non-Jew. (See
                   Chapter 20, paragraph 25.)

intention not
to move object **51.** *a.* On the other hand, an item which, if it belonged to a Jew,
on Shabbath   would be *muktzeh* because its owner put all thought of

[294]

moving it on Shabbath out of his mind (due to the possible involvement of a prohibition) is not *muktzeh* if it belongs to a non-Jew.

b. In the same way, an item intended for sale (see Chapter 20, paragraph 21) by its non-Jewish owner is not *muktzeh*.

52. *a.* Likewise, a table belonging to a non-Jew, on which he put *basis* a *muktzeh* object at the commencement of Shabbath (not *la-davar* for a Jew), may be moved by a Jew *ha-assur*
   1) once the non-Jew has removed the *muktzeh* object from it or
   2) once the Jew has removed it, for instance
      a) in a manner, and with a part of the body, which he would not normally use for that purpose (as to which see paragraph 34 above) or
      b) by means of another article held in his hand (as to which see paragraph 35 above).

   b. 1) This is not the case if the non-Jew put the *muktzeh* object there for the Jew.
   2) For example, if he put his own candlestick on his own table to provide light for the Jew, the table is *muktzeh* and remains so, even after the candlestick has been removed.

53. *a.* 1) Similarly, merchandise which a non-Jewish shop- *goods* keeper takes from his stock, and whose use is a *intended for* permitted one, may be moved and used by a Jew. *sale*
   2) This is so in spite of the fact that the owner of the merchandise is particular not to use it even for his own purposes.

   b. Still, the Jew must be careful not to infringe the prohibitions connected with buying and selling explained in Chapter 29, paragraph 17.

54. *a.* Food which a Jew is not permitted to eat and from which *forbidden* *food and* he is forbidden to derive benefit, such as *chametz* on *clothing*

Passover or fruit which is *orla*, is *muktzeh* even if it belongs to a non-Jew.

b. 1) However, food which a Jew is not permitted to eat but from which he is allowed to derive benefit is not *muktzeh*.

   2) Examples are

      a) cooked meat that belongs to a non-Jew and does not comply with the halachic requirements for consumption by a Jew and

      b) fruit of a non-Jew which still needs to have *t^erumoth* and *ma'asroth* separated from it.

   3) Likewise, the clothing of a non-Jew which contains a combination of wool and linen, and any other item which a Jew is not permitted to use for its normal purpose, but from which he is allowed to derive benefit, is not *muktzeh*.

A NOTE ON THINGS WHICH ARE MADE, OR CHANGE IN FORM,
ON SHABBATH OR YOM TOV

general nature of prohibitions involved

55. a. In certain circumstances, articles or substances which have been brought into existence or have changed in nature or form on Shabbath or Yom Tov may not be moved.

   b. Sometimes it is forbidden to do an act on Shabbath or Yom Tov which creates something new or changes the nature or form of an article or substance.

   c. The laws relating to these two prohibitions are too intricate for inclusion here, and, whenever a situation which may give rise to them occurs, a competent halachic authority should be consulted.

Glossary

(Please note: This Glossary is not intended to give an exhaustive and precise definition of each expression which it contains. It is designed merely to help the reader obtain a *general* idea of the meaning of unfamiliar words he may find in the text. Its use for any other purpose may well be misleading.)

amah (plural *amoth*): A measure of length, 22.7 inches (57.6 centimeters) by one halachic view, 18.9 inches (48 centimeters) by another. In any given instance involving this measure, that view is followed which makes for greater stringency.

aravoth: Willow twigs, used on Sukkoth.

arba kanfoth: A four-cornered garment with a prescribed tassel (*tzitzith*) at each corner, worn to fulfill the biblical injuction to wear fringes on the corners of one's garment.

arba'a minim: Collective name for *ethrog, lulav, hadassim* and *aravoth*.

basis la-davar ha-assur: An article which the Halacha subjects to the same restrictions on handling as a *muktzeh* object that has been placed or hung on it.

carmᵉlith: An area which is not *rᵉshuth ha-rabbim*, but to which the Rabbis applied rules similar to those applying to *rᵉshuth ha-rabbim*.

challa: A proportion of the dough which has to be removed once it is kneaded and which, in Temple times, was given to a *kohen*.

chametz: Food which is made from, or contains, flour and which is leavened. It may not be eaten or kept on Passover.

Chanuka: The Feast of Lights.

charoseth: A mixture of nuts, wine, cinnamon and apples eaten on Passover night.

cholent: A stew, normally containing meat, potatoes, barley and beans, put on the fire before the commencement of Shabbath and left there all night, so that one should be able to have a hot meal during the day.

day: Unless otherwise indicated, or inconsistent with the context, a day, for the purposes of Jewish Law, is regarded as commencing and terminating at what can colloquially be called nightfall.

dreidle: A spinning-top used for playing a Chanuka game.

eiruv: An abbreviation for *eiruv tavshilin* or for *eiruv chatzeiroth*; often used as a general term including both *eiruv chatzeiroth* and *shitufei m^evo'oth*.

eiruv chatzeiroth: The arrangement for permitting the transfer of objects on Shabbath from one *r^eshuth ha-yachid* to another, or within a *r^eshuth ha-yachid* which belongs to two or more adjoining occupiers in common. The expression is often used as a general term including also *shitufei m^evo'oth*.

eiruv tavshilin: The arrangement whereby one is permitted on Yom Tov to make preparations for Shabbath occurring on the following day; also, the food set aside before Yom Tov for this purpose.

ethrog (plural *ethrogim*): Citron, used on Sukkoth.

hadass (plural *hadassim*): Myrtle twig, used on Sukkoth.

Halacha (adjective: halachic): Jewish religious law.

k^eli rishon: The pot or other vessel in which food has been cooked, so long as it retains a temperature of 45 degrees centigrade (113 degrees Fahrenheit) or more, even if it is no longer on the fire.

k^eli sheini: A pot or other vessel into which food is transferred from the vessel in which it was cooked.

k^eli sh^elishi: A pot or other vessel into which food is transferred from a *k^eli sheini*.

k^eli she-m^elachto l^e-issur (plural *keilim she-m^elachtam l^e-issur*): An object which is *muktzeh* because it is used for performing an activity that is forbidden on Shabbath.

kiddush: The blessings recited in sanctification of Shabbath and Yom Tov; often colloquially used for a snack which follows.

kil'ei kerem: Produce which grows from seeds sown within a given distance of vines; the grapes which subsequently grow on those vines.

kohen (plural *kohanim*): A priestly descendant of Aaron, the High Priest.

lechem mishneh: Two whole loaves with which one begins each Shabbath meal.

lulav: Palm branch, used on Sukkoth.

ma'aser sheini: The Second Tithe removed from food grown in what Jewish religious law regards as the Land of Israel. At the time when the Temple stood, it was eaten in Jerusalem; today, one must redeem it in the prescribed manner and may then eat it anywhere.

ma'asroth: The various tithes removed from food grown in what Jewish religious law regards as the Land of Israel.

matza (plural matzoth): Unleavened bread.

mikveh: A ritual bath complying strictly with the requirements of Jewish religious law.

mitzva (plural mitzvoth): A religious obligation or duty.

muktzeh: A term describing objects whose handling is subject to restrictions of various kinds on Shabbath and Yom Tov.

muktzeh mei-chamath chesron kis: Denotes an object, having an appreciable value, which is *muktzeh* because its owner is particular not to use it for other than its intended purpose, lest it be damaged. In most cases, the object's intended use is one that is forbidden on Shabbath.

muktzeh mei-chamath gufo: Denotes an object which is *muktzeh* because it is neither designed nor designated for any use, and is not fit for either human or animal consumption.

muktzeh mei-chamath mitzva: An object which has been set aside for use in the performance of a *mitzva*, and from which it is forbidden, as a result, to derive a benefit.

orla: Fruit which grows on a tree in the first three years after planting.

parve: Refers to food which contains neither meat nor dairy products; also, to a utensil which is used exclusively for food which is neither meat nor dairy.

Pesach: Passover.

reshuth (plural reshuyoth): A term used to denote one of the four categories of place: reshuth ha-yachid, reshuth ha-rabbim, carmelith and mekom petur.

reshuth ha-rabbim: A public thoroughfare meeting criteria laid down by Jewish religious law; such an area is subject to restrictions with regard to the moving of objects into, out of or within it.

reshuth ha-yachid (plural reshuyoth ha-yachid): A place which is enclosed in a manner complying with Jewish religious law, and within which one may carry, but which is subject to restrictions with regard to the moving of objects into and out of it.

Rosh Hashana: New Year.

sechach: The roofing material of a *sukka*.

sefer Torah: A scroll containing the Pentateuch.

sha'atnez: A combination of wool and linen.

shitufei m^evo'oth: The arrangement by which it becomes permissible to transfer objects in, to or from the street on Shabbath.

shofar: Horn blown on Rosh Hashana.

Simchath Torah: The Festival of the Rejoicing of the Law.

siyata di-Shmaya: Help from Heaven.

sukka: The booth in which one resides during Sukkoth.

Sukkoth: The Festival of Tabernacles.

tachshit (plural *tachshitim*): An ornament, or an object which is not an article of clothing but is worn for the purposes of the body.

tallith (plural *tallitoth*): A prayer shawl.

tefach (plural *t^efachim*): A measure of length, 3.8 inches (9.6 centimeters) by one halachic view, 3.15 inches (8 centimeters) by another. In any given instance involving this measure, that view is followed which makes for greater stringency.

t^efillin: Phylacteries.

t^eruma (plural *t^erumoth*): That part which is initially removed from food grown in what the Halacha regards as the Land of Israel, and which, in Temple times, was given to a *kohen*. The plural form, *t^erumoth*, is often used to denote *t^eruma* and *t^erumath ma'aser*.

t^erumath ma'aser: A tenth part which is removed from the tithe designated for the Levite out of food grown in what the Halacha regards as the Land of Israel, and which, in Temple times, was given to a *kohen*.

tzitzith: Fringes which Jewish law requires to be worn on the four corners of a garment.

Yom Tov: The first and last days of the Festivals of Passover and Tabernacles (that is to say including the Eighth Day of Solemn Assembly and the Rejoicing of the Law), the Festival of Weeks and the two days of New Year. The rules which apply to the Day of Atonement are by and large those which apply to Shabbath and not those which apply to Yom Tov.

yom tov sheini shel galuyoth: The second and eighth days of Passover, the second day of Tabernacles, the day after the Eighth Day of Solemn Assembly (known as the Rejoicing of the Law) and the second day of the Festival of Weeks, which have to be observed as Yom Tov by Jews living outside the boundaries of the Land of Israel.

Index

(YT) denotes an entry relating specifically to the laws of Yom Tov.

Index

Baking (*continued*)
  shaping dough, 11:13 (YT)
Balcony, carrying objects on, 17:2
Ball
  games, playing, 16:6
  inflatable, playing with, 16:8
  in a tree, dislodging, 16:7
Banana
  mashed
  —adding lemon juice to, 8:14
  —dividing into small portions, 6:12
  mashing, 6:8; 7:2 (YT); 8:3
  peeling, 3:31
  picking off a bunch, 3:42
  spreading on bread, 6:7
Bandages. *See* Wound
Bank-notes, moving, 20:20
Banquets, selecting food for, 3:63
Basis la-davar ha-assur, 20:46-79
  general definition, 20:46
  intention before Shabbath to move,
    22:22
  moving contents of, 20:58
  prerequisites for, 20:50-56
  status after *muktzeh* object removed,
    20:46; 22:5
  See also Muktzeh
Bathing
  in sea or pool, 14:12
  in therapeutic hot spring, 14:6, 10 (YT)
  See also Washing
Bath salts, adding to water, 14:14
Beads, threading onto cord, 16:21
Beans (uncooked)
  moving, 20:28
  removing from pods, 3:32; 4:13 (YT)
  soaking to find maggots, 4:5 (YT)
Beard, extracting food remains from,
    14:42
Bell, ringing, 16:2, 17
Belt
  going out wearing, 18:29
  inserting into loops, 15:62
  using handkerchief for, 18:47
Belt, rupture or surgical: going out
    wearing, 18:20
Betting, 16:37
Bicycle riding, 16:17
Bifocals. *See* Eyeglasses
Binoculars, using, 16:45
Biscuits. *See* Cookies
Bittul kᵉli mei-heichano, 22:24-27
Bleach, soaking diapers in, 15:4
Blemish, going out with dressing over, 18:19

Blocks, building: playing with, 16:18
Blowing soap bubbles, 16:30
Boat, boarding, 16:38
Boiler. *See* Water heater
Boiling. *See* Cooking
Bones
  moving, 20:26, 27; 21:2 (YT)
  removing from mouth, 20:26; 22:33
  removing from table, 22:36
  separating from food, 3:11-14
  See also Garbage
Boning (fish or meat), 3:11, 12, 13
Books
  moving, 20:80
  rearranging detached pages of, 3:84
  replacing on shelf, 3:81
  selecting from bookcase, 3:69
Boots. *See* Galoshes; Shoes
Bottle caps, 9:17
Bottles
  baby. *See* Baby bottle
  of drink
  —cooling with ice, 10:1
  —selecting from refrigerator, 3:74
  opening, 9:1, 7, 11, 12, 17, 20, 22 (YT).
    See also Opening containers
  plastic, opening sealed, 9:7
Boxes, opening
  by removing gummed paper or tape,
    9:10
  if tied with string, 9:14
  See also Opening containers
Bracelets
  going out wearing, 18:24
  with key attached, 18:26
Braces. *See* Suspenders
Braces (dental), wearing, 18:2
Braiding
  hair, 14:52
  material, 16:36
Bread
  crumbling, 6:11; 7:5 (YT)
  cutting or breaking lettering, 11:8
  putting in soup, 1:59; 5:9
  slicing by machine, 6:11
  spreading foodstuffs on, 6:7, 9; 11:33
  using in *eiruv tavshilin*, 2:10, 13
  toasting, 1:62
  See also Dipping; Frying; Squeezing
Bread label, removal of, 3:31
Brine, pouring off from pickled foods, 3:19
Broken object
  burning a, 22:32 (YT)
  moving a, 20:24, 41, 42; 22:4, 46

Index

Index

Cupboard
  door, *muktzeh* object hanging on, 20:74
  heavy, moving and using, 20:22
  supporting range of burners, moving
    and using, 20:75
Cupple. See Yarmulke
Cups and saucers. *See* Dishes
Curds, separation from whey, 3:20
Curling hair, 14:53
Cushions. *See* Pillows
Cutlery
  arranging on table, 3:79
  mashing with, 6:8, 10, 11, 13, 14
  polishing, 12:24
  selecting with aid of, 3:45
  sorting, 3:78, 80; 12:34
  straightening bent, 12:27
  washing. *See* Dishes
Cutting
  cartons of toilet paper, 9:8
  cheese, 6:14
  food, 11:7-10, 12, 15
  fruits, 5:12; 6:6; 11:12
  hair, 14:41
  knotted cord, lace or ribbon, 15:54
  into letters or designs on food, 11:7-10
  nails, 14:54, 55
  packets along marked line, 9:4
  into peels, 11:15; 16:27
  string
    —of dried fruit, 9:15
    —tied around parcel, 9:14
  thread used to sew up stuffing, 11:36
  vegetables, 6:6; 11:12

Dancing, 16:42
Dandruff, removing loose, 14:43
Dates, removing from a cluster, 3:42
Decals, using, 16:29
Defrosting frozen food, 10:10
Defrosting tray, emptying, 10:11
Dental plate, going out with, 18:2
Designs
  on food, making or breaking, 11:7-15
  on ground, drawing, 16:40
  on seal or wrapping, tearing, 9:12
  on windowpane, drawing, 16:27
Developing film, 16:26
Diapers
  disposable, 15:4
  —with adhesive strip, 15:81
  hanging up to dry, 15:12
  moving when wet, 15:15
  removing excrement from, 15:4

soaking wet or soiled, 15:4
sorting, 3:2
taking off clothesline, 15:18
Dice games, playing, 16:33
Dipping baked food into liquid, 5:9; 8:22
Dirt on garment. *See* Cleaning clothes
Dishes
  dissolving grease on, 12:8
  drying, 12:21
  moving Passover dishes, 20:22
  moving without a purpose, 20:80
  placing dirty dishes in water, 12:2, 3, 8
  sorting, 12:23, 34
  washing, 12:1-20
  —general rules, 12:1
  —heating water for, 12:4 (YT)
  —while wearing rubber gloves, 12:13
  —with bristle-brush-topped liquid-
    soap container, 12:14
  —with dish-washing paste or soap,
    12:5, 6, 7, 14
  —with pot-scourer, 12:10
  —with rubber-bladed scraper, 12:13
  —with scouring powder, 12:9
  —with sponge, 12:11
  —with wet cloth, 12:11
Dish towel
  drying after use, 12:22
  using, 12:21
Dishwasher, use of, 12:35
Disinfectant
  soaking diapers in, 15:4
  soaking fruits or vegetables in, 3:21
Dissolving
  cleaning materials other than soap,
    12:5
  congealed fat or sauce, 1:37
  grease on dirty dishes, 12:8
  ice, 10:1, 2, 3
  ice cream, 10:8
  soap, 12:6
Doctor
  going out with name-tag pinned on,
    18:25
  going out with white coat over clothes,
    18:5
Documents, moving, 20:20
Dog. *See* Animal
Dominoes, playing, 16:34
Door
  moving when off hinges, 20:43
  opening and closing
  —near burning candle, 13:33; 22:15
  —of car, 20:77

Exercise book. *See* Notebook
Exercises, performing physical, 14:38;
  16:39
Extinguishing. *See* Fire
Extracting one item from another. *See*
  Selecting
Eyeglasses
  cleaning, 15:31
  going out wearing, 18:16, 18
  —dark, for medical reasons, 18:18
  —with photogrey lenses, 18:18n
  —reading, 18:16
  repairing, 15:77

Face cloth, washing oneself with, 14:13
Face cream, applying, 14:60
False teeth. *See* Teeth, false
Fan
  electric, using, 13:34, 35
  ventilating refrigerator, 10:14
Farina. *See* Cereal
Fat, melting congealed, 1:37
Feather in hatband, going out with, 18:25
Feeding plate, child's
  attaching to table, 11:41
  warming food with boiling water in,
    1:50
Filing nails, 14:54
Film, developing or making prints, 16:26
Filtering dishwater in sink, 12:16
Fingernails
  cleaning, 14:56
  cutting, trimming or filing, 14:54, 55
  polishing, 14:57
  removing polish, 14:61
Fire
  covered, using, 1:4, 16, 18-23, 32, 33
  covering on Shabbath, 1:18n
  extinguishing
  —general rules, 13:1, 8 (YT), 9 (YT)
  —by letting water boil over, 13:13 (YT)
  flame extinguished, what to do, 1:23,
    28; 13:14 (YT)
  lighting, 13:1, 2-5 (YT)
  lowering flame, 13:1, 9 (YT), 10 (YT)
  raising flame, 13:3 (YT), 5 (YT), 17 (YT)
  uncovered, using, 1:63
  See also Candle; Gas; Paraffin; Pots;
    Smoking; Timer
Firewood, moving, 21:6 (YT)
Fish
  boning, 3:11-13
  chopping, 6:14; 7:6 (YT)

eating "gefilte" (stuffed), 3:15
salted
  —putting into vinegar, 11:3
  —washing to remove salt, 11:4
selecting from mixture of boiled and
    fried, 3:64
selecting from mixture of same variety,
    3:24
"Five-stones," playing, 16:11
Flame. *See* Fire
Flavoring with juice, 5:7; 8:14, 15; 11:38
Flour
  measuring quantity of, 11:28 (YT), 29,
    30 (YT)
  moving, 20:28
  sifting, 4:1 (YT), 12 (YT)
Flute, 16:2
Focusing binoculars, 16:45
Fodder, cutting or trimming, 11:15
Folding
  cloth, 15:44, 45, 46
  clothes, 15:41, 44-47
  paper
  —table napkins, 11:40
  —to make toy, 16:19
Food
  coloring, 11:38
  eating
  —if cooked during Shabbath, 22:12
  —if halachic ruling concerning it
      obtained on Shabbath, 22:19
  —if *t*e*rumoth* and *ma'asroth* wrongly
      taken on Shabbath, 11:17; 22:7
  extracting remains from beard, 14:42
  freezing, 10:4-7, 10
  measuring, 11:29, 30 (YT)
  mixing hot and cold, 1:58
  moving, 20:80
  —if intended for sale, 20:21
  —if one cannot eat it, 11:19; 20:27-35;
      22:12, 33, 54
  —if spoiled on Yom Tov, 21:2 (YT)
  —if *t*e*rumoth*, *ma'asroth* or *challa* not
      yet separated, 11:16; 20:31; 22:12,
      54
  —if thrown into garbage, 20:27
  —if underneath *muktzeh* object, 20:46,
      78
  moving *muktzeh* object to facilitate
      consumption of, 21:3 (YT)
  separating *challa*, 11:16-27, 28 (YT)
  separating *t*e*rumoth* and *ma'asroth*,
      11:16-20, 22-27
  uncooked, leaving on fire, 1:63; 22:12

Index

Going out with (*continued*)
  buttonhole torn, 18:43
  button loose, 15:69; 18:40
  button missing, 18:43
  cane, 18:13, 23; 19:5 (YT)
  coat
  —with attached hood, 18:31
  —with detachable lining, 15:74
  —over one's shoulders, 18:4
  contact lenses, 18:17
  cuff links, 18:29
  decorative buttons, ribbons or fringes
    on garment, 18:28
  a dental plate, 18:2
  "dog-tags," military, 18:22
  a dressing over wound or blemish, 18:19
  earmuffs, 18:4
  eyeglasses, 18:16, 18
  false teeth, 18:2, 15
  food in one's mouth, 18:2
  galoshes, 18:10
  garment to protect clothes from dust or
    rain, 18:9, 10
  gartel, 18:5
  garters, 18:29
  hairpins, 18:8
  hair ribbons, 18:8
  handkerchief, 18:2, 10, 19, 25, 32, 47,
    53; 19:3 (YT)
  identification disc, 18:22
  identification papers, 18:22
  identification tag, 18:25, 44
  insoles, 18:21
  jewelry, 18:12, 23, 24, 26, 27, 42, 48
  key, 18:26, 48, 49
  label or tag in clothing, 18:44
  name-tag, 18:25
  necklace, 18:24
  necktie, 18:29
  one garment over another, 18:5
  ornament, 18:12, 23-28, 42, 48;
    19:3 (YT)
  orthopedic supports, 18:21
  paper tucked in hat to adjust fit, 18:21
  purse, 18:23
  raincoat
  —with detachable lining, 15:74
  —over other coat, 18:10
  —with zipper or buttons for attaching
    lining, 18:31
  rain-hood, 18:10
  reading glasses, 18:16
  rings, 18:24
  rupture belt, 18:20

  safety-pin, 18:29
  sanitary napkin (towel), 18:20
  scarf, 18:7, 10, 29
  shirt-collar stiffeners, 18:29
  spare button on garment, 18:30
  sunglasses, 18:18
  tachshit, 18:11, 12, 24. *See also*
    individual items
  tallith, 18:6, 38
  —with broken chain, 18:41
  torn cord, loop or ribbon, 18:41, 43
  tzitzith, 18:34-38
  walking-stick, 18:13, 23; 19:5 (YT)
  watch, 18:26, 27
  white coat over clothing, 18:5
  wig, 18:7
  yarmulke secured by clip or hairpin,
    18:29
  See also Carrying; Transfer of objects;
    and individual items
Grapefruit
  cutting in half, 5:12
  eating, 5:12
  See also Fruit; Juice; Peeling;
    Squeezing
Grapes
  juice which ran out of, 5:11; 20:32
  removing from cluster, 3:22, 42
  squeezing, 5:4
  sucking, 5:10
  See also Fruit
Grater, using, 6:2, 11; 7:3 (YT), 4 (YT)
Grating, 6:2, 6, 11; 7:1 (YT), 3 (YT), 4 (YT),
    6 (YT). *See also* Grinding
Gravy, pouring on potatoes, 8:19
  See also Fat, melting congealed
Grease, removing. *See* Dishes
Greasing baking tins, 11:34 (YT)
Grinding, Chapters 6; 7 (YT)
  cooked fruits or vegetables, 6:9
  food which does not grow from the
    ground, 6:5, 14; 7:1 (YT), 6 (YT)
  food which grows from the ground, 6:5-
    13; 7:1-5 (YT)
  food which has been previously ground,
    6:11, 12; 7:5 (YT)
  general prohibition, 6:1
  with special implement, 6:2, 3, 11;
    7:4 (YT), 5 (YT), 7 (YT)
Ground nuts. *See* Peanuts

Hadassim
  inhaling scent of, 22:30
  moving, 22:30

Index

Ill. *See* Sick
Immersion in *mikveh*. *See* Mikveh
Infant. *See* Baby; Child
Inflating
 rubber mattress, 15:83
 toy, 16:8
Insect
 exterminating, 12:20
 in food or drink, 3:18, 36, 48; 4:7 (YT), 8 (YT)
 in lettuce, 3:36; 4:8 (YT)
 scale on citrus peel, 3:37
 straining milk to remove, 3:48
Insect repellent
 applying to body, 14:31
 sprinkling on soiled diapers, 15:4
Inserting
 belt into loop, 15:62
 elastic into garment, 15:61
 ribbon, thread or lace into eyelets or loops, 15:59
 shoelaces, 15:60
Insoles, going out with, 18:21
Instant food, mixing with liquid, 8:25, 26
Invoices, handling, 20:20
Ironing, 16:43

Jacks. *See* "Five-stones"
Jam
 spreading on bread, 6:9; 11:33
 stirring into yogurt or cream, 8:16
Jar. *See* Opening containers
Jewelry, going out wearing, 18:12, 23, 24, 26, 27, 42, 48
Jig-saw puzzles, playing with, 16:23
Juice, fruit
 extracting from fruit, 5:1-8, 10-13
 flavoring food with, 5:7; 8:14, 15; 11:38
 straining, 3:53
 sucking out of fruit, 5:10
 which has oozed out of fruit on Shabbath, 5:11; 20:32
 See also Lemon
Jumping rope, 16:39

Kashering
 meat, 11:5
 vessels, 12:28
K*e*li rishon
 cooling food contained in, 1:73
 definition, 1:2
 keeping warm when flame goes out, 1:23
 moving onto flame, 1:22

pouring from, 1:46, 47, 49, 50, 51, 56; 8:19
putting back on fire, 1:17-20
putting into, 1:12, 14, 15, 16, 33, 59; 8:21
stirring, 1:31, 32
taking out of, 1:31-34
transfer from pot to pot, 1:16
transferring to larger flame, 1:21
water heater as, 1:41
wrapping of, 1:68
See also Urn
K*e*li sheini
 cooling food contained in, 1:73
 definition, 1:2
 pouring from, 1:57
 putting food into, 1:53-56, 59
 wrapping of, 1:69
K*e*li sh*e*lishi
 definition, 1:2
 using, 1:57, 58
K*e*li she-m*e*lachto l*e*-issur, 20:5-18
 definition, 20:5, 6
 moving a, 20:7-10, 12
 putting down after permitted use, 20:11
Kerosene. *See* Paraffin
Ketchup, pouring on hot meat, 1:58
Key
 attached to bracelet, going out with, 18:26
 of car, moving, 20:77
 extracting *muktzeh* key from bunch, 20:83
 of house, going out with, 18:48, 49; 19:3 (YT)
 worn as brooch or tie-clip, 18:48
 worn as part of belt, 18:48, 49
Key ring
 with key which is *muktzeh*, 20:83
 with *muktzeh* object attached, 20:82
Kneading, Chapter 8
 general rules, 8:1, 2
 if substances combined before Shabbath, 8:6, 7
 of inedible material, 8:C
 making a thick mixture, 8:8-11, 16, 17, 26
 making a thin mixture, 8:8, 9, 12, 16, 25, 26
 pouring one substance into another, 8:5
 on Yom Tov, 8:B (YT)
 See also Mixing
Knife
 butcher's, moving, 20:19

Index

Mincing. *See* Grinding

Mint leaves, putting into hot drink, 1:53

Mixing

dry items, 8:4

flour with water, 8:5

hot and cold food, 1:58

hot and cold water, 1:51, 52; 14:3, 5

instant powder, 8:24, 25, 26

substances which do not fuse, 8:4

See also Kneading

Modeling with clay, etc., 16:13

Model-making kit, assembling or dismantling, 16:20

Molding, 16:13

Molid, 22:55

Money

finding in street, 22:34

moving, 20:20, 38, 54; 22:34

playing games with imitation, 16:32

Monkey-bars, climbing, 16:15

Mortar, using a, 6:2

Mouse, dead. *See* Animal, carcass of

Mouthwash, rinsing with, 14:36

Moving

an electric fan, 13:35

an electric heater, 13:40

an electric lamp, 13:40

item with *muktzeh* object on it, 20:46-79

items intended for sale, 22:10, 21

valuable objects, 20:19-24

wet garments, 15:15

See also Muktzeh; and individual items

Mud, removing from garment, 15:27, 28

Muff, going out with, 18:4

Muktzeh, Chapters 20; 21 (YT); 22

articles which not everybody would use, 22:46-48

basis la-davar ha-assur, 20:46-79

belonging to non-Jew, 22:49-54

categories, 20:4

covering object which is, 22:24

duration of status as, 22:1-13

—if item became *muktzeh* on Shabbath, 22:8, 9, 10

—if item was *muktzeh* when Shabbath began, 22:1-7, 11, 12, 13

holding child with *muktzeh* object in his hand, 22:40

item intended for a use not permitted on Shabbath. *See K^eli she-m^elachto l^e-issur*

item with *muktzeh* object on it. *See Basis la-davar ha-assur*

items intended for sale, 20:21; 22:10, 21, 53

items mistakenly thought to be *muktzeh*, 22:17-23

items which are not *muktzeh*, but may not be moved, 22:14, 15, 16

items which are not worth much, 22:46, 47

k^eli she-m^elachto l^e-issur, 20:5-18

making it prohibited for an article to be moved, 22:24-27

mei-chamath chesron kis, 20:19-24; 22:4

mei-chamath gufo, 20:25-45

mei-chamath mitzva, 22:28-31

mei-chamath mi'us, 22:42-45

moving *muktzeh* object

—to facilitate eating, 21:3 (YT)

—by means of another article held in the hand, 22:35-39

—with unusual part of the body, 22:34, 37

putting down objects which are, 20:11; 22:33

putting items on object which is, 22:32, 38

repulsive items, 22:42-45

sitting on object which is, 22:32

sweeping away object which is, 22:39

taking non-*muktzeh* article off object which is, 22:38

telling non-Jew to move object which is, 22:41

touching *muktzeh* object without moving it, 22:32

Musical instruments, 16:2

Nail (finger). *See* Fingernails.

Nail (metal), denoted as *muktzeh*, 20:16

Nail polish

applying, 14:57

removing before going to *mikveh*, 14:61

Name-tags, going out with

pinned to clothing, 18:25

stuck or sewn onto clothing, 18:44

Napkins, table

folding, 11:40

wiping one's mouth or hands with, 14:19

Nappies. *See* Diapers

Necklace, wearing in *r^eshuth ha-rabbim*, 18:24

Necktie, tying, 15:58

Needle, extracting thorn with, 20:8

Index

Noisemaking, 16:2, 3

Nolad, 22:55

Non-Jew
  asking him to move *muktzeh* object,
    22:41
  carrying on Yom Tov for, 19:7 (YT)
  cooking for, 2:5 (YT)
  inviting to meal, 2:5, 6
  moving property of, 20:79; 22:49-54
  putting food on stove, 1:26
  repairing *eiruv*, 17:25
  turning on ventilator, 13:34
  tying and untying knots, 15:57

Noodles
  fried, putting into k^eli *rishon*, 1:61
  straining, 3:54; 4:6 (YT)

Notebook, moving a, 20:84

Numbered squares in a frame, playing
  with, 16:24

Nuts
  chopping, 7:4 (YT)
  cracking, 3:31, 38; 4:4 (YT); 20:8;
    21:3 (YT)
  crushing, 7:4 (YT). *See also* Grinding
  shells, handling and clearing away,
    3:38; 20:26; 22:33, 36
  sorting, 3:26

Nutcracker, opening nuts with, 3:38

Nylon stockings, treating runs in, 15:73

Oatmeal. *See* Cereal, cooked

Occupational therapy, 14:38

"Odds or evens," playing, 16:32

Oil
  applying to hair, 14:48
  of lamp, moving, 20:32; 21:3 (YT); 22:2
  pouring
    —on eggs and onions, 8:23
    —into k^eli *sheini*, 1:53
    —on vegetables, 8:4
  rubbing on baby, 14:27, 28

Oilcloth. *See* Tablecloth, plastic

Oil lamp considered as k^eli *she-m^{e}lachto*
  l^e-issur, 20:16

Ointments, rubbing on baby, 14:27

Olives
  pitting, 3:55
  pouring salt water off pickled, 3:19

Onions
  chopping fine, 7:2 (YT)
  removing from mixed salad, 3:23
  salting, 11:1
  skins or peels, removal of, 3:31

Opening containers, Chapter 9
  bags sealed with pliable strip, 9:13
  bottles, 9:1, 7, 11, 12, 17, 20, 22 (YT)
  boxes
    —taped or gummed closed, 9:10
    —tied with string, 9:14
  cans, 9:1-3, 18, 22 (YT), 23
  cartons, 9:3, 5, 6, 8, 10, 12; 16:18n
  jars, 9:21
  parcel or bag tied with string, 9:14
  sealed bags, 9:13, 16, 22 (YT); 15:80;
    16:18n
  seals, 9:11, 12
  stapled bags, 9:9

Opening door or window near burning
  candle, 13:33; 22:15. *See also* Door

Oranges
  cutting
    —letters or designs into peel, 16:27
    —lines to ease peeling, 11:15
    —through markings on peel, 11:10
  peeling. *See* Peeling
  peels, moving, 20:27; 21:2 (YT)
  sorting, from grapefruits, 3:77
  See also Fruit; Juice; Squeezing

Orla. See Fruit

Ornament
  definition of, 18:11, 12, 24
  going out with, 18:12, 23-28, 42, 48;
    19:3 (YT)
  moving coin attached to necklace or key
    ring, 20:38
  See also Going out with

Orthopedic supports, going out with,
  18:21

Oven
  opening door of, 20:76
  putting food in warm, 1:17
  thermostatically controlled, use of,
    1:29, 30 (YT)
  See also Fire; Gas; Stove

Pad, perfumed, using, 14:33

Pages of book, re-inserting detached, 3:84

Painting, valuable: moving, 20:22

Pants and sheets, babies' waterproof
  cleaning, 15:5, 8
  hanging up to dry, 15:11

Paper
  folding to make toy, 16:19
  good quality writing: moving, 20:19

Paper towels, using, 14:21

Papers, commercial, 20:20

Index

Index

Index

Index

Wiping
  cutlery or dishes, 12:21, 24
  face or hands
  —with napkin, 14:19
  —with perfumed towel or pad, 14:33
  hands dirtied with mud, 14:26
Wood, chopping or sawing, 6:1
Wool, removing ends left in new garment, 15:65
Word-building games, playing, 16:23
Wound
  going out with dressing over, 18:19
  tying dressing on, 15:52
Wrapping
  object which gives off scent, 15:76
  pots of food to keep them warm, 1:23, 64-69, 72
Writing
  in dirt, 16:40

non-permanent, 16:22, 27
  on misted window pane, 16:27

Yahrzeit candle, lighting, 13:6 (YT)
Yarmulke
  finding in pocket, 18:53
  wearing with hairpin or clip, 18:29
Yogurt
  mixing with soft cheese, 8:11
  pouring off whey, 3:19
  tearing container top, 9:11, 12
Yom Kippur
  rules of *muktzeh* applicable on, 21:7
  shitufei m^{e}vo'oth and *eiruv chatzeiroth* on, 17:23

Zipper
  going out wearing coat with, 18:31
  using, 15:74

בית מדרש הלכה — מוריה ירושלים תובב"א

עם הספר

הצלחתו המופלאה של הספר "שמירת שבת כהלכתה" במהדורתו הראשונה, אשר הגיע כמעט לכל בית מישראל בכל קצוות תבל, עוררה את הצורך לעיין מחדש בכל ההלכות שהובאו בו במגמה להוציאו לאור מחדש, מוגה ומורחב, שיהא בו כדי למלא את יעודו ולהקל על הלימוד וההתמצאות בהלכות שבת, וכך נתבקשנו ע"י גדולי ירושלים וע"י המחבר הרב הגאון ר' יהושע י. נויבירט שליט"א, לעמוד לימינו ולהיות לו לעזר במשימה קדושה זו. הקדשנו לעבודה זו עמל מבורך של כמה שנים, שפרנו והרחבנו, והיום הזה זכינו בסייעתא דשמיא לברך על המוגמר ולהגיש את הספר מתוקן ומורחב לבית ישראל.

"בית מדרש הלכה—מוריה" נוסד בזמנו במגמה לפעול להפצת דבר ההלכה בעם, בארץ ובתפוצות. במסגרת תכניותיו להוציא לאור סדרת ספרי הלכה לעם במתכונת ספר זה, אשר תקיף את מרבית ההלכות אשר להן נצרך כל אדם מישראל.

ובפתחתו של ספר זה נציב דבר תודה וברכה מעומקא דליבא לכל ידידינו העומדים לימיננו במסירות ובנאמנות, ישלם להם ה' כפועלם מאוצרו הטוב. ותודה מיוחדת למרן הגאון רבי שלמה זלמן אויערבאך שליט"א, שהנחה אותנו והאיר לנו לאורך כל הדרך, והיה לנו לעינים.

והננו תפילה לשוכן מרומים לראות ברכה בעמלנו, לבל תצא תקלה מתחת ידינו. וזכות שמירת השבת תעמוד לנו ולכל המסייעים בידינו לטוב להם ולנו כל הימים, ונזכה לראות במהרה בנחמת ציון וירושלים ובבנין בית מקדשנו ותפארתנו.

כסלו תשל"ט

אשר זלצמן   יעקב וייל

The Distributors' Foreword to the second Hebrew edition

Beit Midrash Halachah—Moriah/Jerusalem

Upon Publication

The wonderful success of the book *Sh^emirath Shabbath K^ehilchathah* in its first edition, which has reached almost every Jewish home in all corners of the globe, has aroused the need for a new examination of the *halachoth* it contains, with the aim of re-publishing it, checked and expanded, so that it should be able to fulfill its object and facilitate the learning of, and familiarity with, *hilchoth Shabbath*. Consequently, we have been requested by the great Torah scholars of Jerusalem and by the author, Harav Hagaon Rabbi Yehoshua Y. Neuwirth, long may he live, to stand at his right hand and be of assistance to him in this holy task. We have devoted to this work the blessed toil of several years, we have improved and expanded, and today we have been privileged, with the help of Heaven, to see completion of the labor and to present the book, corrected and expanded, to the House of Israel.

"Beit Midrash Halachah—Moriah" was originally founded with the object of working for the spread of the word of the Halachah among the people, in Israel and in the Diaspora. Within the framework of its program is the publication of a series of popular books on Halachah, along the lines of this book, which will comprehend most of the *halachoth* that are necessary for every Jewish individual.

At the beginning of this book we state our gratitude and blessings, from the bottom of our hearts, to all our friends who stand at our side with devotion and faithfulness. May Hashem pay them according to their deeds from His goodly treasure-house. Special thanks are due to Maran Hagaon Rabbi Shlomo Zalman Auerbach, long may he live, who has guided us and lit our way and has been our "eyes."

We pray to Him Who resides on high that we may see blessings from our toil and that no faults may result from our work. May the merit of the observance of the Shabbath always stand us and all those who help us in good stead and may we deserve soon to see the consolation of Zion and Jerusalem and the building of our Temple of holiness and glory.

Kislev 5739   *Yaakov Weil*   *Asher Saltzman*

Translation of the Distributors' Foreword to the second Hebrew edition

שמירת שבת כהלכתה

כולל

דיני שמירת שבת ויום טוב

בשם לב לבעיות שהתעוררו בזמננו

(לאלה הנוהגים לפסוק כשיטת הרמ״א)

מאת

יהושע ישעיה נויבירט

מהדורה חדשה, מתוקנת ומורחבת

בית מדרש הלכה — מוריה
ירושלם עיה״ק תובב״א
אך את שבתתי תשמרו כי אות הוא

The title-page of the second Hebrew edition